JEANETTE
63 Su
Ballston Lake, NY
12019

If found, please return to above address. You will be reimbursed for the postage.
Thank you & God Bless you!

SURGERY
of the
SOUL

Portrait of Joseph E. Murray showing the emblems of his career: a skull, representing craniofacial surgery, and a photo of the Herrick twins, representing kidney transplantation. (This portrait, by Herbert Abrams, hangs in the amphitheater at the Brigham and Women's Hospital in Boston, Massachusetts.)

SURGERY
of the
SOUL

Reflections on a Curious Career

JOSEPH E. MURRAY, M.D.

Published for the
Boston Medical Library
by

Science History Publications/USA
2001

First published in the United States of America
by Science History Publications/USA
a division of Watson Publishing International
Post Office Box 493, Canton, MA 02021-0493

© 2001 by Boston Medical Library

FIRST EDITION

Library of Congress Cataloging-in-Publication Data

Murray, Joseph E., 1919–
    Surgery of the soul : reflections on a curious career / by Joseph E. Murray.—
1st ed.
      p. cm.
    Includes bibliographical references and index.
    ISBN 0-88135-255-1
    1. Murray, Joseph E., 1919–   2. Transplant surgeons—United States—
Biography.   I. Boston Medical Library.   II. Title.

RD27.35.M875 A3 2001
617′.092—dc21
[B]   2001020942

All rights reserved. No part of this book may be used or reproduced in any manner whatsoever without written permission of the copyright holder except in the case of brief quotations embodied in critical articles and reviews.

Designed, typeset, and printed in the USA.

Dedication

To my wife Bobby

and

our children—Ginny, Meg, J. Link, Kathy, Tom, and Rick—
and in memory of my mother and dad.

The fruit of silence is prayer
The fruit of prayer is faith
The fruit of faith is love
The fruit of love is service
The fruit of service is peace

—Mother Theresa, "The Simple Path"

"Difficulties are Opportunities."

—Inscription on plaque made by leprosy patient in India

"Now I am well! . . . with the aid of [my friend] 'The Artificial Kidney' and the 'Angels in White' at the Peter Bent Brigham Hospital, there is hope for all with this type of illness. It is so much a miracle that even now I have to press on my abdomen and feel the transplanted kidney to reassure myself that this really happened."

—Edith Helm, the world's longest living organ transplant recipient

There is no higher religion than human service.
To work for the common good is the greatest creed.

—Albert Schweitzer

"I was no longer wanted, . . . rejected by my own mother and family because of heart, hearing, and facial malformation. . . . For years I have seen the pain, sorrow, fear, anxiety, stress, and distrust that confinement in a state hospital inflicts on a human being. . . . I promised myself to be so strong that nothing could disturb my peace of mind. . . . Beauty is not determined by a perfect figure or features—it is determined by the way you respect and honor yourself. I was very lucky to have Dr. Joseph E. Murray—a wonderful human being—for my doctor and surgeon and friend."

—Raymond Francis McMillan, patient

Contents

Acknowledgments ix
Chronology of Events xi
Preface xiii
Foreword xv

PART I	THE EARLY YEARS	1
CHAPTER 1	Charles Woods, Courageous Survivor	3
CHAPTER 2	Life in Milford	19
CHAPTER 3	Life in Medical School	27
CHAPTER 4	Surgical Internship	33
CHAPTER 5	Military Medicine	39
CHAPTER 6	Surgical Residency	45
CHAPTER 7	Virgil Albasi: Civilian Benefits from Military Surgery	51
CHAPTER 8	Private Practice and Research Activities	59
PART II	ORGAN TRANSPLANTATION	71
CHAPTER 9	Richard and Ronald Herrick: First Identical-Twin Kidney Transplant	73
CHAPTER 10	The Expanding Web of Transplantation Surgery	89
CHAPTER 11	John Riteris: First Allogeneic (Non-Identical-Twin) Kidney Transplant	99
CHAPTER 12	The Dawn of Chemical Immune Suppression	105

| Chapter 13 | Mel Doucette: First Cadaveric Donor Kidney Transplant | 115 |

Part III   Reconstructive Surgery   123

Chapter 14	Jay Baloun, Frank Wint, and Dawn Germasian: A Trilogy of Childhood Head and Neck Tumors	125
Chapter 15	Plastic Surgery at Home and Abroad	141
Chapter 16	Walter Murphy: A Surgical No-Man's Land	147
Chapter 17	Marilyn Miele and Jimmy Hickey: The Tessier Legacy in Craniofacial Reconstruction	155
Chapter 18	Travels with Family and Colleagues	165
Chapter 19	Iylene Becker: A Dilemma—Life or Speech?	173
Chapter 20	The Iran Experience: Teaching at Queen's Hospital in Tehran	181
Chapter 21	Lisa Federico and Natalie Kapper: Expansion of the Craniofacial Clinic	187
Chapter 22	Cosmetic Surgery: Not Just a Pretty Face	199
Chapter 23	Raymond McMillan: Surgery of the Soul	207

Part IV   The Later Years   213

Chapter 24	Dr. Joseph E. Murray, Stroke Patient	215
Chapter 25	Nobel Laureate	221
	Epilogue	229
	Endnotes	231
	Chronological Bibliography	237
	Index	249

Acknowledgments

I would like to thank the many colleagues at Brigham and Women's Hospital, Children's Hospital, and Harvard Medical School who enriched my professional career. In particular, I want to thank Dr. Brad Cannon for introducing me to Plastic and Reconstructive Surgery during World War II and continuing to guide me ever since; Dr. Francis D. Moore for his constant inspiration and sound advice during our association spanning more than 40 years; Dr. George W. Thorn, Physician-in-Chief at the Brigham, who originally envisioned treating renal disease by dialysis and transplantation and provided funding for our preliminary work; Drs. John Merrill and J. Hartwell Harrison, who were key members of the Brigham transplantation team; Dr. John Mannick, an early investigator in transplantation and successor to Dr. Moore as Surgeon-in-Chief at the Brigham, for his continued strong support in all phases of my professional life; Dr. Carl Walter, a man whose curiosity and imagination changed medical practice; Drs. Judah Folkman, Aldo Castaneda, and Hardy Hendren of the Department of Surgery at Children's Hospital, for their superb leadership and understanding; Sir Roy Calne for his imaginative use of immunosuppressive drugs in our surgical research laboratory; and Dr. George Hitchings and Dr. Gertrude Elion, biochemists at Burroughs-Wellcome, who first developed immunosuppressive agents and guided us in their use; Dr. Ruppert ("Bill") Billingham, an associate of Peter Medawar and close associate of mine during our early endeavors in transplantation; and Dr. Gustave Dammin, Pathologist-in-Chief at the Brigham Hospital, for the many contributions of his department to the transplant field. Dr. Eugene Braunwald, successor to Dr. Thorn as Physician-in-Chief, read the manuscript and aided in my search for a publisher.

Several deans of the Harvard Medical School also deserve mention here: Sidney Burwell, who was Dean when I graduated and who became

Acknowledgments

an optimistic patient during my early surgical career; George Berry, who helped finance the relocation of the HMS Laboratory of Surgical Research from Building C to Building E in the early 1960s; Robert Ebert, who encouraged our research and clinical work on transplantation; Daniel Tosteson, who restored the quadrangle buildings and landscape to their original pristine appearance and guided and financed the Medical Education Center; and Joseph Martin, who within a few years expanded the medical school campus along Avenue Louis Pasteur.

From the publishing world, several individuals encouraged in this project, particularly two of my friends from Chappaquiddick—Arthur Thornhill (formerly President of Little, Brown and Company) and the late Vance Packard (a successful author). Arthur Klebanoff, a literary agent whom I met at a Harvard Medical School function, was also most helpful and supportive.

Numerous people have played important roles related to my research and clinical work over the years, and I will take this opportunity to mention them here. They include professional colleagues in the fields of medicine, dentistry, physiology, and psychiatry/psychology — Clifford Barger, Benjamin Barnes, Myron Belfer, Alan Birtch, Leo Chylak, Joseph M. Corson, Nathan Couch, James Dealey, Robert Eisendrath, Carla Evans, Robert Goldwyn, Willard Goodwin, Walter Guralnik, John Hall, Alexandra Harrison, Norman Hollenberg, Donald Matson, Roger Moseley, John Mulliken, Nicholas O'Connor, Francine Pillemer, Robert Smith, Stephen Sonis, Willie Stevens, Frank Stuart, Lennard Swanson, Nicholas Tilney, Joseph Upton, Leroy Vandam, and Frank Veith; Research Fellows—Guy Alexandre, Gil Diethelm, Ron Guttman, Ted Hager, Gus Hampers, Alan MacDonald, Ken Porter, Alan Retik, and Ross Sheil; Plastic Surgery Residents—Martin J. Carney, Greg Ganske, Mutaz B. Habal, Pearlman D. Hicks, Jr., Blayne L. Hirsche, George M. Hricko, Elliot Lach, Lucie Lessard, Ronald M. Linder, Thomas D. Mustoe, Douglas J. Ramos, Brooke R. Seckel, Thomas R. Vecchione, and John E. Woods; Surgical Research Laboratory administrators Mary Tilney and Joan Voorhees; surgical nurse Dorothy MacDonald; and social worker Joan Lahey.

I also wish to acknowledge several persons who have worked closely with me during the creation of the book. Julie Varriale served as my first secretary after my retirement from active surgery and helped ease the transition. Sharon Johnson, my first editorial assistant, aided me in the critical initial selection and editing of the patients' stories. Kit Bowry, secretary extraordinaire, provided personal, caring contact with so many of the craniofacial patients, in addition to helping to create a computerized database that made doing research for the book more feasible. Richard Wolfe provided many helpful materials from the archives of the Countway Library of Medicine. Judith Messerle, Countway Librarian for the Harvard Medical and Boston Medical Libraries, and Thomas Horrocks, Curator of Rare Books and Joseph Garland Librarian at the Countway, in tandem with Dr. Leonard Morse and the Board of the Boston Medical Library, made the commitment to publish the book. Kristin Ostheimer was an able library assistant. Neale Watson was responsible for the physical production of the book.

Dr. Anthony L. Komaroff and Ms. Diane Q. Forti were enthusiastic and skilled editors, without whose help the book would never have been completed. Finally, I greatly appreciate the dedication and skillful guidance of Ms. Suzie Brown, who has worked with me tirelessly for the several years it has taken to complete the book.

Joseph E. Murray, M.D.

Chronology of Events

April 1, 1919	Born in Milford, Massachusetts
June, 1936	Graduated from Milford High School
June, 1940	Graduated from the College of Holy Cross
September, 1940–December, 1943	Graduated from Harvard Medical School, Boston, Massachusetts
January, 1944–September, 1944	Completed surgical internship at Peter Bent Brigham Hospital, and Children's Hospital, Boston, Massachusetts
June 2, 1945	Married Virginia ("Bobby") Link in Binghamton, New York
October, 1944–October, 1947	Served on active duty in the United States Army as staff surgeon stationed at Valley Forge General Hospital, Phoenixville, Pennsylvania
December, 1947–December, 1950	Completed surgical residency at Peter Bent Brigham Hospital and Children's Hospital, Boston, including a 6-month rotation at Memorial Hospital, New York City
January, 1951–June, 1951	Completed plastic surgery residency at New York Hospital, New York City
July, 1951	Began practice as plastic and general surgeon on staff of Peter Bent Brigham Hospital and with Dental Service at Children's Hospital
December, 1954	First identical-twin kidney transplant (Herrick brothers)

1952–1975	Assumed directorship of Surgical Research Laboratory at Harvard Medical School
1959	First allogeneic (non-identical-twin) transplant (Riteris)
1962	First cadaveric donor kidney transplant (Doucette)
1962	First International Conference on Human Kidney Transplantation
1964	First report of Human Kidney Transplant Registry
1966	First mid-face advancement operation in U.S.
1962–1976	Visited foreign countries (including India, Iran) to train physicians in reconstructive surgical techniques
1970–1979	Elected Regent of American College of Surgeons
March, 1986	Retired from active surgery owing to a stroke
December, 1990	Received the Nobel Prize in Physiology or Medicine

Awards

1962	Francis Amory Prize of the American Academy of Arts and Sciences
1963	Gold Medal of International Society of Surgeons, Brussels, Belgium
1969	Honorary Award of the American Association of Plastic Surgeons
1970	Ninth Ferdinand C. Valentine Medal and Award, New York Academy of Medicine
1979	National Kidney Foundation Gift of Life Award

Chronology of Events

1980	VIIIth International Congress of Transplantation Society—Dedication to Drs. Joseph E. Murray, John P. Merrill, and Jean Hamburger
1980	Honorary Citizen's Award from the City of Boston on its 350th Anniversary
1981	Clinician of the Year, American Association of Plastic Surgeons
1985	Honorary Fellow, Royal Australasian College of Surgeons
1987	Honorary Award, The Boston Leadership Forum (Greater Boston Chamber of Commerce)
1987	Honorary Fellow, Royal College of Surgeons of London
1988	Honorary Fellow, Royal College of Surgeons in Ireland
1990	Olof Af Acrel Medal, The Swedish Society of Medicine
1990	Nobel Prize in Physiology or Medicine
1991	Medal for Distinguished Service to Surgery, American Surgical Association
1991	Nathan Smith Distinguished Service Award, New England Surgical Society
1992	Bigelow Medal, Boston Surgical Society
1992	Distinguished Academician for 1992, Academy of Medicine of Singapore
1992	Honorary Fellow, Royal College of Surgeons, Edinburgh, Scotland
1992	Honorary Fellow, Royal Academy of Medicine of Belgium
1992	Medallion for Scientific Achievement, American Surgical Association
1993	Elected Member of National Academy of Sciences

1994	Elected Member of Institute of Medicine, National Academy of Sciences
1994	Sabin Award, Americans for Medical Progress
1994	Honorary Fellow, Royal College of Physicians and Surgeons of Canada
1997	Member of Pontifical Academy of Science, Rome, Italy
1997	Honorary Degree, McGill University, Montreal, Canada
1998	Lifetime Achievement Award, Massachusetts Medical Society
2000	Outstanding Medical Award, National Kidney Foundation of Massachusetts

Council and Advisory Committee Memberships

1956–1969	Member, National Research Council, Committee on Tissue Transplantation
1962–1966	Member, National Institutes of Health Surgical Studies Section
1963	Chairman, National Research Council, First Human Kidney Transplant Conference, Washington, D.C. (September)
1964	Founder, International Kidney Transplant Registry
1965	Chairman, National Research Council, Second Human Kidney Transplant Conference, Washington, D.C. (May)
1967–1971	Member, National Institutes of Health Immunobiological Study Section
1969	Member, Ad Hoc Committee Examining the Definition of Death, Harvard Medical School
1969–1970	Chairman, American Board of Plastic Surgery

Editorial Board Member and Editorships

Transplantation Journal
Journal of Plastic and Reconstructive Surgery

Preface

From earliest memory I knew I would be a surgeon. Although there were no doctors on either side of my family, our family doctor, Dr. George F. Curley, was a powerful influence. His "fever powders" always cured our childhood illnesses, and his very presence in our house brought comfort to the entire family. But my basic desire must have been inborn, because whenever an adult asked what I would be when I grew up, I just cheerfully announced, "I'm going to be a surgeon!"

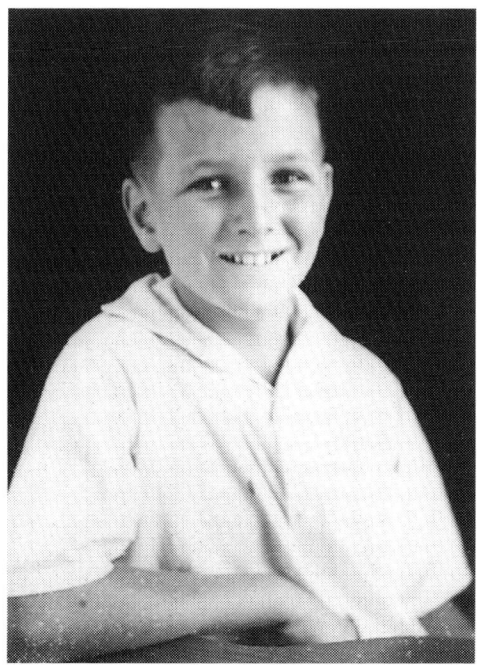

Joe in the third grade.

Foreword

This is a very surgical book: it is a surgeon's story of a surgical career devoted to surgical patients.

Before reading such a book, readers' images of surgery will differ according to their prior experiences with surgeons. For many, this may have been childhood terror at the looming operation for an acute appendix or a hernia, with masked faces and threatening anesthesia machines. Or it might be a teenager's image of gratitude to the surgeon who set and stabilized a skiing fracture, relieving pain and promising a return to the slopes. For many of our older age group, the image of surgery includes the tension of awaiting the biopsy verdict, followed by the apprehension that maybe the tumor cannot be removed.

All this is the stuff of surgery. And all of surgery has one common denominator: one caring person, the surgeon, who applies knowledge and skill to relieve the anguish of disease or injury. The surgeon remains as an indivisible unit of our society, like the ship's captain, the Olympic athlete, or the fighter pilot, who performs with final, solo responsibility and cannot be more than one person at a time. The surgeon is never anonymous, a committee, or a corporation. Only one person makes the critical decisions and takes the crucial steps with helping hands.

Joseph Murray has devoted his entire career to the relief of human suffering through plastic and reconstructive surgery. This has been the focus of his professional life and is the subject of this book. As key chapters unfold, he describes a series of individual patients, their specific problems, and how they were helped by his skill and dedication. These are stories of patients with a very special kind of pain, one that many of us have never experienced: the anguish of facial or bodily distortions that make the beholder turn away. In children, such an appearance makes the child an outcast, vulnerable to isolation and rejection by their classmates, to weeping on the way home from school, to a devastating loss of self-esteem. For a child with an embarrassing facial deformity, simple repair of a lopear or harelip restores self-respect, provides acceptance by peers, and truly heals a wound of the soul. In a remarkable climax to a remarkable story, the final case described is that of the author himself. He tells us what it was like for an active person at the very peak of his career to suffer a stroke.

As we reach the new millennium, ending a century of both hateful cruelty and healing science, the scope of surgery has expanded immensely. Formerly confined to diseases that were acute, focal, or traumatic, surgery now also addresses diseases that are chronic, widespread, and often lethal. These often demand the use of new organs to replace failing hearts, livers, or kidneys; new joints for those crippled by arthritis; microsurgical techniques to repair tiny ear bones or the ultrathin retinal membrane of the eye; new blood vessels for leg, kidney, brain, or heart. Now surgeons often enter the domain of the internist or pediatrician and take on some of their burdens, bringing joyful years of life.

No matter what the surgeon's special knowledge or skill, patients' realities of body, mind, and soul are made of quite the same stuff in everyone. All doctors must respect the living wholeness of each patient. Here, the author describes for us, case by case, the growth and maturation of his skills in plastic and reconstructive surgery based on a series of sentinel cases, starting during his wartime collaboration with Dr. Bradford Cannon and their care of the wounded at the Valley Forge General Hospital in Pennsylvania.

It was no accident or coincidence when, a few years later at the Peter Bent Brigham Hospital in Boston, George Thorn and I asked Joe Murray to perform those first successful renal transplants that led him to Stockholm to receive the Nobel Prize in 1990. Dr. Murray's experimental work in the field of whole-organ replacement had started after his discharge from the Army, when he rejoined the Harvard/Brigham Department of Surgery. At that time, he began his experimental studies of kidney transplantation in the dog, working with Dr. David Hume, who was then in charge of kidney transplant research in our department.

In following this path, Dr. Murray helped create the largest completely new field of biomedical science and clinical art to have originated entirely within this century: organ transplantation. By current estimates, over 600,000 patients worldwide have received transplants of kidney, liver, heart, lung, pancreas, or skin from other human beings. This flow continues to swell at an incredible rate, with an ever-improving record of increased survival and decreased morbidity. Greater progress is restricted only by the lack of donors from our own species. Donors from other species will surely come. For this option to become a reality, we must acquire more knowledge than we now possess.

Some books might tell the story of one person or one idea. This is "A Tale of Three Careers": Joseph Murray the man—husband, father of six, athlete, teacher, and friend to many; Joseph Murray the surgeon—repairing defects of birth, cancer, violence, and war; and Joseph Murray the scientist—a key figure in the history of surgery. He applied both clinical science and surgical skill so that the cells of two people might, through transplantation, collaborate peacefully to make life possible for both when death is imminent for one.

In Chirurgia, Veritas. In Surgery, there is Truth.

Francis Daniels Moore   *September, 2000*
Moseley Professor of Surgery, Emeritus,
Harvard Medical School
Surgeon-in-Chief, Emeritus,
Peter Bent Brigham Hospital
Boston, Massachusetts

PART I

THE EARLY YEARS

CHAPTER 1

CHARLES WOODS
Courageous Survivor

> *Procedure:* Burn treatment
> *Dates of Operations:* 1945–1947
> *Institution:* Valley Forge General Hospital, U.S. Army, Phoenixville, Pennsylvania

MEETING CHARLES WOODS

When I first saw the young aviator, Charles Woods, he had no nose, eyelids, or ears, and his mouth—if you could call it that—was a raw opening. He had been terribly burned, burned beyond recognition and was weak from infection, loss of body fluids, and malnutrition. Burns covered more than 70% of his body, including his entire head and hands.

According to studies of many patients with equally serious burns, Charles Woods should not have lived more than a few minutes after the fire. But it was now six weeks later, Charles had been airlifted over 10,000 miles, and he was still holding on to life. He had arrived at Valley Forge General Hospital, an Army hospital in Phoenixville, Pennsylvania. His fingers and tendons had been fused and encased in fragile, immature scar tissue. His face had been erased by fire. Charles Woods was a human form—one whose age could not possibly be determined from his appearance. In fact, he was 22 years old. What awaited him over the next two years was a series of 24 operations, many conducted with only minimal anesthesia, and unimaginable pain. A team of surgeons was going to try to build him a new face and functioning hands and to give him back his life.

At age 25, I was the most junior member of the team. The questions raised and lessons learned in trying to help Charles would determine the course of the rest of my professional life.

Young aviator Charles Woods before his accident.

CHARLES' STORY

Charles Woods' injuries were anything but routine, and so was the manner in which they were incurred. From early childhood, Charles' life ambition had been to fly. Brought up an orphan in Alabama, he first enlisted in the Canadian Air Force until the United States entered World War II, when he joined the U.S. Army Air Corps. After an illustrious career in Europe and Africa, he returned to the States and requested further duty. He was then sent to Burma and assigned to fly the "Hump" into China, ferrying supplies for the Allies' Flying Tigers to help the Chinese army fighting against the Japanese in Mainland China.

Flying the Hump meant filling the huge containers attached to the bottom of his airplane with a cargo of 28,000 pounds of aviation fuel and then flying that fuel from Kurmitola, India, where he was stationed, to Lulaing, China. There was nothing direct about the route. The Himalayan Mountains boast some of the most treacherous terrain in the world, and that distinction does not end at the mountaintops. The steep, jagged peaks did strange things to the surrounding air, and Charles would find himself wrestling surging updrafts, then suddenly fighting to break free from powerful wind shear. Add to these conditions weather that was often inclement and an airplane made cumbersome by a heavy load of fuel, and you have the potential for disaster.

But that was not the way Charles saw it. He flew the Hump every day, untroubled by the rigors. Flying was what he wanted to do and, in a way, flying the Hump was flying at its best. It required every bit of concentration and skill he had, and Charles proved his abilities with the completion of every safe passage. This held true for as long as he was the one in control of the plane.

At 22, Charles was young to be an instructor pilot responsible for training other pilots. But his "natural born" flying abilities were recognized early by his superiors, and Charles advanced quickly—as much out of need as of talent. Fighter-bomber pilots in Europe experienced substantial losses. Their average combat life expectancy was 56 flying hours. With every mission, 11 percent of the planes were lost. With pilots normally flying two missions a week at the height of the bombardment, a pilot's life expectancy was 30 days. For those pilots flying the Hump month after month, the average loss was 100 percent of the planes every 90 days. As Charles recalls,

> I tried not to think about it. I accepted it as part of my job, and when I was told to fly, I flew. And I flew a lot. We averaged from 140 to 150 combat hours each month. In comparison, a commercial airline pilot in the United States today is grounded after 100 hours. I remember being so sleepy when flying that airplane that at times I hoped we would hit a mountain. I was so tired that even *eternal* rest seemed preferable to no rest at all.
>
> There is a strong camaraderie among fighter pilots worldwide, but our casualties were so high that the pilots in our group tended to keep to themselves. With hindsight, I realize that we didn't want to risk becoming friends with someone only to have him disappear the next day. We did little socializing at the Officers Club; we were just too tired. We ate, we slept, and we flew.

On December 23, 1944, Charles was preparing to take the trip he'd made hundreds of times before. But this time he had a passenger. Captain Stalmacher would be flying first seat as pilot-in-training to test whether he could fly the tricky passage on his own.

> I had a habit of saying a simple prayer before each takeoff: "Dear God, please be with us." The day I took off with Stalmacher . . . , this prayer was more fitting than I could know. Stalmacher made a fatal error on takeoff. Mistakenly thinking the plane was airborne, he applied the brakes to stop the wheels from spinning. Getting the plane airborne was now out of the question. One hundred and twenty mph was the minimum requirement to get off the ground, and Stalmacher's act lowered the speed to 90 mph. We had slightly over 100 yards of runway remaining. I knew we'd "bought it." I remember telling myself that if I could only stay conscious, I could get out of this mess.
>
> I assumed command and took the only prudent course of action available: I pulled power and put my entire body weight against the brakes. Stalmacher and I both fought the controls as the plane plowed into the soft dirt at the end of the runway. The plane fishtailed, then slowed to a near stop before crossing paths with the sharp branches of a fallen tree. I yelled a warning to the flight crew, "Let's get out of here." But it was too late. The fuel tank was pierced, and a single spark was followed quickly by an explosion. The plane and all of us inside it were instantly enveloped in flames.
>
> I felt a first blast of heat, then my nerve endings must have seared because I lost all feeling. I knew what I had to do and I did it. I stayed calm and kept my eyes shut tight, hoping to protect them. I felt for the small Plexiglas window beside me, opened it and twisted through and slid down the fuselage. The plane was tipped over on its wing. I could hear the big old propeller still ticking over, and I knew I had to stay clear of that. I landed hands-first in a puddle of flaming gasoline, then ran until I could no longer sense the intense heat from the plane. Natives rushed out to help put out the fire that was consuming me. I discovered much later that they helped themselves to my watch and wallet as payment for their troubles.

As was the case with many aviators during World War II, Charles had removed his helmet and gloves prior to take-off because they impeded his fine-motor control. The consequences of that action were frightfully severe. When he was suddenly engulfed by flames, his face and hands were unprotected. They were severely damaged, and his life hung in the balance.

The Long Trip Home

Charles was given some medical treatment in Burma, and plans were made for his return to the United States for follow-up care and more definitive surgical treatment. Military transport had progressed to the point that Charles could be moved quickly. Already a hero because of his courageous flying record, he was granted coveted Priority One status. Even so, his transport took six weeks. "I was so weak," Charles says. "I could only fly one day, then I'd have to rest up in a hospital somewhere for a week."

One of those rest stops was in Calcutta, where he was put in a corner to die. "I kept telling them that if they'd just send me to the United States, I would live," says Charles. Finally, after two weeks, they sent him on his way. But the trip home almost ended in Cairo. "It was there they took me off fluids," Charles remembers, and his voice still retains barely controlled rage as he describes the experience.

> They kept pumping water into me, and I was so weak and sick I kept throwing it right back up. One of the more junior doctors told the nurse to take me off fluids. It was like signing my death warrant. I begged for water. I tried to explain why I needed it. Fluids were oozing out of 70 percent of my body. I quickly dehydrated. With no saliva in my mouth, I could no longer speak. I slipped in and out of consciousness. I dreamt of deserts, and mirages without water. It was a nightmare then, and I still have nightmares about it to this day. Finally the more senior charge doctor returned, stunned to see what had happened to me. He placed a teaspoon of water in my mouth, and again gave orders for fluids. He was the one who had the sense to assign a full-time nurse to travel with me to the United States. Even so, I continued to deteriorate on the endless flight over.

Military transport planes were not designed to cradle their passengers in comfort. The rough ride took its toll on Charles, and when he finally arrived at the Army hospital in Pennsylvania, he was teetering on the edge of life.

Taking Care of Charles

The surgical team charged with the care of Charles Woods was made up of Dr. James Barrett Brown, Dr. Bradford Cannon, Dr. Andrew M. Moore, and me. Drs. Brown and Cannon supervised Dr. Moore, who was responsible for Charles' day-to-day care on the Officers Ward, and I assisted Andy. Some of the things we had to do were obvious. Top priority in the treatment of burns is making sure the airway is kept clear. Because burns of the breathing tubes—the trachea and bronchi—and lungs cause so much swelling of the air passages, a burn victim can suffocate within minutes. Once a functional airway is established, the chief threats to life are fluid imbalance and infection. Replacement of skin is critical for controlling both.

The first order of business for Charles, in addition to controlling infection and limiting fluid loss, was to cover the burned areas with skin as rapidly as possible. This involved taking (or "harvesting") pieces of healthy skin from an area of the patient's body that had not been burned (called the "donor site") and transferring them to the burned area. Such transplants are called skin "autografts" because the transplanted tissue is from the same person and will therefore not be rejected by the immune system. Technically, the only other possible kind of autograft would be tissue obtained from a patient's identical twin. In fact, years earlier, Dr. Brown had published a report describing the first successful skin graft in which the donor and recipient were identical twins. Unfortunately, Charles had no twin.

In some cases, using a burned patient's own skin is not possible, for example, if the person's burns are so extensive that not enough healthy skin remains for harvesting. Even if enough healthy skin is available, the patient may be too sick to undergo autografting. This was surely the case with Charles, who was far too malnourished and debilitated from infection to withstand the operation required to harvest the skin grafts we needed. As a stopgap measure, Dr. Cannon decided that we would use skin grafts from a cadaver, and he called the next of kin of a recently deceased patient to get the necessary permission for the donation.

Tissue transplanted from one individual to another is called an "allograft." I had little hope that this type of graft would survive for long, since it was well known that an allograft recipient's immune system eventually rejects transplanted tissue such as skin. For the first seven to

10 days after skin is transplanted, an autograft and an allograft look the same: pink, healthy, and viable. However, after 10 to 14 days, the allograft starts to fray around the edges, and within a week or so it begins to shrink until it disappears completely. In contrast, the autograft not only maintains its original size, but it starts to expand around the periphery and creep out in all directions, ultimately covering a much larger area than it did when first transferred.

In Charles' case we were forced to use an allograft, meaning that we could hope to buy only 10 to 14 days before we would have to find another solution to the problem of coverage. But, to our amazement, the allograft continued to serve adequately for about a month. During that crucial reprieve, Charles' nutritional status improved and the infection subsided. We were then able to start replacing the now failing allograft with skin taken from unburned parts of Charles' own body. Because his burns were so severe, total coverage required many operations.

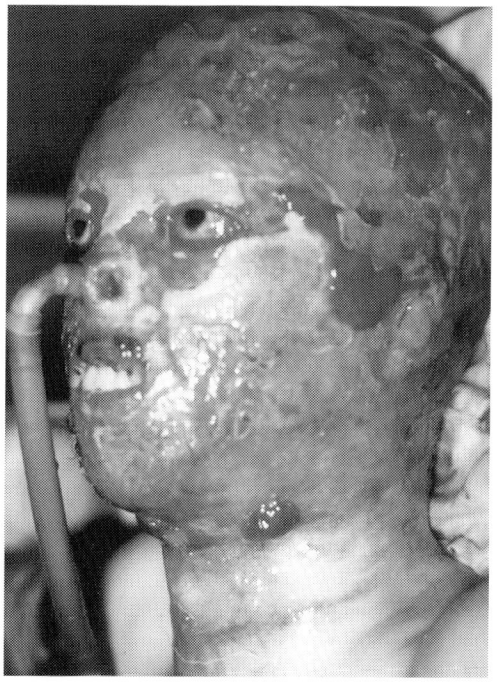

The anesthesia was given through the tube coming from Charles' right nostril. Nasal intubation was rare in civilian life but routine at Valley Forge General Hospital.

Our team developed an efficient operating routine. While either Dr. Brown or Dr. Cannon worked to restore Charles' facial features, Andy and I used tweezers to position the little squares of new skin on the hands. All newly placed skin had to be covered with dressings, which were replaced each day. These daily dressing changes were painful but necessary to prepare the recipient sites for subsequent skin grafts. What we were doing was analogous to planting seeds, optimally preparing the "soil" to accept and "grow" the precious pieces of skin.

After weeks of dressing changes and several additional skin donations from the cadaver, Charles' wounds began to heal, and he began to gain weight. Soon all the burned areas had healed. By that time we knew that he would live but his injuries would still result in a devastating number of surgically challenging deformities—more than any of us had ever seen.

"Reconstructing" Charles

When planning for Charles' long-term reconstruction, we gave highest priority to replacing his eyelids. Since the unprotected eyes were in danger of infection and subsequent loss of vision, careful dressings, antibiotics, and ointments had to be used to protect the eyes 24 hours a day to prevent irritation, further injury, and drying and destructive loss of the cornea. We released the scar contractures of his eyelids by cutting across the fibrous tissue, allowing the lining to drape over the eyeball itself. Skin grafts from unburned areas around his collarbone (the clavicle) were used to cover the areas exposed by the incisions and to reconstruct both upper and lower lids. The color match was satisfactory, and the pliable tissue allowed Charles to open and close his eyes. This use of clavicular skin to cover the eyelid surface was just one of many outstanding medical innovations developed during World War II.

We performed these early operations under general anesthesia. At one point, mid-operation, Charles' heart stopped. Because we had such trouble restarting it, we wor-

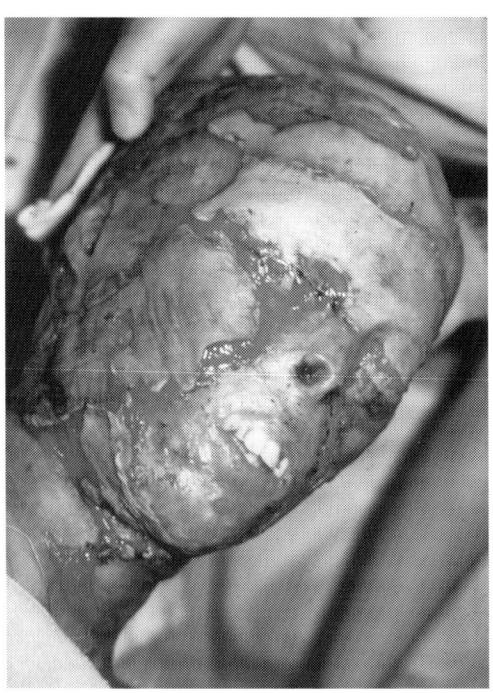

Operating room photo showing skin allograft already in place. According to Dr. Cannon's logbook, Charles underwent a total of 24 operations.

ried about the risk of using general anesthesia again. Instead, we tried to get by using as little anesthesia as Charles could stand in the form of local anesthetic or sometimes no anesthetic at all. Consequently, every operation Charles underwent from then on caused our courageous patient considerable pain. I remember one procedure involving the eye in which we could use only numbing drops. We strapped his arms down with sheets and had two nurses lie across his body to keep him still. Although the operation was mercifully short, Charles moaned for well over an hour afterward.

About a month later, after we had repaired Charles' eyes, we turned our attention to releasing the scars around the corners of his mouth. Conceptually, this step was intended to enlarge the surface area of skin covering his face to allow the underlying muscles and nerves to function better so that Charles could open and close his mouth. We did this in stages. Since burn scarring contracts the skin in all directions, we had to incise the scars on both sides of his face, from the corners of his mouth all the way up to his ears (or rather to his ear canal, since both ears had been burned off).

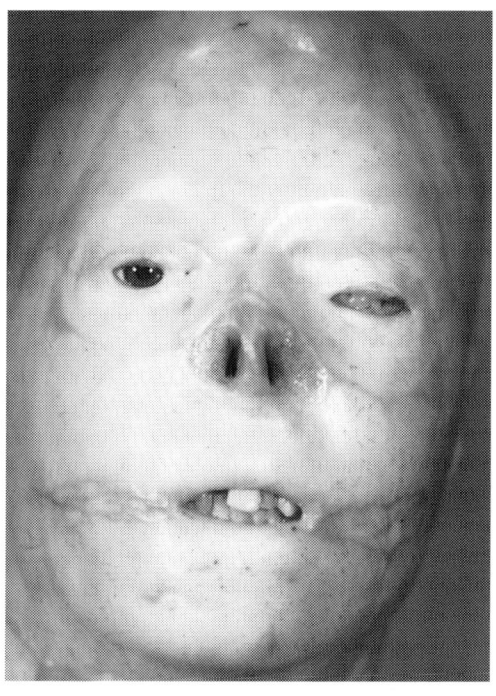

The burned areas are shown covered completely with new pieces of skin. The eyelids have been partially reconstructed to protect the corneas. The nose has not yet been rebuilt, and the mouth is tightly constricted due to loss of a flexible "skin envelope." As part of a multistage procedure to expand the skin envelope, autografted skin has been inserted in the horizontal scarred areas at the sides of the mouth. Various skin autografts form a patchwork of still immature tissue grafts.

Cutting these thick scars was somewhat like cutting an elastic band. Once the cut is made, the freed ends retract, leaving a crater of raw tissue that must be filled in and covered. To achieve this, we obtained multiple pieces of skin from Charles' flank and the hairless parts of his thighs.

The next priority was to create a new nose for Charles. This was done using a rectangular flap of arm tissue, roughly 4 × 7 inches. Unlike the small pieces of healthy skin that could be removed from the unburned areas of Charles' body to cover the burned areas, the flap of tissue from his arm could not be detached immediately, since the tissue required a steady blood supply to remain viable. As we attached the loose end of the arm flap to Charles' face, we had to position the donor arm close to the point of attachment and secure it there until the skin from the flap "took" and started to attract its own blood supply. In Charles' case, this process took 22 days. Finally, the flap that would become his new nose could be cut free from its anchor on his arm.

After about nine months, Charles' eyes had healed to a point where the bandages could be removed. Understandably, one of the first things Charles asked for was a hand mirror. But despite his several requests, there was a surprising absence of compact mirrors in the nurses' pocketbooks. Finally, he dragged himself to the bathroom mirror. As a surgeon, I was able to look at the misshapen mass that was then Charles' face and envision what I knew it could be. But Charles did not have the training to perceive it that way. What he saw must have alarmed him— an uneven patchwork of skin, a tiny hole of a mouth, and a mound of flesh for a nose that looked like a three-year-old child's first attempt at molding clay. Whatever Charles thought, he said nothing. Instead, he just dragged himself back to his bed, curled up, and went to sleep. It was a sensible response, for he would need all the rest he could manage to make it through the months-long reconstruction process.

Using our now standard operating routine, the four of us continued to work as a team. While either Dr. Cannon or Dr. Brown fashioned Charles' nose, Andy and I began reconstructing what was left of his hands. He had lost the tips of all his fingers and both thumbs. It was during these operations that I learned the difference between fine and gross surgical reconstructive maneuvers. Knowing when to use one or the other was an important judgment call. In Charles' case, Dr. Brown's instructions were clear: "Just try to release all of those bones and tendons that are entrapped and create as much raw surface as you can. Give as much motion as possible." So Andy and I would cut away through layers of scar tissue that was devoid of identifiable normal anatomic structures. We did our best to create finger-like structures from the bones and muscles of the palms of the hands and then covered all the exposed surfaces with skin taken from wherever we could find an intact donor site.

"I knew that I wouldn't be able to eat for a week after each of those operations," Charles remembers. Determined not to become addicted to drugs, he gritted his teeth through the pain. A typical course of morphine administered at our hospital was one shot every 4 hours, for a total of 6 shots per day. Charles prides himself on never having had more than four shots per day throughout his entire stay at Valley Forge.

Charles Goes Home

After 24 operations and a year and a half spent at the hospital, Charles was pronounced "healed." He had eyelids to protect his eyes, could eat, and was able to use his hands for most functions. Charles' recovery was made possible by a combination of many things. Good medical care, to be sure, but equally important was the efficiency of the military transport system in getting him halfway around the world, and the good sense of those in charge to assign him to a hospital equipped and prepared to care for him. In Charles' case, these logistics of patient management were critical to his survival. Overriding all of this, however, was Charles' determination to live, and his strong faith in God.

Charles returned to Alabama and became a successful businessman. Recognizing the need for homes for returning veterans, he parlayed a small loan and his building know-how into a thriving construction business. He later recognized the importance of the then new medium of television and saved enough money to buy a television station. To this he soon added another, until he owned more than a dozen stations throughout an area that stretched from the mid-South to the West Coast.

In a way, Charles' story has come full circle. He is now involved with setting up a system whereby the latest medical information and technology will be available worldwide 24 hours a day via three uplinks: one in San Diego, California; one in Charlottesville, Virginia; and a third in San Tau, China, where Charles was honored 50 years later by the Chinese government for his efforts on their behalf during World War II.

Over the years, I have seen Charles more or less regularly. He would on occasion return to the Boston Veterans Hospital, where Dr. Cannon and I would make small improvements in some of his scars and enhance the function of his eyelids, mouth, and hands. As plastic surgery techniques advanced, we offered to refine his appearance, but Charles didn't feel it was necessary. With characteristic good humor, he remarked, "Oh, they could put me in some eyebrows, and they could make me some ears, and they could give me some lips that work better. But I'm so used to myself it's not worth the trouble now." Today, when asked whether he would like his original face back, Charles responds with an emphatic "NO!" He contends that he has learned much and benefited greatly from his ordeal.

Charles continues to have an impact on medical knowledge. In 1989, Dr. Cannon and I invited him to give a talk to the first- and second-year Harvard Medical School students. He began his speech by telling them they were among the most fortunate persons on earth, with a tremendous future before them. As he retold his dramatic World War II story, he was not in the least bit heroic, stressing instead the need to keep one's head in time of crisis. (As impressive as his many military medals are, Charles told me recently that they didn't mean much at the time they were awarded: "We didn't pay much attention to the decorations back then. They'd send you a certain medal for so many missions or something like that, and you'd stick it in your baggage and wouldn't hardly give it a thought because almost never did you see anybody wearing a medal overseas. You wore your wings and your rank and that was it.") His story had quite an effect on the open-mouthed students. Here was a 67-year-old man who, though severely disfigured, had obviously been successful in both business and his personal life, an ebullient optimist who unabashedly relied on God for everyday guidance.

A recent photo of Charles, in all his glory.

Charles has never considered his appearance a handicap. As a matter of fact, he points out that it has proved useful in at least one respect—no one ever forgets meeting him. "They always know me at the bank," he jokes. Sometimes his competitors assume that he's not very bright, which has given him a certain advantage. According to Charles, one of his greatest satisfactions was realizing that his competitors had tried to cheat him and were thus treating him as an equal.

When Charles asked one of his young sons what his friends at school thought of their father, he steeled himself for what he expected to be unkind words. But they never came. "They think you're magic, Daddy," his son said to him. And reflecting back upon his incredible recovery, I realize that some part of that statement must be true.

The Impact of Charles Woods on My Life

As with any discipline, surgery is always building on lessons learned in the past. All the surgical procedures that we performed on Charles Woods previously had been pioneered by others—in some cases, centuries earlier. For example, when we used a flap of tissue from Charles' arm to rebuild his nose, we were using an established reconstructive technique first described by Tagliacozzi in the late 1500s. During that period in Italy, a common form of punishment for crimes such as stealing or adultery was to slice off the offender's nose. Not surprisingly, a group of skilled technicians devised ways to reconstruct the missing appendage.

Although the field of reconstructive surgery was not new, Charles Woods was my introduction to it. At the time, the rebuilding of the face and other external parts of the body to correct deformities was not highly regarded within academic surgery and thus had relatively few practitioners. Most surgeons removed or repaired diseased organs *within* the body. Yet caring for Charles Woods instilled in me a fascination for reconstructive surgery. Charles became the first of hundreds of patients whom I was able to help through reconstructive surgery—people with terrible deformities, either from birth or through some accident later in life.

Charles Woods set the course of my professional life in another way. In caring for Charles, we used skin from a recently deceased person to temporarily cover his burns. Although this was a well-established technique, it was new to me—and it had a lasting impact. Charles was my introduction to the use of tissues from one person to save the life of another. As in Charles' case, the only tissue that had ever been transplanted from one human being to another was skin, and that worked only briefly. In fact, basic scientists were pessimistic about the feasibility of human transplantation. For example, in his book *The Biological Basis of Individuality*, Dr. Leo Loeb categorically stated that transplantation between individual humans would never be possible. Although his thesis was accepted as dogma by some, it did not seem irrefutable to me. Surgeons by nature tend to be optimists.

I began to wonder whether it would ever be feasible to go beyond skin. Would it someday be possible to remove a healthy internal organ from a recently deceased person and transplant it into a person in whom that organ was failing? Might we eventually harvest one of a pair of vital organs, such as a kidney, from a healthy person and transplant it into a person who would otherwise die? The challenge posed by such questions was obvious. The immune system rejects tissue that it recognizes to be foreign, and the transplanted organ would not last. Yet, in the case of Charles Woods, the skin transplanted from another person had surprised us by lasting nearly a month before being rejected.

That was a puzzling observation. I now believe that Charles' weakened physical condition probably depressed his immune system and therefore postponed rejection. At the time, however, I had no idea why the transplanted "foreign" skin had lasted. One thing was clear, though, and the notion kept returning: perhaps the immune response could be controlled! Perhaps there were tricks we could learn that would one day allow us to prevent the rejection of transplanted organs. As I continued to ponder that possibility, my career began to take a new direction.

In his book *The Art of the Soluble*, Sir Peter Medawar, Nobel Laureate and the acknowledged dean of transplantation biology research, stresses the importance of picking the right subject for research. As it turned out, I had picked an appropriate subject. In Boston, Massachusetts, on December 23, 1954—10 years to the day after Charles Woods was enveloped by a ball of fire in Kurmitola, India—our team transplanted the first internal organ, a kidney, from one living human being into another.

Thus, Charles Woods led me to pursue both reconstructive surgery and what has become the field of "transplantation surgery"—the two fields that have been my life's work. I feel blessed to have had a career full of trying to solve puzzling intellectual challenges and of helping patients. Charles is aware of the role that he inadvertently had in the history of

Charles 40 years later, completely healed, talking with Harvard Medical School students. His hands had been made sufficiently functional to allow him to return to flying, which he only recently gave up at the age of 70.

human organ transplantation and even now, whenever he hears of a successful transplant, he feels a certain satisfaction: "I feel I had a small part in it, just by laying still on that table and letting Dr. Murray cut on me."

I am pleased to have been able to help my patients, but so often my patients have given me much more than I have given them. Such was the case with Charles Woods. First, he taught all of us who cared for him how a will to live can overcome enormous odds. There is no scientific explanation for his nearly miraculous survival, and there does not need to be. Second, Charles taught us about physical and emotional courage. For two years, he suffered unimaginable pain. On occasion, he moaned or cried, but he never complained. Charles also taught us about a deeper kind of courage. We reconstructed what we could of his body, to the point where he could function normally—could eat, could talk, could blink his eyes, and use his hands to fly an airplane again—but he still looked like no one you have ever seen. When we were through, Charles looked in the mirror, walked out into the world, and built a life full of accomplishment and happiness.

As remarkable as he is, Charles Woods is not alone. Since caring for him, I have cared for hundreds more like him: people struck down by misfortune, people who make a life for themselves with enormous dignity. This book is not just the story of my life. This book is also about them.

CHAPTER 2

LIFE IN MILFORD

THE MURRAYS AND THE TAFTS

My grandfather, James Murray, was born in Milford, Massachusetts, in 1855. Pa Murray was of South Irish stock. I remember him only as an old man shuffling along with a cane. Dad often said he wished I had known his father before his stroke, when he was young, strong, and vigorous. I thought of Pa Murray often during my recovery from a totally unexpected (and still unexplainable) stroke at the age of 67. Fortunately, unlike Pa Murray, my recovery was rapid and almost complete.

An old map of Milford shows the Murray farm on Silver Hill in the northern end of town, near Hopkinton. As a child I often hiked and sledded there, and I have fond memories of exploring the crumbling one-room schoolhouse Pa Murray had attended as a boy. At the opposite end of town was the Taft family farm. Here, in a modest, unpretentious house filled with love, fun, and laughter, my grandmother, Theresa (Taft) Murray, and Pa Murray had raised seven children. Their fourth child, William A. Murray, was my father. Ma Murray was also born in Milford, in 1859. Her family had come to the United States from Wolverhampton, England, one generation earlier. I remember her as being lean, quick-moving, and always upbeat. In fact, cheerfulness was a quality inherent in all the Murray aunts and uncles.

Because of financial constraints, Dad never went to college, but instead went directly to Boston University Law School after graduating from Milford High School. No matter how often my sister Norma and I would try to reassure him that he was as thoroughly educated as anyone, he always felt the void of having missed that undergraduate experience and would wistfully yearn for the camaraderie and self-assurance of those with more established credentials.

Dad read the classics voraciously. His preferred subjects were travel, inventions, mythology, the classics (novels and orations), Greek and

The Murray family in the mid-1920s. From left to right: Mary Norma Murray; William A. Murray, Jr.; Mary DePasquale Murray (my mother); me; William Andrew Murray (my father). The sailor suit is strangely inappropriate, since 15 years later I was denied entrance to the Navy.

Roman histories, and biographies by the score. His favorites were Washington, Lincoln, and Supreme Court Justice John Marshall—his personal idol. Sunday night was Dad's reading night, and since I was the youngest child I had a chance to spend that time alone with him during my high school years. We had wonderful discussions on as many topics as we had books in our library. For my high school graduation gift, Dad presented me with Marshall's four-volume biography of George Washington, and it remains on my desk to this day.

Like President Harry Truman, Dad more than compensated intellectually for his lack of a college degree. He became a highly educated student of the classics, a wise judge, a conscientious public servant, and a loving father whose guidance and influence on my life have never ended. He and mother were determined to give their children "the best education in the world." Many years later, I felt their presence when I stood at the podium in Stockholm to accept the Nobel Prize in Medicine. In some sense I felt I was fulfilling their dreams.

The DePasquales

My mother's parents were born in Italy. Her father, Antonio DePasquale, came from San Marco, near Foggia, where he served for 3 years in compulsory military service in Garibaldi's Army. Her mother, Maria Vitale, came from Santa Croce del Sannio, near Benevento in the foothills of the Apennines. After 19-year-old Antonio and 17-year-old Maria were married, they boarded a ship headed for America. Assigned to steerage class, they shared close quarters with the cattle for 29 days. Nametags tied around their necks "introduced" them to Antonio's older brothers who were waiting for them at Ellis Island. Thus began my grandparents' life in America.

Antonio and Maria first lived in Providence, Rhode Island, where my mother, Mary, was born on February 27, 1891 (the month and day of Henry Wadsworth Longfellow's birth, as she was always quick to point out). She was the second of six children: three boys and three girls. When Pa DePasquale later joined the large Italian community of workers in the quarries, the family moved to Milford. He was a remarkable entrepreneur, managing a series of disparate enterprises simultaneously: he ran a sand and gravel business about a mile from his house, was a successful undertaker, and operated a soft-drink processing plant on the first floor of their home. The third floor was rented out to another family.

As a child, I was fascinated watching the bottles of orangeade hurtle through the automated machinery. I was allowed to take as many bottles as I wanted, provided I drank them all. I was up to the challenge, though I recall having to make frequent trips behind the garage to relieve my bladder.

Ma DePasquale was quiet, kindly, always busy, and usually dressed in black. The vigil light constantly glowing in her bedroom intrigued me. Although she spoke English well enough, I suspect she was never comfortable using it. Whenever she and my mother conversed, it was in Italian.

My mother, Mary DePasquale Murray, was energetic, bright, and ambitious. One of her special talents was her superb penmanship, which lasted until she died at age 93. At one point, while she was still in high school, her father added an insurance business to his numerous other ventures, and he commandeered her to translate and transcribe the Italian of the insurance applicants into legible, grammatically correct

English. She completed her four-year high school course in three years and received a scholarship to Pembroke (now Brown) University. However, Pa DePasquale must have imperiously ruled the roost, because he would not allow her to accept the scholarship. Instead, he had her commute 12 miles by trolley to Normal School (now Framingham State College). Considering this missed opportunity, it is not surprising that mother enrolled my sister Norma in Wellesley College just days after giving birth to her. Twenty-one years later, Norma graduated from Wellesley with the Class of '37.

After graduating from Normal School, Mother began teaching grade school in Milford, proud to be the first woman of Italian extraction to teach in the public school system there. One of her young pupils was Nicola Sacco, of "Sacco and (Bartolomeo) Vanzetti" fame. These two Italian immigrants were convicted of killing two payroll guards in South Braintree, Massachusetts, in the summer of 1921. The trial, conducted in the nearby Dedham Court House, resulted in the execution of these two men and engendered a controversy over the fairness of the proceedings and questions about their guilt that persist to this day. Years after the event, Mother vehemently challenged the charges brought against her former student, saying that such a well-behaved child could never have grown up to become a murderer!

Mother also taught English to the Italian immigrants enrolled in Milford High Night School. Dad had just started his law practice and, being in need of extra income, applied to be her assistant. He often joked that he ended up being her "assistant for life."

My mother loved politics and was active on both a national and a local level. Although she attended every Democratic National Convention from 1920 through 1976, she declined the nomination for Secretary of State of the Commonwealth of Massachusetts for fear of creating an unnecessary split in the party. For years she served on the Milford School Committee, and she worked vigorously for repeal of the Prohibition (18th) Amendment, driving around town with a "Repeal The 18th" sign attached to her license plate. This was ironic because, except for an occasional glass of wine with meals, she never drank, and Dad was practically a teetotaler. Years later the Massachusetts Legislature passed a special resolution honoring Mother for her contributions to the Commonwealth.

My Beginnings

I was born in Milford in 1919. Life there was simple in the best sense of the word. Mother and Dad always helping the less fortunate and less educated, whether it was showing them how to obtain citizenship or to get credit from the local banks or helping them understand civic regulations. Father would often work for free or would charge only a token fee. My older brother Bill, who joined Dad's law office after graduating from Harvard Law School, was appalled when he would come across Dad's old bills to clients for such paltry sums as $5.25 or $6.50. In spite of this, we never felt threatened financially, because we had always lived frugally. Even during the Depression we were fine; my parents' meager income was constantly being supplemented by persons coming to our door, home-grown food in hand, as payment and gratitude to my parents.

The election of Franklin Delano Roosevelt in 1932 brought a renewed sense of optimism. As they were viewed at the time, Hitler and Mussolini were just two rather comical overseas dictators of no real importance to us. Lindbergh had made the first trans-Atlantic flight in 1927, but flying was so new that the sight of an airplane in the sky warranted comment. Our town had the typical local politics, but the perspective of my fellow students and me was that, regardless of ethnic and religious differences, Milford was a unified and self-contained community.

I attended Milford public schools all the way through high school, as had my father, mother, brother, and sister. All my schools were never more than a pleasant half-mile walk through the town park. I marked the change of seasons as I trudged to and fro, never ceasing to enjoy the brilliant colors of autumn, the crunch of snow and ice in winter, and the shadows of welcome leaves on the path come springtime.

Among my happiest memories are those days spent in spontaneous play outdoors with my friends and classmates. The town park was the common playground for pickup games of football and baseball, though baseball was the king sport. St. Mary's High School was our arch rival, and the Memorial Day game between Milford High and St. Mary's was a big town event, drawing a crush of spectators. In summer, we cooled off with swims at North Pond and Lake Nipmuc and, in direct opposition to our parents' wishes, the quarries. In winter, we played ice hockey on Louisa Lake, Hopedale Pond, or any place that happened to have a good hard surface.

Salutatorian of my high school class and a good all-round athlete, I was an avid reader of all types of books, but I gravitated particularly toward biography and medicine. My favorites were *Arrowsmith* by Sinclair Lewis, *Microbe Hunters* by Paul De Kruif, *Man the Unknown* by Alexis Carrel, *American Doctor's Odyssey* by Victor Heiser, and *Memoirs of a Small-Town Surgeon* by John Brooks Wheeler (Harvard Medical School Class of 1878). Wheeler's book I liked especially. I snatched glimpses of the impressive marble quadrangle of Harvard Medical School on those days when I accompanied my father to his Boston law office and became convinced that Harvard would be the ideal medical school for me.

In preparation, I attended Holy Cross College and graduated with honors in 1940. Dr. Worth Hale, the legendary one-man admission committee at Harvard Medical School, asked during my interview why I had chosen to attend Holy Cross rather than Dartmouth or Harvard, where I had also been accepted. When I explained my desire for a college education with a strong liberal arts component combined with science, he telegraphed his approval with an almost imperceptible nod. I was elated to be accepted into the medical school one week later.

During the spring of my senior year, I recorded some of my private anxieties in a journal:

> I've been thinking about my future. At first, I never thought I'd be successful. I had doubts about being admitted to [medical] school, always figured so many fellows around here were so much better than I. But they were rejected and I was accepted. So I can't be too bad.

Medical school was the beginning of, in the words of my wife Bobby, a very "curious career." She was right. My career has been curious, in many respects. For example, I gave up a successful career as a transplant surgeon in favor of working on craniofacial problems in children. In addition, many coincidences and chance affiliations helped shape my career. But above all, my own curiosity—defined as "careful or anxious to learn; eager for knowledge; given to research or inquiry, habitually inquisitive; prying"—played a key role in my development as a surgeon.

My career has also been blessed. The patients you are about to meet were selected because each one's medical condition provided the opportunity for a specific advance in surgical knowledge or technique. On a more personal level, they were chosen because they enlarged my understanding of my role as a physician. These individuals taught me much, and I am indebted to them as well as to the hundreds of other patients who are not described here but whom I have had the privilege of knowing. In the final analysis, they were responsible for teaching me what it really means to be a doctor.

Chapter 3

Life in Medical School

Inside the Marble Quadrangle

The curriculum at Harvard Medical School was stimulating and satisfying, yet not at all what I had anticipated. I had assumed we would be taught medicine in a linear, lockstep fashion. First we would learn anatomy, pathology, and physiology. To this we would add pharmacology, bacteriology, and preventive medicine. Finally, we would apply all this newfound knowledge to patients in hospitals and outpatient clinics. Naively, I had thought that medicine would be taught as a trade, with a dash of humanity thrown in.

And while I knew that research was a fundamental part of that "trade," I did not expect it to be an important part of my medical career. I would do what was necessary to complete the obligatory research papers, but frankly I was worried about being smart enough to graduate. I did not want to divert any energy or time from my main goal, which was to follow the example set by our beloved family doctor, Dr. Curley, and become "a good doctor."

Imagine my surprise, then, to find myself fascinated with the research my second-year pathology instructor, Valy Menkin, was conducting on inflammation. As I looked at his slides under the microscope I was intrigued to see different types of cells accumulate in one site but not in another. What caused them to act in different ways? This was my first realization that basic research could be so interesting and satisfying. My curiosity was piqued and I was hooked!

The Boylston Society was an organization for Harvard medical students. We would meet monthly to present and discuss papers we had written. During my fourth year of medical school, I entered the following revealing note about my eagerness to pursue new concepts:

November 5, 1943

Working on my Boylston Society paper, I became much encouraged and enthused in reading the books around the library. I love to look up the original articles and to trace ideas through the literature. Reading gives you such great ideas and new approaches to any problems. I want to, some day, read up on old surgical operations for ideas which, although impractical then, now will be useful in conjunction with chemotherapy [then a totally new concept] and other developments. There are so many ideas in them and so much to learn about that the days are too short.

Helped by two of my faculty advisors, Dr. Joe Meigs, a surgeon at the Massachusetts General Hospital, and Dr. Arthur Hertig, a pathologist at the Boston Lying-In Hospital, I selected for my paper the Papanicolaou ("Pap") smear, which was at that time a revolutionary use of cytology—in this case, the microscopic examination of cells gently scraped from the cervix—to permit early detection of uterine cancer. In a very satisfying follow-up to presenting this paper, I was able to introduce this technique to the Peter Bent Brigham Hospital during my surgical internship the following year.

Wartime Students

Medical school changed for everyone on December 7, 1941, the day the Japanese bombed Pearl Harbor. All the medical students across the country were drafted, and our courses were accelerated to get us into military service as quickly as possible. Marching and drilling were added to the core curriculum of classes and clinics.

Those of my fellow classmates who joined the Navy immediately received a commission and an impressive officer's uniform. Since I required glasses for myopia, I had no choice but to join the Army. My status as a medical student did not carry as much weight with this arm of the military. Along with all those who signed up with me, I was given the rank of "Private First Class" (PFC).

We lowly Army privates were quartered in a section of Vanderbilt Hall dormitory on Longwood Avenue that had been converted into barracks. These accommodations were a far cry from Room #204, my former four-bedroom, two-bath suite located in the more luxurious wing of the Hall. Early each morning, before classes, we drilled and marched in the parking lot. Those of our Navy buddies not still lying in bed or eating a leisurely breakfast hooted at us from the windows of their more palatial dwellings.

However, I do not remember harboring any hard feelings about the incongruity of the situation. We were all so immersed in our studies and in the war effort that the differences did not seem important, and medical school life continued to be rich and full. Symphony Hall and the Isabella Stewart Gardner Museum were within walking distance, squash courts were available for daily exercise, and our Sangerfest singing group met weekly. Bicycle trips (automobile travel was limited because of wartime gas rationing), club dances, and evening sails on the Charles River added to the variety. A membership at the Public Sailing Club on the Back Bay Esplanade cost only $5.00 for the entire summer.

Meeting Bobby

Just a few months shy of graduation, I met Virginia "Bobby" Link. Several classmates and I held an entire row of season tickets for the Saturday night concert series of the Boston Symphony Orchestra. On any given night some of us would be there solo and others would be there with dates. We never knew ahead of time just what the makeup of our group would be. One night I happened to sit next to Bobby, the date of my classmate Alphonse (Al) Meyer. Bobby was vibrant and extremely attractive. After maneuvering her to the corridor during intermission I discovered she was a serious music student. I was a frustrated musician then (and still am) and had made a poor attempt at piano lessons at the New England Conservatory of Music during my second year of medical school. My teacher must have needed the money badly to take on such an inept and unprepared pupil.

That night back in my room in Vanderbilt Hall I announced to my roommate that I had met the girl I would marry. Bobby's musical abilities, combined with her other charms, had clinched the deal! Bobby, on the other hand, may not have had similar thoughts. Dressed as I was in my standard Army khakis, I paled next to Al in his fancy gold-braided Naval Ensign uniform.

I ran into Bobby several times that fall at medical school parties and dances. She was often, but not always, with Al. I would make sure to seek her out for talks and touches. I recall a group picnic at Jerry Goldthwait's

The far left of the photo shows Bobby and me sitting back-to-back at a party with the Harvard Medical School singing group. Al Meyer is right in front of Bobby, but I am close by.

home in Medfield when she and I rested against each other's back as we sang and drank beer. It felt so good. And it still does!

An Introduction to Surgery

Although I enjoyed all my medical school courses, surgery was the most thrilling and challenging. We spent our final two years rotating through selected Harvard hospitals, mainly Children's, Massachusetts General, and Peter Bent Brigham. As a fourth-year student I got to care for a wide variety of patients and scrubbed in on surgical operations as much as possible.

It was during an elective month in Pediatric Surgery at Children's Hospital that I observed plastic surgery for the first time. Dr. Donald MacCollum was operating on babies with cleft lips and palates, and Drs. Ladd and Gross operated on deformities of the aorta, heart, intestines, and genitalia. The Brigham was where I took my fourth-year rotation in internal medicine. The newly appointed young Physician-in-Chief, George W. Thorn, ran a stimulating service that emphasized endocrine, cardiac, and renal diseases.

Francis D. Moore (left) and George W. Thorn.

I chose the Massachusetts General Hospital (MGH) for my fourth-year surgery rotation because I planned to seek my surgical internship at the Brigham and thought exposure to surgery at the MGH would be broadening. The Chief Resident in Surgery during my rotation there was a dynamic, skilled, articulate fellow named Francis D. Moore. Prophetically, Drs. Moore and Thorn turned out to be crucial influences on my career for six decades.

Since medical school courses were being accelerated to fulfill the military's need for surgeons, our class completed the usual 4-year curriculum in 3½ years and graduated on December 31, 1943. The class assembled in the Vanderbilt Gym to hear the address by Harvard President James Conant. With the exception of two classmates classified as 4-F (for physical disability), we were all dressed in our service uniforms. The day after graduation I began my surgical internship at the Peter Bent Brigham Hospital.

CHAPTER 4

Surgical Internship

Since it was wartime, the senior surgical staff at the Peter Bent Brigham Hospital had been reduced, because practically all able surgeons, including the Surgeon-in-Chief, Dr. Elliott C. Cutler, were overseas serving on the Harvard Units.[1] This left behind a skeleton staff of older surgeons.[2] The vigorous Chief Surgical Resident, James B. Blodgett (Harvard Medical School Class of '37), carried a particularly heavy load as both outstanding surgeon and teacher.

House Pup

It was January of 1944, and I lived upstairs in the hospital, in a tiny room in an area called "the crow's nest." My dad occasionally dropped by for quick visits and would often give me a check for $10 or $15. I simply added it to the others I had yet to cash. I had no need for money and no time to get to the bank even if I had wanted to. Meals were supplied, and my time was fully occupied. Any free time I did have was late at night, when I could often be found on the squash courts. I thoroughly enjoyed the vigorous exercise, and the anticipation of it motivated me to finish my chores on time.

I loved being a surgical intern. It was a chance to test one's personal judgment, to prioritize daily duties, and to decide when to call for help and when to "go it alone." I found myself living the life of the heroes from my childhood readings. The physician John Brooks Wheeler had written so fondly of his days as a "house pup," and I found myself walking in the same footsteps he described. And I, too, answered to the call of "pup." Like young dogs, we needed training, but our superiors combined both firm discipline and caring to turn us into competent, sympathetic physicians. It was a bit like the spankings my father sometimes gave me. They didn't hurt because I knew he loved me; likewise, the Brigham staff had our future welfare at heart.

A pup's job, as I soon learned, began early—5:30 A.M. being the typical wake-up time. The first chore of the day was to sharpen the hypodermic needles used to draw blood and collect urine specimens from the patients on our service. There were no "IV" nurses back then, so we were forced to master the skill of inserting intravenous needles into even the most intractable veins. Specimens were carried to the clinical lab, which was accessible only via an outdoor corridor known as the "Pike." The outpatient department of the old Peter Bent Brigham Hospital was actually referred to as the "ODD" for "outdoor department." In winter we understood why, as we hugged the inner walls to avoid the blowing snow. Although technicians ran the tests on the specimens, we interns were responsible for the results. It was a matter of pride to get all the findings entered into the patient records before afternoon rounds.

Interns were also responsible for selecting the surgical instruments for the next day's operative schedule. Woe to anyone who failed to include the necessary instruments on the surgical tray! We served as first or second assistants on major cases and, when appropriate, were assigned to act as operating surgeon.

Most general surgical operations at the time were excisional. Not once during my internship did I see a skin graft or any plastic surgical procedure. In fact, at that time, plastic surgery at Harvard Medical School was dismissed as inconsequential and beneath the level of the real "blood and guts" surgeons. I would spend much of my career trying to change that viewpoint.

The Real Challenge: Courting Bobby

We medical students shared an unspoken oath not to move in on friends' dates. But since Al had gone to St. Louis for his internship, the way was clear for me to date Bobby. This was easier said than done. Repeated phone calls to her always yielded the same result: "I'm sorry Joe, I'm busy." I used to make these calls from a phone in the lab, and the constant rejection got to be a running joke with the technicians and nurses there.

But persistence paid off, and finally we hit upon a time we both were free. We double-dated with a fellow intern, Jack Lowery, who had an old Ford. On a snowy Saturday night Jack, his date, and I drove to the Student's Club on the Fenway to pick up Bobby. We made quite an entrance as Jack pulled up to the building, slammed on the brakes, and executed a perfect 360-degree skid. Bobby hopped in and off we went. I was dog-tired and remember only that I drank too many beers.

The second date was similar. Bobby didn't even know my last name until our third or fourth date; she thought it was "Murdock." I may not have known it myself, so anxious was I during those rare free evenings to celebrate my release from hospital chores.

That spring our affection blossomed. It's still a mystery to me how Bobby and I managed to detect each other's inner selves. We'd walk on the Fenway and Esplanade, along the Charles River, and visit the Arnold Arboretum, where we first kissed. Sometimes she would visit me at the hospital. Once while watching me play tennis in the annual MGH-Brigham match, she was embarrassed when Dr. Norbert Wilhelm, the hospital president, asked her if she was Joe Murray's wife.

At that time my future was so uncertain that I never took any steps toward making a permanent commitment. When I put Bobby on the train to Binghamton, New York, where she went to spend the summer at home, I hoped she would be back in Boston come September to resume our friendship. But my time horizon extended no farther than that.

Bobby and I wrote back and forth that summer of 1944, and we began to address issues that we had been hesitant to discuss in person. I remember that in one letter Bobby brought up the subject of our religious differences. We were both beginning to think long-term, even though my future was completely uncertain.

Roadblock to Stepping Stone

That fall, just as I was completing my last month of internship at the Brigham, Bobby returned to Boston to resume her music studies. As it turned out, it was I who would not be in Boston come September. I was crushed to learn that my surgical training would not be extended beyond nine months. Of the six interns, only two—Dave Hume and Phil Walker—were selected to stay for the second nine months. Even though I had worked hard, I was upset to think that my performance had not been good enough. Dr. Orvar Swensen, Jim Blodgett's successor as Chief Resident, sensed my disappointment and called me up to his room one afternoon to reassure me that I had performed superbly, reaching the top in every category. Years later, after the war, I learned that I had been passed over simply because I was not married. Both Phil and Dave were married and each had a newborn child. Like so many apparent setbacks in life, this roadblock proved to be a stepping stone, because my intervening service in the military ended up determining my entire professional career.

As it turned out, Dr. Francis C. Newton, the acting Surgeon-in-Chief, must have made a special note in the file about me, because when Dr. Elliott Cutler returned from overseas in 1945, he wrote me a personal letter promising me a residency position as soon as I was discharged, no matter when that might be. At the time Dr. Cutler was aware that he had advanced prostate cancer, and he felt a real sense of obligation to make sure all his "boys" were taken care of after he passed away. As it turned out, I was not able to take advantage of Dr. Cutler's thoughtfulness. By the time I received his letter, I was "frozen" in the military by direct order of the Surgeon General.

Meeting Bobby's Parents and Making the Commitment

I was not at all looking forward to going into active duty and leaving Bobby, who would be living in a community house in Cambridge with men and women from the U.S., England, and South Africa. If the situation turned threatening, I would not be around to take on the competition.

My first temporary army assignment was to the Newton D. Baker General Hospital in Hagerstown, Maryland. En route, I joined Bobby in New York, to meet her parents. Their farm was about 10 miles out of Binghamton—a beautiful drive over rolling hills. When I arrived, Bobby's mother was baking chocolate pie (now a Murray family favorite) in the kitchen of the farmhouse. That pie smelled great. Bobby always said the reason I married her was because her mom made such a good pie.

I first met Bobby's father, George T. Link, at the Binghamton Club for lunch. We hit it off right away. He had been born in Chicago and came to Binghamton in his mid-teens when his father's business, the Link Organ Company, relocated. This company was the forerunner of Link Aviation Company, founded by him and his brother Edwin A. Link. Edwin invented the Link Trainer, the flight simulator that played a major role in the training of American and British pilots during World War II.

As was by now our custom, Bobby and I did a lot of walking and talking during that brief visit. On one of those walks, on a crystal-clear autumn day in 1944, with the leaves at the peak of their beauty, we found ourselves high on a hill overlooking the Chenango River. As we sat on the hillside and watched a train puffing up the valley in the distance, we decided to get married. How we had the courage, I do not know. Our future was still so uncertain, even though active military duty at least guaranteed me a salary.

My dad was especially concerned about my ability to make a living and support a family. His doubts were understandable. The whole internship/residency program was unclear to him. His only understanding of the way a doctor made a living was through private practice. After all, that was how our beloved family doctor, Dr. Curley, had done it. Dad knew no other role model; for that matter, neither did I.

Bobby and Joe Murray
June 2, 1945

June 2, 1945. Bobby and I were married in St. Christopher's Catholic Church in Hinman's Corner, New York, near Bobby's family farm in Binghamton.

CHAPTER 5

Military Medicine

In the six weeks I spent at Baker General, I had an opportunity to learn the inner workings of an army hospital. This was followed by another six weeks of military medical training at Carlisle Barracks in Pennsylvania. There we learned military organization, regulations, map reading, hiking discipline, and maneuvers. Crawling on my belly with live bullets passing overhead was the closest I ever came (and ever care to come) to physical danger.

Isadore Rosenberg, a classmate of mine at Harvard Medical School, and I drove from Carlisle to Fort Dix, New Jersey, to pick up our permanent assignments. I was understandably nervous. Now that Bobby and I had decided to get married, the thought of leaving her weighed heavily on my mind. While I was standing in line, awaiting my permanent assignment, I could not help but overhear the Sergeant-in-Charge from the Women's Army Corps (WAC) assigning each and every person in front of me to overseas duty. I approached the front of the line with trepidation. Just as I stepped up to the desk, a phone call came in. The WAC answered and said, "Oh yes, I'll see about it." She looked up at me and said an assignment had just opened up at Valley Forge General Hospital in Phoenixville, Pennsylvania. "Would you like it?" she asked me. "Yes," I almost shouted, hardly believing my good fortune.

Valley Forge General Hospital

Valley Forge General Hospital was one of eight regional plastic and reconstructive surgical hospitals in the Zone of the Interior (that is, the Continental U.S.). Plastic surgical and burn centers were being organized around the country, and Valley Forge was known to be one of the best. The Chief of Plastic Surgery was Colonel James Barrett Brown,[3] Chief Consultant in Plastic Surgery for the entire Army Medical Corps. He had served in Britain[4] during the early years of the war but returned to the U.S., realizing that he could be more useful ensuring high-quality care for the wounded. He joined Valley Forge General Hospital in June of 1943.

Lieutenant Bradford Cannon[5] from the Massachusetts General Hospital (MGH) was Assistant Plastic Surgical Chief. Dr. Cannon was a former trainee of Dr. Brown in St. Louis. While working at the MGH, he had worked with Drs. Oliver Cope and Francis Moore caring for the victims of the devastating fire at the Cocoanut Grove nightclub that occurred in Boston on the night of November 28, 1942.[6] More than 400 persons lost their lives in that disaster, but in helping its victims, doctors learned much about burn treatment. The fundamental principles of burn care they established during that fateful period proved invaluable to us at Valley Forge.

Brad Cannon was renowned for his extraordinary accomplishments at MGH. I will never forget the first time I met him. When Wally Reed,[7] second-in-command in anesthesia, brought me to the operating room for the introduction, Dr. Cannon was cordial but understandably preoccupied with the procedure at hand. When a male nurse came in and announced, "Lt. Cannon, the Commanding Officer wants you to attend a Discharge Committee meeting," the esteemed Dr. Cannon responded, "Tell the C.O. to go to hell! I'm operating!" The message was relayed to the C.O. a bit more diplomatically, but it was an unforgettable introduction to this precious man. He and his wife Ellen have been Bobby's and my closest personal friends, mentors, advisors, and confidantes for more than a half century.

Together, Drs. Brown and Cannon ran the most productive and efficient plastic surgical unit that I have ever seen. The right combination of talent, spirit, and courage coalesced at Valley Forge and made a dramatic impression on us surgeons who had the privilege of working there. There was a real sense of camaraderie, which came from the high level of respect we had for our patients and a feeling that we were all working together for a common cause. Surgeons were brought in from across the country to help care for the patients, many of whom came to us directly from the front lines. Because of this, severe cases were the norm.

Hundreds of patients arrived with every conceivable type of injury. The daily operating schedules were chock full of exciting challenges: bone grafts to jaws and skulls; restoration of eyelids, ears, and noses; repair of ulcers and cavities in extremities requiring innovative migration of pedicles of skin and soft tissue from one part of the body to another. (Pedicles are stalks of tissue that remain attached to their original site at one end and are connected to a flap of tissue at the other to provide a blood supply until the flap can be transferred to the injured site.) Occasionally, a patient would be admitted for a purely cosmetic procedure. When that occurred, I enjoyed observing.

In many ways, Valley Forge was a community unto itself. It had its own movie theater, bowling alley, and even a weekly radio broadcast. Anyone who happened to tune in to that broadcast on January 14, 1947, would have heard the interview with Virginia McCall, a volunteer artist who painted plaster casts[8] of the patients' faces and did a series of drawings illustrating the main procedures being carried out. She worked closely with the patients and the doctors and described the contrast between our military hospital and a civilian hospital: "There is no hushed atmosphere. Our long corridors are filled with young men constantly coming and going. There is a good deal of laughter, and the wit and humor are some of the best I have ever heard."

Brad and Ellen Cannon in 1997.

Since so many of the surgeons were about the same age as the patients, there was no doctor/patient barrier; these men were both patients and friends, with a real sense that we were all in this together. Even though many of the men had severe injuries, the overall mood was high-spirited, and the patients never let their high regard for us doctors interfere with their sense of fun.

Many of the patients had been fighter pilots—a breed so entirely apart that membership in that select club seemed to override all else, even nationality. I remember hearing the story of a well-known British "ace" who had been shot down over France by the Germans. His custom-fitted leg prosthesis had been damaged in the plane crash. So impressed were the German captors with the pilot's record that they somehow managed to contact the Allied Air Force who, on a bombing mission from England, air-dropped a replacement prosthesis for the prisoner.

When the pilots on my ward learned I was engaged to Bobby Link, whose uncle, Edwin Link,[9] had invented the Link Trainer and whose father had developed the business, my status was greatly elevated. Once the news got out, I was no longer "Lt. Murray" but rather "Bobby Link's fiancé."

When I first arrived at Valley Forge, I was assigned arbitrarily to the urology service under Major Frank Boland. He was a fine surgeon who graciously advised me that there was no future for me on his service and suggested I try to get onto the plastic surgical service, where "the action" was. It happened that a mild scarlet fever epidemic broke out on the plastic service at that time and threatened to shut it down. They needed someone—any warm body—to act as "Infectious Disease Control Officer," a formal title to describe what was basically scut work. This I knew how to do. Contrary to standard military advice ("Never volunteer for any job"), I stepped up and volunteered for the position.

The duties consisted of taking daily throat cultures and obtaining white cell blood counts on every doctor, nurse, technician, and attendant. Col. Brown thought it all nonsense. It probably was, but even he had to obey orders. Through our brief but daily interaction, he came to know me by face and by name.

Shortly afterward, a new ward had to be opened to care for the increasing census. This additional ward, Ward 19, was located in the back of the hospital, a long way from Wards 3, 4, 5, and 6, where Drs. Brown and Cannon and the senior surgeons worked. When Dr. Cannon asked me if I would be ward officer for Ward 19, I was delighted to be assigned anywhere and thrilled to finally have patients of my own! I was now officially "part of the action."

As ward officer I was responsible for 90 to 100 patients. When new patients arrived from the European, African, or Pacific Theaters, I would review their records, do physical examinations, and suggest treatment. When in doubt, I phoned for advice or took the patient to Dr. Brown or Dr. Cannon for evaluation. At the end of each afternoon, Dr. Cannon integrated the information from all five plastic surgical wards to form the next day's operative schedule. Those schedules were full.

We ran three operating rooms in order to keep up with demand, operating five days a week from 8:00 A.M. to 3:00 P.M. Two operations were performed in each room, so there were six operations taking place simultaneously. By the end of the day, it was typical to have performed 20 to 25 operations. This level of activity required precision teamwork. Each operating room had one separate supply table that was loaded with sterile surgical instruments for both operating teams. At the end of each operation, the used instruments were taken away to be washed and resterilized, then quickly returned to active duty on the supply table. With just 5 to 10 minutes between operations, it was efficiency at its best.

Since Drs. Brown and Cannon were the only experienced plastic surgeons on the service, they rotated from operating table to operating table to supervise neophyte plastic surgeons, such as Andrew M. Moore (Andy), Milton Edgerton (Milt), and myself, as well as general surgeons such as Carl Lischer and Gene Bricker.

Married Life

After our marriage, Bobby and I moved to Pennsylvania. Our first home was in Birchrunville, a little town along the Lancaster Pike surrounded by Amish and Mennonite communities. Because of wartime gas rationing, I would ride the 20 miles into work with one of the technicians from the hospital. Those were happy summer mornings, driving over the rolling hills beyond Kimberton, Pennsylvania, sharing the road with the horse-drawn buggies.

Bobby often joined me in the hospital to help out with patient care, trying to be—as she jokingly puts it now—the "dutiful wife." During the hot summer months, with no air conditioning on the wards, she suffered through the unpleasantness of changing numerous wound dressings, a task made even more unpleasant by the fact that it was early in her first pregnancy and nausea was a frequent accompaniment.

The friendships we formed at Valley Forge were rich and, as it turned out, long-lasting. One of those friends was Andy Moore,[10] another 9-month surgical intern who had graduated from the Barnes Hospital Program at Washington University in St. Louis. I first met him at Carlisle Barracks (we platooned alphabetically). Andy was in charge of the Officers Ward at Valley Forge, and he and his wife Peggy, a lovely Valley Forge nurse, became two of our closest friends. The four of us matured together in both marriage and military medicine.

Many of us were married within a few months of each other, socialized together at the Officers Club, and shared informal meals at each other's homes. The play "Oklahoma" was currently being staged, and we would often break into song (some of us more in tune than others), joining in that familiar refrain, "Oh the cattle are standing like statues." It was the best of worlds—the chance to work with bright individuals during the day, under intense and challenging circumstances, then to relax together in the evenings. Bobby and I have often commented that starting married life in the army under wartime conditions had a stabilizing effect, because it forced us to appreciate every day together. Yet the possibility of overseas service loomed, as colleagues were often shipped out at a moment's notice.

Of course it was at Valley Forge that I met Charles Woods (Chapter 1), was first introduced to the field of plastic surgery, and first began to think about the problem of transplanting tissues from one person to another. It was there that I met a most remarkable group of colleagues: Drs. Brown, Cannon, Moore, and Edgerton (and I), each of whom went on to serve as President of the American Association of Plastic Surgeons, the world's oldest plastic surgical organization, as well as Walter Graham, Benjamin Fowler, Daniel Riordan, Don Eyler, and J. Willam Littler, who ultimately served as presidents of the Society of Hand Surgery. They taught me surgery, they taught me teamwork, and they taught me that there can be no surgery without teamwork. For the rest of our lives we learned from one another and pursued careers filled with challenges and successes. But for me, and perhaps for each of us, the recognition we would receive later in life did not mean as much as the experiences of those early days together at Valley Forge—learning our craft, working as hard as we could to help those injured men, playing and relaxing together, and beginning married life at the same time. As I write this, a lifetime later, the memories of those days remain fresh and vivid.

CHAPTER 6

SURGICAL RESIDENCY

After the victory over Japan was declared on August 15, 1945 ("V-J Day"), the ranks at Valley Forge General Hospital thinned out considerably. Drs. Brown, Cannon, Lischer, and W.B. Davis were released from duty, and even Milt Edgerton, who had arrived at Valley Forge after I did, got to go home. Casualties continued to trickle in, however, so some surgeons were needed to remain on duty to care for them.[11] Since Andy Moore and I had by now extensive plastic surgical experience, the Surgeon-General declared us both "essential" and our status was frozen indefinitely.

Although being promoted to Major was some compensation, I was anxious to return to Boston and resume my "real" life. After all, I had only nine months of internship under my belt, and I needed at least three or four more years of general surgical training before I could even begin to make a living in civilian life. At that time a position in any surgical residency program was difficult to obtain, and there were quite a number of capable young surgeons returning from the war, all of them vying for a relatively small number of appointments.

The Brigham, my hospital of choice, was a particularly coveted spot, and I was concerned that by the time I was released from Valley Forge there would be no position open for me in Boston. I was gratified to receive the letter from Brigadier-General Elliott Cutler, Surgeon-in-Chief at the Brigham, assuring me that there would always be a place for me there whenever I was free to leave Valley Forge. Still, the letter did nothing to alter my situation. It seemed I would never be released from duty. Even though the lifestyle at Valley Forge was pleasant, it represented a holding pattern. I was not advancing my career, and even my father was concerned. From time to time, he would ask, "When are you going to hang out your shingle, Joe?" I had no answer for him.

Dr. Cutler was sympathetic to my plight and anxious to fulfill his promise to me. As his prostate cancer progressed, his pleas to the

Surgeon-General on my behalf became more urgent. Finally, he sent me a letter, saying, "I can't understand it. The Surgeon-General refuses to release you." Although Dr. Cutler died while I was still at Valley Forge, his promise was honored. When I was finally released in November of 1947—more than two years after V-J Day—I was accepted back at the Brigham to complete my surgical residency.

Returning to the Brigham

Being able to return to the Peter Bent Brigham Hospital was worth the wait. The dynamic, caring, and intellectually stimulating environment was everything I had hoped it would be. I cherished the experience, much as I had my earlier experience as an intern, except this time around no one dared call me "pup"!

I was appointed Assistant Resident in Surgery under the new young Surgeon-in-Chief, Dr. Francis D. Moore. At this time, Dr. Moore was starting his monumental lifelong study on "The Metabolic Care of the Surgical Patient," so I became familiar with his research. I also learned much from my contact with his clinical practice, which included patients with burns, breast cancer, and problems related to the gastrointestinal, metabolic, nutritional, and endocrine systems.

The Brigham surgical residency program included a three-month rotation in neurosurgery with Children's Hospital, our neighboring facility. During my rotation, the chief neurosurgical resident became ill. Since the service was short-staffed, I was asked to fill in as temporary Chief Neurosurgery Resident for an additional three months. This extra exposure gave me experience with brain tumors, cerebral vascular problems, and congenital defects that proved useful in my craniofacial work 25 years later (see Part III).

Memorial Hospital, New York City

To round out the Brigham surgical residency program, Dr. Moore arranged for a six-month exchange program with Memorial Hospital in New York City. Connected with the Sloan-Kettering Cancer Institute, Memorial was a major cancer center known for innovative radical surgical resection. Accordingly, it attracted large numbers of cancer patients to its several surgical services. For example, the Head and Neck Service alone performed six to ten major cancer operations daily.

Memorial proved to be an incredible learning environment for me. I participated in as many operations as possible during the six months I was there. At any one time, the wards would be filled with patients who had a variety of cancers of the head and neck, such as tumors of the lip, tongue, palate, jaws, tonsil, pharynx, larynx, and thyroid. Since some cancers grow rapidly and others grow slowly, it was not uncommon for identical treatments to produce varying results. Even those cancers that looked the same under the microscope behaved differently, depending on their anatomical site.

Knowledge of these differences dictated how I carried out the physical examination. With sensitive, almost "seeing" fingertips, I was able to distinguish between metastatic lymph nodes and the adjacent nerves and muscles. Tumor classification became second nature, and each cancer became as individual as the patient afflicted with it.

Surgery at Memorial was "modified assembly-line" style, with emphasis on quantity and technical skill. Patient examinations were carried out in outpatient clinics or private offices. The surgical residents had little say in decisions about the actual surgery, but they operated daily, either independently or with a senior staff member present in the operating room.

The famed Dr. Hayes Martin, Chief of the Head and Neck Service, presided over the weekly conferences with dignity and respect. He was a kindly, soft-spoken, tall, gray-haired man from the Midwest. Although an early enthusiast of the use of x-ray therapy, Dr. Martin later became discouraged by the relatively poor results. But with the advent of antibiotics, controlled anesthesia, and improved nutritional and fluid support, radical surgical excision had become safer, and he embraced it with almost missionary zeal as the best way to treat head and neck cancer.

As Dr. Martin and his cadre of five or six superb general surgeons performed surgical resections, I stood silently by watching them treat gaping postoperative wounds with only the simplest of surgical methods and dressings. Some patients were sent back to the wards unable to swallow, talk, or keep from drooling. Like most major hospitals of the time, Memorial's policy was to delay reconstructive surgery for at least one year to be sure the cancer had not recurred. To consider surgical reconstruction immediately following resection was akin to heresy.

My time on Dr. Martin's service was an epiphany. I soaked up every possible pearl of information and under his guidance received some of the best instruction of my career. However, though I respected him completely, I could never endorse his strict policy of delayed reconstruction. Why perform an operation intended to cure yet not reconstruct, especially since the operative site was right under your eyes, almost crying out for repair? I knew from my days at Valley Forge that a planned reconstruction could be done in a relatively short time with little added risk.

In Dr. Martin's defense, neither he nor his staff had any experience in basic reconstructive surgery. Many had just returned from the service, and the lessons learned during the wartime plastic surgical experience had yet to percolate into the civilian surgical world. Although the surgeons at Johns Hopkins *did* support the concept of immediate repair, their opinion was not shared.

The general reluctance to reconstruct was understandable. Most cancer surgeons at the time were general surgeons. They had a deservedly low regard for plastic surgeons, who usually performed simple cosmetic surgery rather than major reconstructive surgery (such as we had performed on Charles Woods [Chapter 1]). Furthermore, some plastic surgeons used inferior surgical techniques, which then required repeat procedures. In short, plastic surgery did not have a good reputation.

Over the years my surgical mentors, Dr. Bradford Cannon and Dr. Francis D. Moore, taught me not to be impatient or outspoken. As a young, inexperienced surgical resident visiting New York from "Hahvahd," on the lowest step of the residency hierarchy, I intuitively guarded my tongue in the operating room and in conferences. If asked, I would suggest treatment options, but I realized that to interject my opinions would have been presumptuous and might have needlessly antagonized the staff.

So I kept quiet. But every evening I'd go up to my small room on the upper floors of the hospital and spill forth into my diary all the thoughts I had held back during the day. Bobby and the two children were staying in Florida with her parents, so I had unlimited, uninterrupted time in the evenings to reflect upon the day's events. My room faced south overlooking midtown and lower Manhattan, and as I sat writing, I would watch the twilight turn to night and the lights of the city spread out before me—a beautiful sight, conducive to quiet reflection. I would write detailed notes about the operations and conferences of that day. By the end of the evening I would have the steps of each operation "down cold." If I didn't, I knew I could use some time the next day to clarify any confusing stages of the procedure.

When I finished my writing, I would on occasion visit the patients recovering on the wards to check for possible complications or complaints. Though I was unaware of it at the time, those quiet, contemplative evenings laid the foundation for the deep-seated satisfaction I would have over the years in the care of patients with head and neck cancer.

The New York Hospital

I finished my rotation at Memorial on June 30, 1950, then returned to the Brigham to complete the final four months of my residency in general surgery. By then I knew I was going to be a career plastic surgeon. I had passed my certification for the American Board of Surgery, but the American Board of Plastic Surgery decided that, in spite of my wide experience in military plastic surgery, I still needed an additional year of civilian plastic surgery to meet their requirements for certification. Brad Cannon was able to obtain for me another six-month residency, this time with Dr. Herb Conway,[12] a plastic surgeon who was establishing himself at New York Hospital. The remaining six months of the plastic surgery requirement I could fulfill working in Boston as Brad's "preceptee" in plastic surgery.

New York Hospital was located at East 68th Street, directly across York Avenue from Memorial Hospital. Thus, just a few months after I'd left New York, I went back to the same area to begin yet another residency. My sister Norma and her husband, Tom Ervin, also lived in New York, and we saw them regularly. These were formative years in the new television industry, and Tom had just been made head of the legal department and executive vice-president at RCA-NBC—a position he would hold for 25 years. It was good to have family in New York, but it wasn't enough. I couldn't bear another six months away from Bobby and the children. By now we had two daughters, Ginny and Meg, and were expecting our third child. Through the help of a college classmate, we were able to obtain an apartment in Mount Vernon, only 10 minutes away from New York Hospital.

For the first time Bobby and I detected a glimmer of our future family lifestyle. Ginny and Meg were lovable and full of fun; they accompanied me each morning across the field to the railroad station. Work and family were thus reunited.

CHAPTER 7

VIRGIL ALBASI
Civilian Benefits from Military Surgery

> *Procedure*: Intraoral cancer excision with immediate reconstruction
> *Date of Procedure:* February 21, 1951
> *Institution:* New York Hospital, New York City, New York

The word "cancer" is always frightening, and this was especially so 45 years ago, when effective surgery, chemotherapy, and individualized x-ray therapy were in their infancy. Cancer does not define a circumscribed or homogeneous entity; it is merely a general term to describe the uncontrolled growth of cells from any organ of the body.

Cancers vary widely in their biological activity, from the innocuous basal cell skin cancer to rapidly growing lethal cancers that may occur anywhere. In the head and neck area, some cancers in the nasopharynx are detected only by their spread to a lymph node in the neck. The behavior of cancer cells can vary even when they involve the same type of gland. For example, some thyroid gland cancers are relatively innocuous, whereas others are lethal within months. For all cancers, however, the unfortunate common denominator is that they show no concern for the well-being of the patient. They just want to grow and grow, nibbling away at the healthy tissues of the host. The presence or absence of cancer beyond its site of origin, or the presence of distant spread (metastases), is a critical factor in deciding how much tissue to resect and what to leave behind.

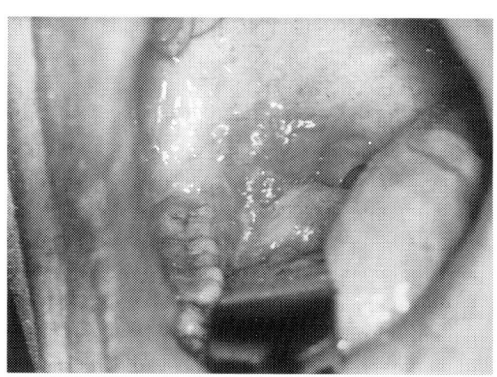 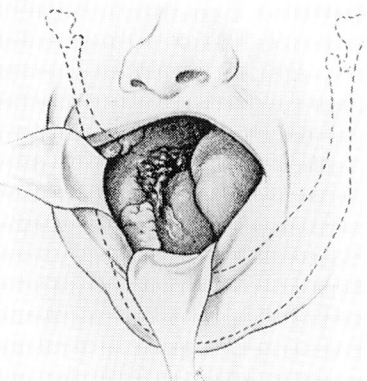

Mr. Albasi's cheek and lower lip have been retracted to reveal cancer that has spread from behind the lower molars to the floor of the mouth and onto the tongue. The sketch shows more clearly the location of the cancer.

Meeting Virgil Albasi

When Mr. Albasi walked into the outpatient dental clinic of the New York Hospital on a snowy day in February 1951, he unknowingly offered me the opportunity to combine the experiences I gained doing military surgery with my training in the treatment of cancer. A sturdy, rugged 69-year-old man of Italian extraction, Mr. Albasi reminded me of my maternal grandfather, "Pa DePasquale." His chief complaint was painful swallowing and soreness in the back of his mouth.

Examination of the area revealed an ulcerated mass, 5 by 7 centimeters in diameter, that extended from his right tonsil onto the tongue and floor of his mouth and was attached to the underlying lower jawbone. I detected no masses in either side of his neck—a favorable sign, since this type of cancer most often spreads to the lymph nodes in the neck. We removed a piece of tissue under local anesthesia and, as we suspected, microscopic examination (biopsy) confirmed that it was indeed squamous cell carcinoma.

Cancers like Mr. Albasi's are called "primary" because they originated in the site where they are first detected. When they do spread, it is usually by invading adjacent structures in a predictable pattern. The first level of invasion often involves nearby lymph nodes, which act like sinkholes, trapping circulating cancer cells and bacteria to prevent their rapid spread to the rest of the body. Only rarely do squamous cell cancers of the head and neck metastasize to distant organs such as the lung or liver. If the primary cancer is not completely removed surgically (excised), it can spread and ultimately cause death as a result of infection, nutritional deficiencies, or bleeding. Since Mr. Albasi's cancer had not spread, his was an ideal case for demonstrating how an adequate excision could be followed by immediate reconstruction.

A Chance to Prove Myself

Although I had held the post of Chief Surgical Resident in Plastic Surgery at New York Hospital for less than two months, Dr. Conway gave me total responsibility to plan and perform the operation on Mr. Albasi. Dr. Conway knew of my Valley Forge and Memorial Hospital experiences and had often observed me operating. He also approved of my care of patients and respected my judgment. I in turn welcomed his confidence. This was my chance to combine the best techniques in both cancer surgery and facial reconstruction and to demonstrate what I had seen and done so often at Valley Forge.

Two options existed for Mr. Albasi's treatment: surgery or x-ray therapy. (It was the early 1950s, and the use of chemotherapy was just beginning to be tested in patients with lymphoma and leukemia.) The course of action was up to me. Should we aim for cure or settle for palliative care only? Could we keep Mr. Albasi comfortable if his cancer recurred? Would a radical excisional operation, even if curative, leave him a "facial cripple," drooling and having difficulty swallowing and speaking? Such radical treatments are almost oxymorons, since the so-called "cured" patients often end up as homebound recluses.

Balancing all these factors, I concluded that wide surgical resection of the primary tumor with simultaneous reconstruction of the jawbone would give Mr. Albasi the best chance for cure along with optimal function and appearance. Because of the large size and location of the primary tumor, we decided to remove the lymph nodes in the right side of his neck, even though they were not enlarged on palpation, because of the chance that undetected malignant cells might have spread to these nodes. Since this operation would be a first of its type for New York Hospital, I wanted it to go smoothly, with no complications or surprises. I therefore spent considerable time with the surgical team preparing for the operation, reviewing each stage, and highlighting areas of potential difficulty.

As plans were completed and the scheduled day of the operation neared, Dr. Conway asked if I could postpone the procedure for a few days. Although he wished to observe the operation, he would be out of the hospital that day. But I firmly refused. Everything had been carefully planned, and the patient's family had been alerted to the potential hazards and complications as well as the chance of failure. Mr. Albasi was ready, and so was I. Although Dr. Conway was an imperious, intimidating man, unaccustomed to hearing the word "no"—certainly not from a brash young resident—to his credit, he acceded and gave me the freedom to go ahead on my own.

Make Way for the Anesthetist

During an operation for cancer of the mouth, the logistics can be awkward because both the surgeon and the anesthetist compete for space in the constricted area of the mouth and nose. The anesthetist needs access to the patient's airway, while the surgeon needs freedom of motion and unobstructed vision. Because these requirements are equally important, the operating room must be set up to accommodate both operators. As might be imagined, this can result in a bit of juggling and jostling for position.

Thorough preoperative planning is key to minimize fatigue and ensure that all members of the operating team have the space and equipment they need. On the day of Mr. Albasi's surgery, I arrived in the operating room early to check the details. I positioned the overhead and side lights, adjusted the sitting stool to the right height, and rotated the operating table 180 degrees to position the patient's head away from the bulky mechanical equipment below. This unconventional arrangement troubles anesthetists, who wish to have complete control when it comes to positioning the patient. Although I understood their point of view, as the surgeon I needed to be able to adjust to the changing circumstances of such a complex operation without constantly bumping my knees against the metal wheels and handles that protruded from the controls beneath the table.

Over the years, as anesthetists and I each argued for our preferred set-up, negotiations could become heated. On more than one occasion, I was known to suggest that perhaps the anesthetist would be happier working out in the corridor. Fortunately, improvements in operating room equipment (and my temperament), along with better means of anesthetic control, have eliminated such conflicts. Back then, however, each operation had to be planned carefully so that logistical problems would not jeopardize proper care.

Now, with my active surgical career behind me, I recall with gratitude the men and women anesthesiologists with whom I have worked over the years. Today, when we get together, we still chide each other and chuckle over our personal idiosyncrasies. Some operations, especially those in their innovative stages (Chapters 7 and 9), lasted for 14 to 16 hours, yet I cannot recall a single complaint being made by any member of the anesthesia team.[13]

A FIRST-RATE OPERATION

Mr. Albasi's operation began with the creation of an opening in the trachea (tracheotomy), performed under local anesthesia, followed by general anesthesia via the tracheotomy tube that was inserted through his mouth and down into the lung. To gain access to the cancer, I exposed the entire neck area with a sequence of long, gently curving incisions. The *en bloc*, or solid block, excision was started as far from the primary cancer as possible to encompass the greatest number of lymph nodes within

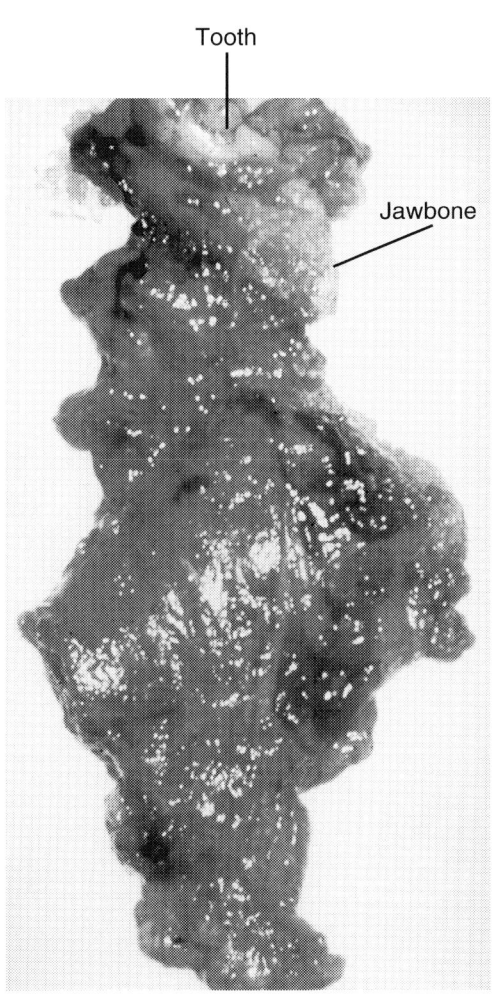

The excised en bloc specimen, which includes the cancer, part of the tongue, and part of the right jawbone with several teeth still in place. The lymph nodes and muscles of the neck, from the ear to the clavicle, are attached.

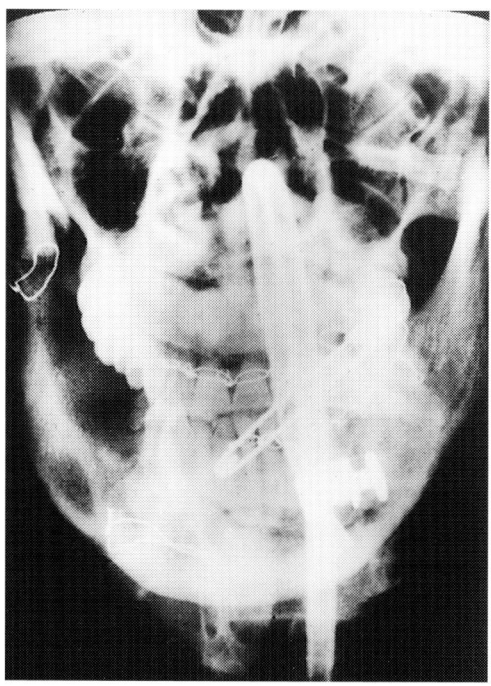

Postoperative x-ray (frontal view) showing where the hip bone graft was used to replace the surgically created gap in the right jawbone. Wire sutures hold the bone graft in place. At the end of the operation, a rubber feeding tube was secured with a safety pin and metal clamp.

the specimen. Once this mass of lymph nodes was detached from the underlying muscles and nerves but still attached to the jaw, the lower lip was incised from the midline down to the point of his chin, thus connecting the lip and upper neck incisions. The lower lip was now free to be hinged back on itself like a page in a book, exposing all the intraoral structures on the right side.

The primary site of the cancer could now be clearly seen and was easily excised. I cut completely around the tumor and then transsected that part of the jawbone directly beneath the tumor mass, allowing the primary tumor, regional lymph nodes, and underlying jawbone to be removed as a unit. This "excisional" phase of the operation took about three hours. Mr. Albasi's condition continued to be excellent, so everything was in place for a tidy reconstruction.

We had removed no skin during the operation but had excised a goodly portion of his tongue, cheek lining, and floor of the mouth. To replace the lining, we mobilized flaps of adjacent tissues and migrated them into position. The two cut ends of the jawbone were then smoothed off, and loops of stainless-steel wire were inserted into holes drilled at each end for later use.

Meanwhile, another surgical team obtained a 10-centimeter segment from Mr. Albasi's hip bone to replace the segment of jaw that had been removed. The iliac crest of the hip bone serves as a reliable pinch-hitter for all sorts of surgical reconstruction, especially for the face and

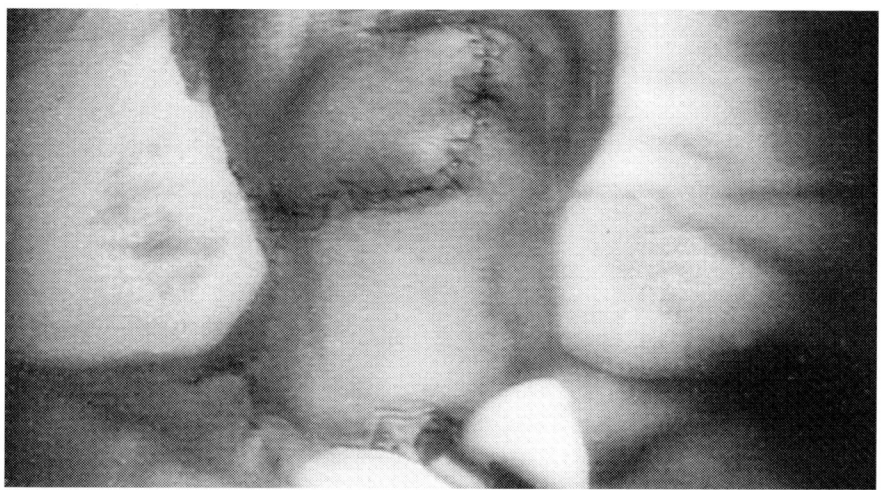

At the completion of Mr. Albasi's operation, the three incisions that allowed access to the tumor and reconstructive sites are visible. Anesthesia was administered via a hole in the trachea.

skull. The hip donor site regenerates within a few months, and the bone graft can become solid in six weeks.

Holes were also drilled in each end of the bone graft, so the wires previously inserted in the cut ends of the jawbone could be passed through them, firmly securing the graft into the 10-cm gap. Next, we brought together (occluded) the upper and lower teeth and fixed them in this position with wires. This type of surgery might be considered "carpentry" at its finest. Mr. Albasi had a particularly healthy set of teeth, and I noted with satisfaction when we finished that his upper and lower teeth meshed perfectly.

Mr. Albasi left the hospital after a couple of weeks and returned six weeks later to have the dental wires removed. He was able to chew, eat, swallow, and speak without undue difficulty. I received Christmas cards from him every year until his death some 21 years later at the age of 90.

The success of this operation reflected well on our team but also on Dr. Conway. I presented Mr. Albasi's case at surgical grand rounds, following the presentation of a gastrointestinal operation by the chief resident in general surgery. Although the two cases were similar in magnitude, the surgical chief resident had been assisted by a member of the senior staff. After my presentation, Dr. Conway was quick to point out that his resident had been able to plan and perform the entire operation independently.

A Second-place Showing

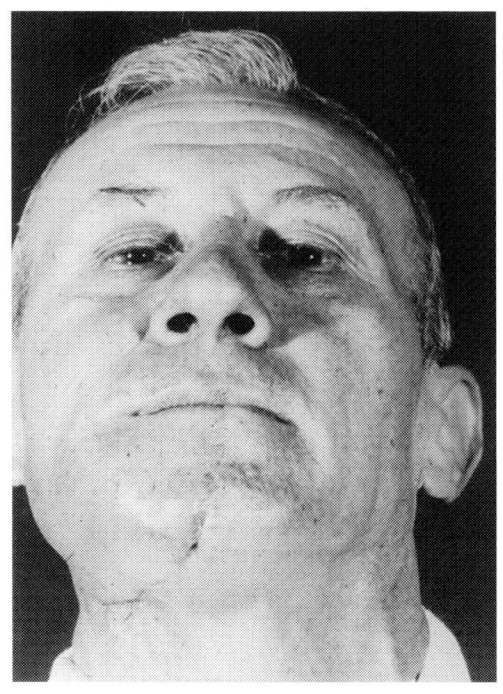

Mr. Albasi six months after his operation.

When Dr. Conway and I published Mr. Albasi's case, along with several others, in the journal *Cancer*,[14] those familiar with the situation were amused to see Dr. Conway's name listed as first author. This convention never bothered me, since getting the information published was more important than top-billing. I was grateful to Dr. Conway for giving me the opportunity to perform the operation "solo," and it was a privilege for me to be his coauthor.

The operation on Mr. Albasi represented a significant milepost in my surgical career. During the bone grafting portion of the operation, I had sensed the disapproving spirit of Dr. Hayes Martin, just across the street at Memorial Hospital, hovering over my shoulder. Nevertheless, my experience at Valley Forge had convinced me that my approach to Mr. Albasi was the correct one. The total success of the procedure gave me confidence that I was a capable surgeon in terms of technique and skill in planning both the operation and the patient's postoperative care. More importantly, it demonstrated a new method of treatment that was of enormous benefit to the patient and became the prototype for the subsequent care of those with head and neck cancer. Dr. Martin must have come around to my way of thinking, for it was he who asked me a few years later to become a founding member of the Head & Neck Society, of which he was the first president.

CHAPTER 8

Private Practice and Research Activities

On July 1, 1951, I finally started a private practice in Boston. Dr. Bradford Cannon took me on as a clinical associate and gave me space in his office at 330 Dartmouth Street. At that time I was a total unknown in Boston surgical circles; in fact, I had only three private patients in that first year of practice. However, Dr. Cannon kept me busy. I made hospital rounds with him, observed him with his office patients, and scrubbed in his surgical operations, all the while being careful not to usurp the place of the assigned general surgical residents.

Dr. Cannon was the plastic surgical consultant to two Veterans Administration Hospitals: the West Roxbury VA, which treated a large number of patients with spinal cord injury, and the Cushing VA[15] in Framingham, which had been an army plastic surgical hospital during World War II. Dr. Cannon and I attended weekly plastic surgery clinics at these two hospitals and both assisted and taught general surgical residents there.

In addition to these plastic clinics, I attended the weekly tumor clinics at both VA hospitals to begin to establish myself as an excisional and reconstructive surgeon specializing in head and neck cancer. Even though I sat quietly through dozens of presentations, commenting only when it seemed appropriate, I was appalled by the lack of experience and knowledge about these types of cancer. Even the consultants—the supposed "specialists"—were ill-informed. Often the operative resections were poorly planned. Not enough attention was given to achieving optimal surgical exposure, and there was little or no thought of reconstruction. Postoperative complications were frequent. Occasionally, I would express my frustrations privately to Dr. Cannon. But he repeated the advice he had first given me at Valley Forge (and would repeat to me throughout my career): "Keep a low profile and never criticize."

One day, after I had been attending these tumor conferences for several months, I was asked about the best way to treat a patient with an extensive tongue cancer that invaded the jawbone. The case was similar to that of my patient Mr. Albasi at New York Hospital (Chapter 7), so I laid out a straightforward plan for excision with immediate reconstruction. At the end of my comments, the Cushing VA's Chief of Surgery, Dr. Henry Faxon, responded, "Why not give the young fellow a chance to show what he can do?" I was delighted at the opportunity, although I suspected that Dr. Cannon might have privately alerted Dr. Faxon to my frustrations. Using the same treatment plan that had worked so well for Mr. Albasi, I resected the tumor and lymph nodes and used a bone graft to replace the excised portion of the jawbone. The operation was a total success.

When I returned to the Cushing VA Hospital in Framingham a week later, I received a hero's greeting. No one could believe a patient could undergo such an extensive operation and have an uncomplicated recovery. From then on, Dr. Faxon assigned all head and neck cancer cases to my supervision and care, and my specialized practice was launched. Subsequently, when the Cushing Hospital was moved to Boston and was renamed the Boston VA Hospital, I became the head and neck cancer consultant there as well as at the West Roxbury VA Hospital.

Within just a few years, I had acquired hundreds of head and neck cancer patients and began to publish articles describing many of these cases. I also worked with Dr. Cannon at the Crippled Children's Program (now called Services for Handicapped Children), which he had established along with Dr. Varastad Kazanjian, the dentist and later physician.[16] Although Children's Hospital would have been the natural home for this program, Dr. Cannon was not permitted to practice there because he presented too great a threat to Dr. MacCollum, the one-man plastic surgical presence at that hospital. The MGH would have been the next best site, but Dr. Kazanjian was not particularly welcome there either, because he was considered by many to be "just a dentist." Therefore, Mt. Auburn became the hospital of choice, to the benefit of all involved. The generous cooperation among the staff at Mt. Auburn was well suited to Dr. Cannon's multidisciplinary program. Doctors, dentists, nurses, speech therapists, and social workers all worked together—a refreshing contrast to the rather territorial behavior found in some of the larger hospitals. It was at Mt. Auburn that

I had my first experience operating on children with congenital problems involving the face and extremities.

My interest in children had begun when I was a fourth-year medical student under Dr. William E. Ladd at Children's Hospital. I had been impressed as I watched him operate on an infant's imperforate anus; his hands were so big they covered the entire operative field. As I was walking with him one day in the old Hunnewell building, a bright little girl about eight years old came bounding down the stairs and greeted this tall, white-haired rock of a man with a big bear hug. He explained that he had treated her for esophageal atresia (a congenitally blocked esophagus) early in his career. Using skin grafts and pedicles (connecting stalks of tissue) from her chest, he had constructed a substitute passageway. I had marveled then at his skill and imagination; now I realize that he served as a role model for me as a pediatric plastic surgeon.

Being Dr. Cannon's associate did not completely occupy me in my fledgling Boston medical career. Realizing it would take some time for my career to get off the ground, I made a special effort to make myself known at other hospitals, among them Boston City Hospital, Newton-Wellesley, St. Elizabeth's, Framingham Union, and Chelsea Naval Hospital. Thanks to Dr. Francis D. Moore, I had admitting privileges at the Brigham as a general surgeon with a special assignment in plastic surgery. Since the Brigham had no plastic surgery service, there was no patient pool. A one-hour weekly visit from Dr. MacCollum, the plastic surgeon at Children's, was considered sufficient to meet the Brigham's plastic surgery needs.

For a while my talents were not utilized simply because most of the medical and surgical staffs did not understand the full scope of plastic surgery. Dr. Donald Matson was the exception. He had acquired extensive neurosurgical experience during the war and went out of his way to consult with me on combined reconstructive problems. In fact, Don was later instrumental in getting me on the active staff of Children's Hospital.

The Kidney Transplant Program at the Brigham

Dr. George Thorn, the Physician-in-Chief of the Peter Bent Brigham, had established the kidney transplant program in order to study and treat end-stage renal disease. Dr. Thorn's major clinical interests were hypertension, renal and adrenal disease, diabetes, and endocrine and metabolic disease. By this time, he had already developed and used hormonal replacement for adrenal insufficiency. Knowing that high blood pressure was somehow related to or caused by kidney disease, he envisioned the need to develop a functional "artificial kidney" (i.e., renal dialysis) as a temporary substitute for patients in renal failure. In the late 1940s, during grand rounds at the Brigham, I was astounded to hear Dr. Thorn say, "The best way to treat hypertension is to remove both kidneys." The entire audience gasped, but clearly he had planted the seed for a renal transplant program.

In the pursuit of his strong interest in hypertension and renal disease, Dr. Thorn invited Dr. Willem Kolff from the Netherlands to come to the Brigham to demonstrate the dialysis machine he had designed during his forced confinement by the Germans during World War II. When Dr. C.W. Walter, a Brigham staff surgeon with engineering experience, improved one of the couplings on the rotating dialysis drum used by Kolff, the "Kolff-Brigham Kidney" was born. First used at the Brigham in 1948, it set the stage for kidney transplantation itself. When Francis D. Moore became the new Surgeon-in-Chief in 1948, he shared Dr. Thorn's enthusiasm for pursuing the possibility of treating kidney failure with transplantation. With the strong leadership of Drs. Thorn and Moore, the program became totally integrated, with physicians, surgeons, pathologists, radiologists, nurses, and social workers all working cooperatively to make the renal transplant program a success. Hospital administration was equally supportive.

A "Bunch of Fools"?

Once I became a staff member at the Brigham, I wanted to become involved in some aspect of the top-quality research taking place at the Surgical Research Laboratory.[17] True, with the exception of my paper on the Pap smear, written for The Boylston Society when I was a fourth-year medical student, my research background was slim. The fledgling renal transplant program was particularly fascinating and piqued my interest. The biological problem of donor-recipient kidney incompatibility was similar to that of the skin graft incompatibility that had so intrigued me while I was stationed at Valley Forge General Hospital.

My decision to join the renal transplant group hinged in large part on my complete respect and admiration for their work. But there would also be real benefits to studying the biology of rejection in the kidney as opposed to the skin. Rejection of a kidney graft could be detected more accurately by the abrupt cessation of urine than by the gradual dissolution of a piece of transplanted skin. Moreover, connecting the artery, vein, and ureter of a kidney presented a more technical surgical challenge than placing a skin graft.

At that time, the concept of organ transplantation was so revolutionary that it was generally deemed not worth pursuing. At best, it was considered a problem for basic scientists to solve. One of my closest friends, a professor at Harvard Medical School, took me aside and said, "Joe, don't get involved in that. It will never work, and you may ruin your whole future."

The work being done at the Brigham was considered a fringe project, even by many of those who should have known better. When one of our research fellows dared to ask his chief if he could come to Boston to work with us, he was warned about that "bunch of fools down there." This response was not malicious, just short-sighted. Indeed, on theoretical grounds, there were at least four valid concerns that led many knowledgeable scientists and doctors to argue that transplantation was doomed to fail:

First, there was the question of the transplanted organ's blood supply. One cannot remove an organ from a donor animal, or from a human donor, without interrupting its connection to the blood vessels that nourish it. At least for several hours, this organ would be deprived of its circulation until the surgeon could reattach it to the major vessels in the recipient, thereby restoring blood flow through the organ. Would the organ be damaged by this temporary disruption of its blood supply? *No one knew.*

Second, another fluid besides blood flows through the organs. This fluid, called "lymph," flows through its own network of vessels and is responsible for removing cellular wastes. Unlike blood vessels, however, lymphatic vessels in the transplanted organ are not large, like arteries and veins, so they cannot be reconnected to lymphatic vessels in the recipient. Thus, lymph flow could not be reestablished in the donor organ. Would the transplant be able to remain healthy without its lymphatic supply? *No one knew.*

Third, the nerves leading to and from the donor organ would also be severed on its removal. New nerves would not immediately grow from the recipient into the transplanted organ, so its connection to the host's nervous system could not be restored quickly, as would be true for its blood supply. Could the donor organ function properly once it was transplanted without such innervation? *No one knew.*

Finally, there was the problem of rejection. The threat to survival of the donor organ posed by the host's immune response to this foreign "invader" loomed before us as the most difficult problem to overcome. At this time science was only beginning to understand the concept of immunity and how the immune system might attack the foreign organ.

Thus, it was not surprising that well-informed and experienced members of our profession regarded any attempt at organ transplantation as a "fool's errand." Still, theories about how to overcome these potential risks can be tested. The question was whether it was worth trying. We believed that it was.

Despite the fact that many bench scientists (meaning those who work in the laboratory and have no contact with patients) considered our decision to test our belief in transplantation was folly, we decided to persevere in our efforts for what we considered good reasons. We were doctors faced with desperately ill, dying patients for whom there was no other recourse. The technique of kidney dialysis was still in its earliest stages. In fact, it could be effective for only short periods of time, to help people through periods of temporary kidney failure. The technique of chronic kidney dialysis, developed a few years later by Dr. Belding Scribner at the University of Washington, in Seattle, was at that time unknown. Thus, it was nearly a certainty that these patients would die. We felt we had to try transplantation. Extensively burned patients required skin allografts (Chapter 1); patients with end-stage renal disease required either dialysis or new kidneys. It was as simple as that.

So I remained undaunted by the disparaging remarks made about our transplant group and eagerly joined George W. Thorn, Physician-in-Chief, and Francis D. Moore, Surgeon-in-Chief—the leaders of the so-called "bunch of fools" who made up the Brigham renal transplantation team.

Perfecting the Surgical Technique

Although our team was eager to test the viability of human transplantation, we *would* have been foolish if we simply removed a kidney from a healthy person and implanted it into another person who was dying of kidney failure without thinking through how to overcome the obvious obstacles to success. The problem had to be approached systematically and—as is often the case in medical science—required experiments involving animal models first.

We started by transplanting kidneys between dogs. Dogs (even "pure" breeds of dogs) are as genetically diverse from one another as human beings are; hence, we knew the problem of immune rejection would also occur in dogs. However, by using dogs we could at least test the surgical techniques that we would ultimately need to use in humans, such as the effect on the donor organ of severing its nerves and blood and lymph vessels after its removal from the host.

The first member of the Department of Internal Medicine to be assigned to work on the transplantation program was Dr. John Merrill, as head of Nephrology. At first, Dr. Merrill was not enthusiastic about his assignment. He was uncertain about its success, afraid that it would prove to be a waste of time. But it was very hard to say "No" to Dr. Thorn.

The first surgeon to participate in the kidney transplant program was Dr. David M. Hume,[18] a vigorous and talented physician. Since medical school, Dave had been keenly interested in the relationship between two adjacent parts of the brain, the hypothalamus and the pituitary, which serve as master glands for endocrine function. When I joined the Brigham transplant program, he was only too happy to transfer responsibility for the animal kidney transplants to me, although he wished to remain in charge of the patient transplants. It wasn't until he was called to serve in the Korean War that I assumed responsibility for both the animal and human programs.

Our goal with the animal studies was to achieve a standardized, predictable kidney transplant operation in the dog that would be adaptable to humans. First, we had to find the best location for the transplanted kidney. To eliminate the possibility of immunological rejection, we would surgically remove a dog's kidney and then "transplant" it back into a different location in the same dog's body. I tried several different anatomical sites and finally decided that the best one for implanting the donor kidney was low in the abdominal cavity, behind the appendix, between the hip bone and the bladder. In this location the vascular anastomoses, or joining of two blood vessels, could be performed with excellent visualization, and the ureter could be conveniently implanted into the bladder.

These notes from my journal hint at the evolution of my thinking:

10/22/51

Harvard Lab for Surgical Research—abdominal transplant of kidney with Ed Harris. Good techniques of exposure and anastomoses.

11/6/51

Tuesday, 6:00 A.M. Off to the slaughterhouse to investigate sheep kidneys. [I wanted to see if sheep would be better experimental animals.]

4:00 P.M. Explored kidney [in the dog]. Anastomoses in the vein and artery perfect. The kidney must be reversed to allow vein to be posterior and the ureter anterior. Thus the artery becomes inferior. On to the office [at 330 Dartmouth Street].

By the summer of 1954, as a result of these experiments, several animals had survived for years with solitary, life-sustaining renal autografts. These animals behaved normally in every way. Nephrologists sent over from Dr. Merrill's lab, using the most sensitive tests available, could not detect the slightest diminution of kidney function. These animal experiments were critical to the ultimate success of our renal transplant program because I knew with certainty that a transplanted kidney, temporarily deprived of its blood supply and lacking nerves and lymphatics, could, in the absence of an immunological barrier, function normally indefinitely. That was a revelation and most encouraging.

Before he left for Korea, as part of Dr. Thorn's team under Benjamin F. Miller, Dave Hume had actually tried an experiment that provided some basis for optimism. He removed kidneys from recently deceased people (no living, healthy donor was put at risk) and attached them to the vessels of the thighs of nine patients with kidney failure under local anesthesia to minimize risk. Although no one expected this third (thigh) kidney to survive permanently, the hope was that it would serve as a "bridge," providing tempory function until the patient's own kidneys could repair themselves. In one instance, the thigh kidney continued to function for almost six months before the patient died of renal failure. The success in this case was evident in the patient's biochemical

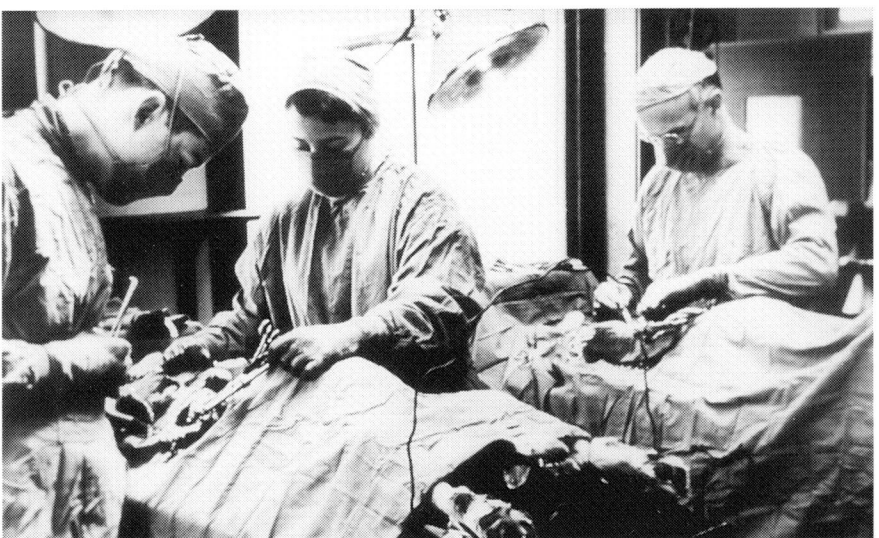

Operating in the lab with Dr. Nathan Couch (left). Assisted by a lab technician (center), he and I (right) are swapping canine kidneys in an experimental protocol designed to study alterations in the donor kidney in dogs.

profile, results of tests that evaluated kidney function by measuring blood levels of natural substances controlled by the kidneys, such as potassium and other minerals. This experience suggested that, at least in some patients, the immune system's rejection of the transplanted organ might not occur immediately, which would buy some time.

Despite these encouraging results, we still felt we had more to learn about how to overcome the problem of immune rejection. Therefore, we could not justify removing donor kidneys from living, healthy human beings. Such a procedure would subject these healthy donors to surgical risk, although the potential recipients, who were dying of end-stage renal failure, and their families might be willing—even eager—to try. Indeed, many candidates for transplantation expressed to us that even if the transplant didn't succeed for them, we might learn something that would help someone else in the future.

Thus, we faced a real dilemma. We had perfected a surgical technique in dogs—a predictable, dependable operation—and believed that it should also work in humans. But without human trials, we could not

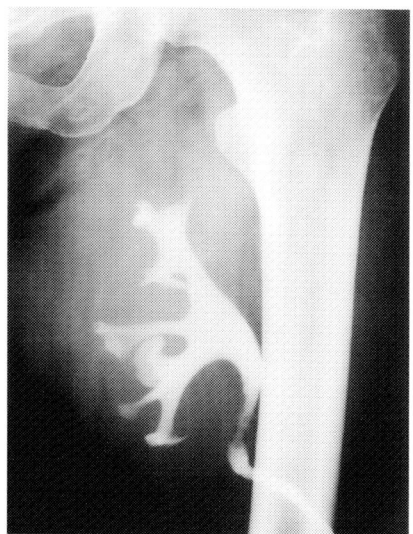 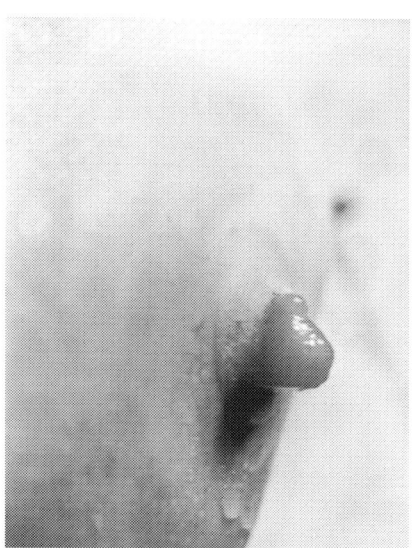

Left panel: X-ray of an allografted human kidney transplanted into the thigh of a 21-year-old man. Urine produced by the kidney normally empties into the bladder (a sac in the lower abdomen), where it is stored. It reaches the bladder through a natural tube called the ureter. Dye (which appears white on this film) has been injected through the ureter and shows the tree-like structure within the kidney.

Right panel: In this patient, however, the ureter has been redirected through the skin and carries the urine out of the kidney and into a plastic bag glued to the patient's thigh.

prove our hypothesis. And we could not conduct such trials until we were sure we could minimize the risk of immune rejection.

By a remarkable stroke of luck, an opportunity to do just that presented itself. Even more remarkably, years later I discovered a somewhat prophetic event in Christian hagiography. In the 4th-century, Saints Cosmas and Damian, twin brothers, transplanted a limb from a black prisoner to a white recipient—an event portrayed in a number of classic paintings. I have examined such paintings in museums and galleries all over the world, and Cosmas and Damian are always depicted as identical twins.

Perhaps the fates long ago envisioned that an understanding of the nature of twinning would shed light on the biology of human transplantation and saw fit to offer us a clue to help solve our dilemma. Because identical twins not only look alike but have body tissues that are genetically identical, an organ transplanted from one identical twin to the other would not be rejected. In 1937, Dr. J. B. Brown had demonstrated that a person could accept a skin graft from his or her identical twin, with no sign of immune rejection. We assumed that this ought to be true of any transplanted organ, not just skin. Thus, if we could find two identical twins, one with kidney failure and one without, we could test our surgical technique without putting the healthy donor twin at unnecessary risk, and chances would be good that the donated kidney would survive in the recipient. Late in 1954, the Herrick twins entered my life.

PART II

ORGAN TRANSPLANTATION

CHAPTER 9

RICHARD AND RONALD HERRICK
First Identical-Twin Kidney Transplant

> *Procedure:* Identical-twin kidney transplant
> *Date of Operation:* December 23, 1954
> *Institution:* Peter Bent Brigham Hospital, Boston, Massachusetts

On October 26, 1954, Richard Herrick was admitted to the Peter Bent Brigham Hospital with a diagnosis of chronic nephritis, a life-threatening inflammation of the kidneys. His physician had referred him as a possible candidate for a renal transplant, using as the donor Richard's genetically identical twin brother Ronald. Our optimism at the prospect of transplanting a kidney from one twin to another was tempered initially by Richard's difficult behavior as a result of his illness. He was disoriented, exhibited psychotic behavior and, in general, made life hard for the attending doctors and staff. The physicians' notes tell the story:

10/27/54

> Since admission patient has been extremely uncooperative. Has knocked over infusions, has been restrained, has been moved to side room because of loud outbursts. Restless, cursing all members of the House Staff.

The nurses fared no better than the physicians:

10/28/54

Rather a difficult p.m. . . . Is extremely uncooperative. Behavior erratic and unpredictable. Bit nurse on hand while bed linen being changed. . . .

Dr. E. M. Kudarduskas, a psychiatrist called in to evaluate Richard, put such behavior into context:

When seen on October 27 and 28th, prior to dialysis, patient showed a varying disorientation as to time, place, and person. Was periodically disorientated. During his excited stages he would pull out his indwelling urethral catheter and would struggle against doctors and nurses, accusing them of attacking him sexually. Impression: toxic psychosis reaction superimposed on a paranoid personality. Offhand, I feel the patient will recover from his psychosis with the use of medications and removal of toxic agents by dialysis.

In spite of these problems, we continued systematically to work our way through all the procedures necessary to ensure the success of the operations. To test the true genetic identity of these twin brothers, we performed 17 formal genetic tests, only one of which—the reciprocal skin grafts—provided indisputable evidence. After four weeks a skin graft from Ronald to Richard showed no sign of rejection.

I even went so far as to arrange for Ronald and Richard to be fingerprinted at the local police station so we could compare the markings. It hadn't occurred to me that news reporters might be hanging around the station in hopes of getting a scoop. Imagine my surprise when, driving home that evening, I heard on the car radio that Brigham doctors were planning a daring operation. The Herricks' fingerprinting made headlines the next day, and the press began requesting daily bulletins from the hospital. With this news leak, the pressure on all of us increased.

Richard's condition was deteriorating, and although we were able to control the symptoms with judicious fluid balance, medications, and dialysis, we knew we were running out of time. His failing kidneys were beginning to cause his heart to fail as well.

Twin's Life May Hang on Fingerprint Today

A fingerprinting at 4 p.m., today at Roxbury Crossing police station may save the life of a 23-year-old Marlboro man seriously ill in Peter Bent Brigham Hospital.

The fingerprinting is to determine whether Ronald Herrick of East Main street, Marlboro, is the identical twin or merely the fraternal twin of Richard Herrick, critically sick with a kidney ailment.

If the fingerprints of Ronald, when they are taken this afternoon, match his brothers, Ronald can, if he desires, donate a kidney that may save Richard's life.

If the fingerprints do not match, it still is not definite that the two boys are only fractional twins. Doctors then will be forced to rely on a skin graft the size of a thumbnail they made from Ronald to Richard five weeks ago.

So far the graft has stuck, which would indicate the twins the kidney from an identical twin will serve to help permanently a patient with nephritis, the disease which Richard is suffering.

At the suggestion of a Peter Bent Brigham physician, The Herald attempted last night to find the doctor who delivered the Herrick twins June 15, 1931.

Both of the Herrick parents are dead.

Dr. John P. Merrill, chief of the Kidney Research Laboratory at Peter Bent Brigham, said last night that a kidney transplant never before has been attempted between identical twins.

He emphasized also that even if Ronald and Richard turn out to be identical twins the operation may not take place. Richard already may be too sick to survive the shock of serious surgery.

Richard, the twin in the hospital, was recently discharged from the Coast Guard. Ronald is a freshman at Worcester State Teachers College. Both live with an uncle and aunt, Mr. and Mrs. Leander Herrick, at the Marlboro address.

Headline appearing in The Boston Herald several days before the kidney transplant operation.

Like many twins, Richard and Ronald were best friends. They spent their childhood together on the family dairy farm in Rutland, Massachusetts. At the outbreak of the Korean War in 1950, each signed up for a different branch of the military service. Ronald was sent to Germany as a soldier in the Army, while Richard joined the Coast Guard and was stationed in the U.S. Their mother had died while the boys were in high school, and their father died while they were in the service. Both were discharged late in 1953, and the two brothers had planned to move to Marlboro, Massachusetts, to live with an aunt and uncle. But while waiting for Richard to join him, Ronald received a letter saying that Richard was being detained at the Marine Hospital in Chicago for care of chronic kidney disease. Their grandfather, a general physician, told Ronald what the disease was and added that there was no known cure. One of their aunt's relatives had also died from nephritis, so the situation seemed hopeless. As Richard's condition grew worse, he was transferred to the Public Health Service Hospital in Brighton, Massachusetts, to be nearer the family.

Richard's death seemed imminent. "We knew he wasn't going to make it," remembers Ronald. Along with their older brother Van and younger sister Virginia, Ronald visited Richard in the hospital almost every day. At one point, Van was particularly distressed by Richard's condition and asked Richard's doctor, Dr. David C. Miller, whether he could donate one of his own kidneys to try to save his brother's life. At first, Dr. Miller told him it was impossible, but then remembered that Ronald and Richard were identical twins. He had heard about the pioneering work going on at the Brigham and immediately called us. With the family's consent, Richard was quickly transferred to our Kidney Research Laboratory. As Ronald remembers,

> I had heard of such things, but it seemed in the realm of science fiction. For the first time, we began to feel the faintest glimmers of hope. My Aunt Virginia, Uncle Lee, Van, Virginia, and I were caught up in the enthusiasm, but I felt a knot in the pit of my stomach. What was it I was about to do?
>
> When it became clear that Richard would die without one of my kidneys, I did some serious soul-searching. I mean, here I was, 23 years old, young and healthy, and they were going to cut me open and take out one of my organs. It was shocking even to consider the idea. I felt a real conflict of emotions. Of course I wanted to help my brother, but the only operation I'd ever had before was an appendectomy, and I hadn't much liked that.

Medical and Ethical Issues

Any form of medical treatment is a balance between intended good and potentially adverse effects. For the healthy donor, however, there is no physical benefit. For us surgeons who had been taught to make sick persons well, subjecting Ronald, a healthy human being, to an extensive surgical procedure required a basic qualitative shift in our thinking. To this extent, we were compromising the physician's injunction to "do no harm." Therefore, we had to assume that the low risk to Ronald was justified by the expected benefits for Richard. Only after a series of consultations involving experienced physicians within and outside the Brigham, clergy of all denominations, and legal counsel did we feel comfortable offering the option of transplantation to Richard, Ronald, and, by extension, their family.

The Brigham kidney transplant team, which comprised Drs. John P. Merrill (Head of Nephrology), J. Hartwell Harrison (Chief of Urology), Gustave Dammin (Pathologist-in-Chief), and me, met several times with the Herrick family members to discuss calmly and in detail the preparations, anesthesia, operations, possible complications, and anticipated result of the transplant. We advised neither for nor against the operation; we merely presented the facts as thoroughly as possible and left it for the family to decide, encouraging them to ask any and all questions, no matter how irrelevant they might seem.

"What is the life expectancy of a person with one kidney?" they asked. We approached insurance companies for their actuarial tables and discovered that there was no increased risk from living with one kidney. One person in a thousand is born with a solitary kidney, which is usually detected incidentally on medical examination for other purposes or after accidental loss of their only kidney.

"What are the chances of subsequent disease affecting the remaining kidney?" they asked. We explained that the most common types of renal disease affect both kidneys simultaneously. The most critical conditions affecting a solitary kidney are cancer and trauma, both fortunately rare.

Once the Herricks and the surgical team made the decision to proceed with the transplant, an additional professional burden was imposed on Dr. Harrison,[19] who would be removing Ronald's healthy kidney (a procedure known as a nephrectomy), because his patient was expected to survive normally. In contrast, I was performing the transplant on a patient otherwise doomed to die. The moral and ethical ramifications of this decision weighed heavily on all our minds.

Henry M. Fox, Chief of Psychiatry and one of the doctors monitoring the case, expressed his thoughts in the patient record:

11/4/54

Saw this patient today and discussed the entire situation with the house staff. This is a very complex problem and there is much to be said for and against asking him to donate a kidney. In my opinion, this is primarily an ethical problem. I think we have to be careful not to be too much swayed by our eagerness to carry out a kidney transplant successfully for the first time (i.e., to succeed in having it take permanently). It seems to me, furthermore, that the potential recipient's mental state is a subsidiary issue. The important question would seem to be whether we as physicians have the right to put the healthy twin under the pressure of being asked whether he is willing to make this sacrifice. I do not feel that we have this right in view of the potential danger to the healthy twin as well as the uncertainty of the outcome for this patient.

Dr. John P. Merrill, who was on the medical service, head of the Kidney Research Laboratory, and my co-leader of the transplant team, was keenly aware of these issues and wrote in the record:

11/29/54

We are now faced with a situation (in the recipient) in which the immediate prognosis is certain. The advent of congestive heart failure (CHF) makes it imperative that we decide whether to attempt a homograft [an inexact term that eventually was more precisely referred to as an 'isograft'] taken from his identical twin. The hypertension and CHF make this more difficult and the prognosis uncertain even if the graft functions well. If it does, and hypertension remains, removal of the diseased kidney is indicated. Dr. Murray feels that if the skin graft remains well healed after four weeks the probability of identity is excellent. He (Richard) will return in one week. In the meantime, we will investigate other legal, technical and moral aspects.

This thoughtful consideration of the potential consequences of the transplant contrasts with medical resident E. Robin's enthusiastic note: "Informed that patient has a twin (identical) and possibility of transplant from brother to patient exists. This is an exciting prospect and all stops should be pulled to promote this project."

At the conclusion of our last preoperative group discussion, Ronald asked whether the hospital would assume responsibility for his health care for the rest of his life. Dr. Harrison replied, "Of course not." But he immediately followed this declaration with a question: "Ronald, do you think anyone in this room would ever refuse you care if you needed help?" Ronald paused, then realized that his future health care depended upon our sense of professional responsibility rather than on legal assurances.

Once Ronald had made up his mind, there was no turning back. Unbeknownst to us, it was Richard who had second thoughts. He wrote an urgent note to Ronald on the eve of the operation: "Get out of here and go home," it said. But Ronald would not be swayed, and in a return note he told Richard, "I am here and I am going to stay." With that, we entered uncharted territory.

A Dry Run

Richard had reached the final stage of his disease and was close to death. But before we could attempt any operation, he had to be metabolically stable—that is, there had to be proper levels of minerals and acid in his blood; otherwise, his chances of surviving any surgical procedure would be greatly diminished. Fortunately, thanks to the "Kolff-Brigham Kidney," we were able to achieve this with dialysis. However, in those days the dialytic process caused a large internal fluid flux, upsetting the balance of ions in the blood and possibly causing serious cardiac irregularities. To avoid this risk, we had to coordinate the timing of the dialysis and the operation itself.

To be as cautious and thorough as possible, Dr. Francis Moore and I were anxious to do a "test run" using a cadaver to ensure that a transplanted kidney would fit comfortably in its new site. When experimenting on the dogs in the lab, I had ample time to try out a variety of sites before settling on the best one. In Richard's case, I would have no second chance. The kidney I was transplanting was the only compatible kidney in the entire universe! I did not want it to fail for any reason—especially for a reason I had neglected to anticipate.

I left my name with pathology departments all across the city, with instructions to alert me the minute a patient died so I could use the cadaver for a trial run of the operation. Each day was one of anxious waiting, both at the office and at home. My daughter Ginny, who was eight years old at the time, recalls not being able to use the telephone for days for fear we'd miss the critical phone call. Richard's condition was continuing to deteriorate, and I feared we'd lose him if we didn't operate soon.

December 20th was cold and snowy. Bobby and I were home, preparing for a Christmas party for about 75 friends and neighbors. I was in charge of making the eggnog and was just about to get started when the phone rang. It was the Brigham pathology department, calling to tell me that a cadaver was available. I handed Bobby the eggnog ingredients, kissed her goodbye, and left immediately.

I anxiously drove the icy roads into the city and met Franny Moore in the postmortem room. I'd brought all the necessary instruments, and together we went through the entire operation, trying to think of every possible surgical mishap. The whole procedure took only a couple of hours, and I arrived home to share the last of the eggnog with the few remaining guests. The Herrick operation was scheduled for three days later.

December 23, 1954: The Operation

As I drove in to the hospital early on the morning of December 23rd, I listened to the news report about the impending operation on the car radio. If not the eyes of the world, certainly the ears of those in Greater Metropolitan Boston would be tuned in to what we were about to do. I felt as prepared as I could be.

The operation began at 8:15 A.M. Throughout I was in constant communication with the donor team in the adjacent room. By 9:50 A.M., the blood vessels supplying Richard's donor kidney had been isolated and exposed but were still attached. When I was completely prepared, I took a deep breath and gave Dr. Harrison the go-ahead to sever the blood supply to one of Ronald's damaged kidneys. From that moment on, timing was critical. At all costs, the time between cutting off the blood supply to the donor organ and reestablishing it in the recipient (the "ischemic time") had to be as short as possible.

Dr. Francis Moore carried the severed donor kidney into the room at 9:53 A.M. Wrapped as it was in a cold, wet towel and set in a sterile stainless-steel basin, it seemed a humble transport for such precious cargo. Now we had to reestablish blood flow as rapidly as possible, which meant pumping fresh arterial blood into the donor kidney and removing the "used" venous blood.

We could not let Richard's blood flow into his new kidney until we had attached his native vessels to the donor kidney vessels (artery to artery and vein to vein). For this reason, clamps had been placed on two of Richard's arteries supplying his kidney and his leg. We began by attaching (anastomosing) the renal artery of the donor kidney to Richard's external iliac artery at 10:10 A.M. and completed the connection 30 minutes later. Joining the donor renal vein to Richard's external iliac vein took a bit longer and was completed at 11:15 A.M. Although I was well aware of the time ticking away throughout the procedure—everyone was—I could only continue to work carefully and systemati-

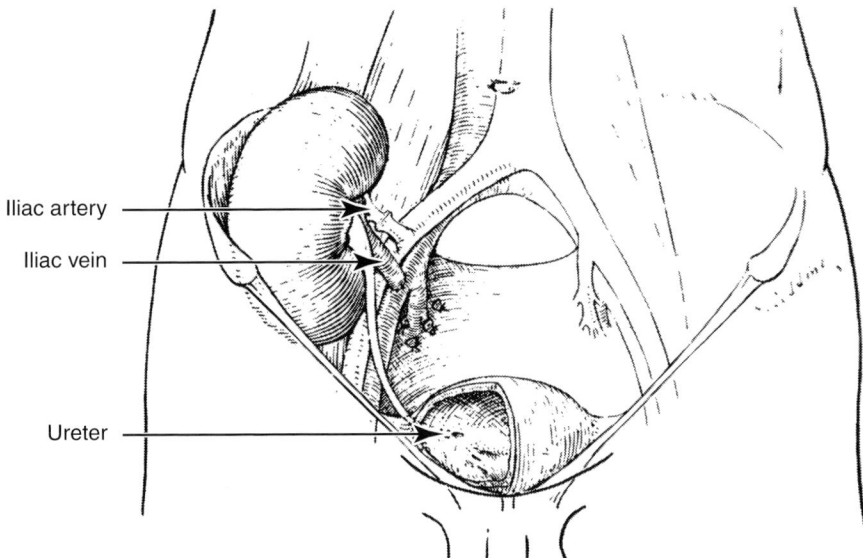

The donor kidney has been placed within the abdominal cavity of the recipient. The intestines and appendix (not shown) remain within their peritoneal sac but have been pulled back with retractors to allow better visibility of the operative site. The recipient's iliac artery brings fresh blood into the new kidney via its renal artery, while the recipient's iliac vein returns used blood to the patient via the kidney. The ureter carries urine from the kidney to the urinary bladder.

cally and, at all costs, efficiently. We would know soon enough whether I had succeeded.

There was a collective hush in the operating room as we gently removed the clamps from the vessels newly attached to the donor kidney. As blood flow was restored, Richard's new kidney began to become engorged and turn pink. The donor kidney had been without blood flow for total of 1 hour and 22 minutes. There were grins all around. We removed the remaining clamp from the common iliac artery approximately 10 minutes later and immediately noted pulsation in Richard's right foot.

The kidney lay comfortably in its new site, pulsing with blood and showing pinpoint areas of bleeding on the surface. Urine flowed so briskly from the ureteral catheter that it had to be mopped up from the floor. Judging by that measure, the kidney was working perfectly. We next implanted the free end of the ureter, which was spurting urine, into the urinary bladder. Thus, the normal flow of urine was restored.

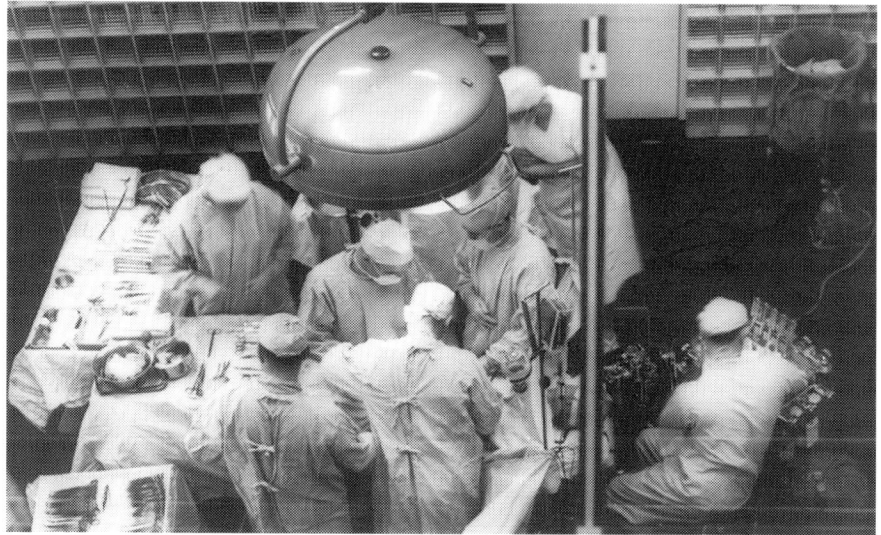

The first identical-twin kidney transplant operation, performed on December 23, 1954.

Postoperative Course

Once both patients had recovered from their respective operations, we realized there were still several hurdles for Richard to surmount. When one reaches the summit of a high mountain, it can be a bit deflating to realize that one is not truly safe until the return journey has been completed.

Dr. Merrill and I had an honest and understandable difference of opinion about whether or not Richard's diseased native kidneys should be removed. I wanted both kidneys out immediately, since I believed that leaving them in place would pose a high risk of infection or of transmitting disease to the new kidney. But Dr. Merrill firmly believed that Richard should keep at least one of his native kidneys. His reasoning was that it could act as a sponge, absorbing any harmful substances that might remain. In addition, he felt that if the transplanted kidney failed later on, the native kidney might have recovered sufficiently to resume functioning. Even though I strongly disagreed with him, his reasoning was plausible, so I deferred to his judgment, since he was the expert on kidney function and disease.

Nevertheless, I was disturbed by this division within our related professional disciplines. How does one solve such a dilemma? I sought

Dr. Moore's opinion. After consideration of both sides, he felt I should acquiesce, since the decision was more in the domain of the medical service than the surgical service. However, he suggested that I include a note in the patient's record expressing my views, which I did:

1/29/55

Since operation five weeks ago, Richard has done very well. The wounds healed rapidly, his transplant has functioned immediately and continuously. The course of the future is unknown and the best method of future treatment is a matter of conjecture only. In my opinion, his future longevity depends entirely on his transplant as an "all or none" phenomenon. Either the transplant will take or it will not. Therefore every possible and theoretical mode of protecting this transplant should be taken as soon as possible.

Potential dangerous factors to the transplant are hypertension and urinary tract infection. His blood pressure today on serpasil is

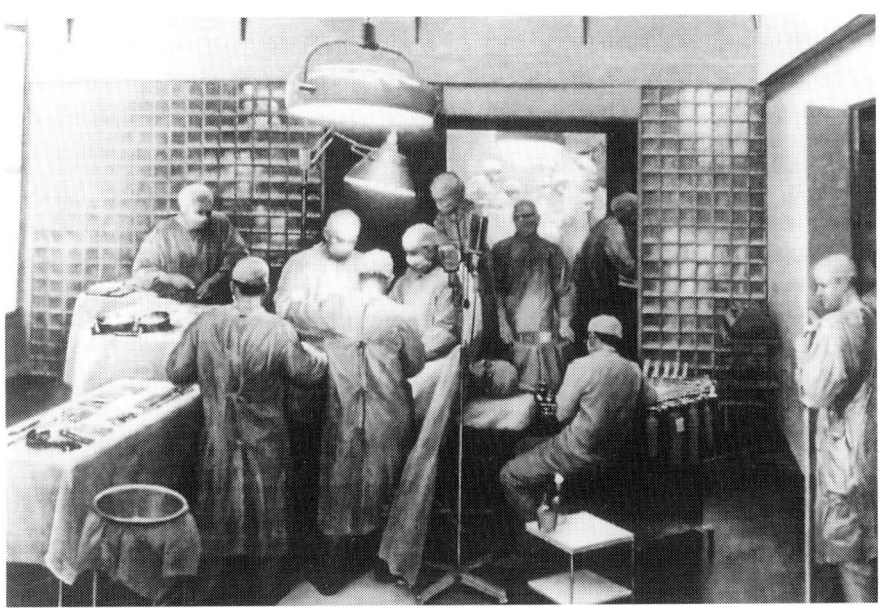

Oil painting by the artist Joel Babb showing the kidney transplant operation. Unveiled in 1997, the painting now hangs in the main lobby of the Countway Library of Medicine at Harvard Medical School in Boston.

Ronald Herrick (left) and Richard Herrick toast to each other's good health 10 months after the successful transplant.

160/104 and the diastolic has been constantly in the 100 range. The last urine culture is positive, and presumably from his own kidneys. Removal of his own kidneys potentially will help both of these latter conditions, and therefore ought to be started as soon as possible. I would much prefer to do the nephrectomy next Monday or Tuesday rather than send him home on an anti-hypertensive drug. However, no one knows the proper answer and when an honest difference of opinion exists a compromise is acceptable.

After discharge, Richard continued to thrive. Because function of the donated kidney was so good, Dr. Merrill felt removal of the diseased kidneys was reasonable, but only one at a time. Richard underwent a left nephrectomy on March 29, 1955, and a right nephrectomy on June 20, 1955. He subsequently married his recovery room nurse, and they had two children. Richard died in 1962, eight years after the transplant, from recurrence of his original kidney disease in the transplanted kidney.

John and I learned from our joint experiences with several more identical-twin transplants that recurrence of the original disease could be prevented by pretransplant removal of both diseased kidneys followed by the use of appropriate cytotoxic drugs.

ONE OPERATION AMONG MANY

I am often asked whether, at the time of the Herrick operation, I was aware of its historic significance. Although I knew the operation was potentially momentous, in truth, I treated it as just part of the week's work. Two days prior to the transplant procedure, I had repaired a double cleft lip, resected a recurrent cancer of the mouth, corrected protuberant ("lop") ears in a child, and closed a burn of the buttocks. And two days after the operation, on Christmas Day, I was in the Newton-Wellesley Hospital Emergency Ward, suturing a laceration of a child's forehead. To the individual patient, *any* operation is momentous. As such, one prepares for each case as it comes, thinks about it ahead of time, and anticipates and identifies trouble spots that could waste time or lead to complications. In that sense, the Herrick operation was no different from any of the other procedures that surrounded it.

A friend who is aware of my religious convictions asked me whether I prayed before the Herrick operation. I replied, somewhat reluctantly, that I did not alter my daily pattern in any way; I consider every day to be a call to prayer. I later learned that Bobby had had the children kneel down the night

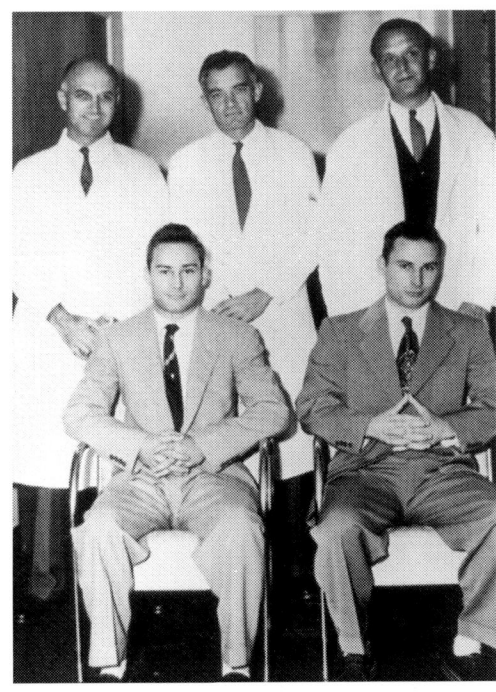

Front row (left to right): Richard Herrick, kidney transplant recipient; Ronald Herrick, kidney donor. Back row (left to right): The Brigham transplant team: Joseph E. Murray, surgeon for the recipient; John P. Merrill, nephrologist and co-leader of the team; J. Hartwell Harrison, urological surgeon for the donor.

before the operation and say special prayers, explaining to them, "Daddy's doing an important operation." The importance of this venture was very real. I won't say that I offered any special prayers for the success of the Herrick transplant; all I know is that I drove into Boston the morning of the operation determined to do the very best work possible. According to the popular theologian Thomas Merton, one's work should be "a wordless prayer."

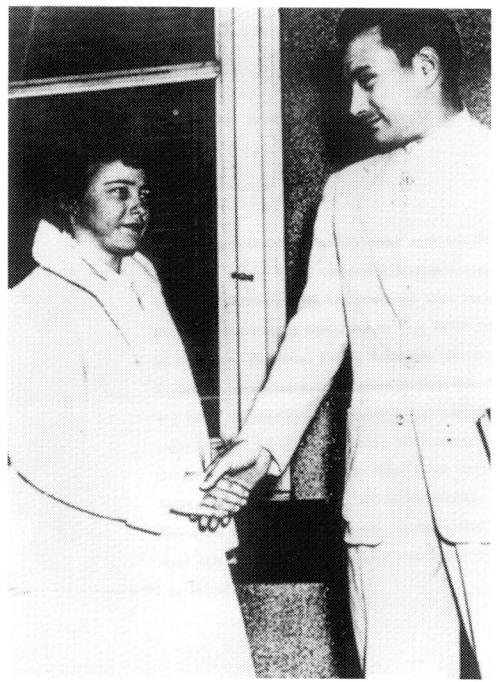

Richard Herrick greeting Edith Helm in May of 1956. Edith was the third identical-twin transplant recipient and the first transplant recipient to go on to complete a successful pregnancy. She is the longest-living transplant recipient in the world. She and her donor, Wanda Foster, continue to have normal renal function, and both are now grandmothers.

Ripple Effect

Dr. Moore later said that if the operation had failed, it could have set the field of transplantation back a decade or more. Even though eight years later, Richard did succumb to renal failure, the operation's early and complete success was a tremendous shot-in-the-arm to all of us everywhere who were working in the field. Basic scientists were impressed, and even my doubting colleagues admitted it was a great step forward. There were those who dismissed the event as a one-in-a-million occurrence and not something that would add greatly to the store of medical knowledge. They argued, correctly, that there would be very few identical twins like the Herrick brothers, so this advance would not benefit the majority of patients with renal failure. But in my view they failed to understand that this was just the first step. The purpose of this operation was to see whether we could solve several *other* sizable obstacles to kidney transplantation besides immune rejection. This we had done.

The overall reaction around the world was one of buoyed hopes. We had demonstrated that organ transplantation could be life-saving, but we had to make organ transplantation a solution for all, not just for those whose immune systems were identical. Much laboratory work remained to be done, and we would have to find collaborators to help us. Specifically, we had to select one or more of the following goals:

- To alter the donor kidney in some way to make it acceptable to the recipient.
- To alter the recipient to reduce the strength of the immune system's attack on the transplanted organ.
- To develop tests of compatibility between donor and recipient, so that when the two were not identical twins, surgery would be performed only when the chances of success were greatest.

These would be the goals we would pursue for the next 20 years of my career. If we could not achieve them, then our success with the Herrick twins would be just a curiosity, a footnote in the history of medicine. Still, this breakthrough was heady stuff indeed. I was only sorry my dad, who died in October of 1953, had not lived long enough to see it happen.

CHAPTER 10

THE EXPANDING WEB OF TRANSPLANTATION SURGERY

Tremendous publicity had surrounded the Herrick kidney transplant. In fact, the media attention transformed me from a relatively unknown Boston plastic surgeon to a well-known and respected transplant surgeon. However, not all of the attention was good, and not all of it was accurate. In fact, there was considerable misattribution about who had performed which aspects of the surgery. Although the Brigham news release did mention me, it ranked me third in the line-up after the more established Drs. Merrill and Harrison. *Time* magazine credited Harrison with performing the transplant, while other publications gave Merrill the credit. This was understandable, since Merrill was a nationally known nephrologist involved in the medical care and dialysis of patients with kidney disease. However, the misunderstanding was still distressing to me. When directly asked, Merrill and Harrison did acknowledge that I was the one who had performed the transplant operation on Richard.

As a surgeon still trying to make my mark, this lack of personal recognition was frustrating. But once again, Brad Cannon advised me to keep my dismay to myself. "It will all turn out well in the end," he assured me. "Just continue with your lab work and publications."

WIDENING THE SCOPE

Twenty years after Richard Herrick became the first successful kidney transplant recipient, Sir Peter Medawar, now studying the immunology of cancer, referred back to that pivotal time:

> Physicians will arise who feel just as much at home in the laboratory as in the cancer ward. Just one brilliant break is needed, akin to the

first brilliant kidney transplant in the Peter Bent Brigham Hospital in Boston, and then recruits will come forward by the hundreds.

From *Pluto's Republic* (Oxford University Press, 1982, p. 158)

Medawar hoped that what had occurred in the field of transplantation would also occur in the field of cancer. Recruits did come forward "by the hundreds." The Herrick operation had rekindled the interest of clinicians and researchers worldwide who were already involved in transplantation as well as stimulating others to start programs of their own. The field of organ transplantation exploded. Basic scientists, immunologists, pathologists, hematologists, and embryologists became aware that clinicians were in the forefront of an expanding scientific discipline.

Preparing the Soil

We had assumed that the Herrick identical-twin situation—one twin healthy and the other dying of renal failure—would be a "once-in-a-lifetime" event. But to our great surprise other sets of twins with the same problem appeared at a rate of about one or two a year. Edith Helm, an identical twin transplanted in May 1956, subsequently had children and grandchildren, as did her twin donor, Wanda Foster. Today, 45 years later, both have normal renal function. Edith is the world's longest living recipient of an organ transplant.

Although we were buoyed by each success, we were also frustrated that the success was restricted to such narrow genetic confines. We were determined to find a way to break the immunogenetic barrier and make transplantation feasible for anyone. Intuitively, we felt it could be done; we just didn't know how. Neither did anyone else in the world, though not for lack of trying. As young and otherwise healthy patients died around us, and protocol after protocol failed, we grasped at any source of encouragement.

To our good fortune, the basic science of transplantation biology was just beginning to explode. In particular, the work of Sir Peter Medawar and others indicated that under certain circumstances the immune system would tolerate foreign tissue. As is so often the case, research that had been performed years before, but had not been fully understood at the time, provided the necessary insights.

In 1779, John Hunter had reported to the Royal Society of Medicine in England on the intriguing condition of "freemartin" twin cattle, in which the male offspring is normal but the female is sterile. He was curious about this "experiment of nature" that had been described as far back as Greek and Roman times. More than 125 years after Hunter's presentation, F.R. Lillie[20] did more than write about this anomaly; he rolled up his sleeves and went to work to find out the explanation. When he dissected the placentas of these twin cattle, he noted that the blood supplies of the two fetuses were fused early in embryonic development. This allowed the male hormones to enter the female twin's bloodstream and influence her sexual development.

This observation lay dormant for 30 years until Ray Owen decided to see whether there were any immunological consequences of Lillie's finding. Owen discovered that each of the twins had two distinct types of red cells circulating, without adverse or harmful consequence, in their bloodstreams: their own red cells and those of their twins. Theoretically, this was a biological impossibility. The red cells of one twin should have been recognized as foreign by the other, since the twins were not identical, and therefore these "invaders" should have been attacked by the host's immune system. But instead, these red cells were tolerated, even many years later. One possible explanation was that the cattle were exposed to the red cells of their twin early in life—indeed, before they were born. That very early exposure led their immune systems to "think" that the twin's red cells were really their own.

The discovery of this "naturally existing immunological tolerance" stimulated zoologists Peter Medawar, Rupert Billingham, and Leslie Brent to try to recreate the same condition experimentally. When they injected newborn mice with cells from a genetically different strain of mouse, the recipient mice, as adults, were able to accept skin grafts from the donor mice without rejection. They had thus produced in the lab what nature had produced in freemartin cattle—immunologic tolerance. In their landmark article "Actively Acquired Tolerance of Foreign Cells," published in 1953 in *Nature* (Vol. 172, p. 603), Billingham, Brent, and Medawar acknowledged that Owen's work was decisive in providing a scientific basis for the new study of "transplantation biology."

Owen later performed experiments that closed the circle. He succeeded in crossover skin-grafting in these cattle, proving that in becoming tolerant of the twin's red blood cells, the cattle had also become tolerant of other tissues (skin), and that transplantation across genetic barriers was indeed also possible in higher animals than mice.

In 1962, the brilliant Czech biologist Milan Hašek[21] reported findings that were biologically similar to those reported by Medawar's group in mice. As a result of intermingling of fetal blood in parabiotic ducks (meaning that the ducks shared a common circulation of blood in the egg, before birth), Hašek and his wife Vera noted that these ducks were able to accept skin from each other after they were born. Their outstanding work was presented and recognized at several of the New York Academy of Science Transplantation Conferences in the mid-1960s. These conferences ran through the mid-1970s, at which time several of us formed The International Society of Transplantation. The group still meets biennially and attracts several thousand participants.

A Fertile Field

Under Dr. Moore, I was Chief of Plastic Surgery at the Brigham (an honor-by-default, since I was the ONLY plastic surgeon). In addition, I was in charge of the surgical aspects of the transplant program, working closely and productively with my brother-in-arms, Dr. John Merrill, who was in charge of its medical aspects.

I am convinced that the Brigham was the first to succeed in human kidney transplantations because our program was totally integrated under the leadership of Dr. George Thorn, Physician-in-Chief, and Dr. Francis Moore, Surgeon-in-Chief. I organized weekly, hospital-wide conferences attended by the core lab groups of Drs. Merrill, Moore, and Pathologist-in-Chief Gustave Dammin. Nurses, psychiatrists, radiologists, and social services personnel attended, as well as research fellows, residents, and interns. Visitors from all over the world would participate, and members of various departments in the medical school quadrangle, including physiology, microbiology, anatomy, and pathology, also contributed to our discussions. This cross-section of talent and experience enriched the meetings. In the true, Greek sense of the word, the Brigham was a "university," providing an arena where people could come together to think freely and explore ideas and possibilities. The result was a rich, complex learning program in which we all participated and from which we all benefited.

Dog Days

I selected dogs as the experimental transplant model in order to concentrate on a laboratory test system that paralleled the human situation as closely as possible. In the dog, renal allotransplants (from unrelated donors) follow a relatively constant course; although they function immediately, they fail after only 3 to 7 days. Despite hundreds of transplants with various protocols, the longest survival time I was able to achieve was 15 days. In sharp contrast, kidney autografts (i.e., kidneys retransplanted in the same individual), prepared the same way as the allografts, persisted indefinitely with excellent function (Chapter 9). The work of Medawar and others had shown that immune tolerance was possible, but only under circumstances we could not possibly reproduce in human beings who needed organ transplants—that is, exposing the potential recipient, while in the womb, to the tissues of a potential donor who would years later be called upon to donate his or her tissue. Thus, these experimental breakthroughs in transplantation biology were of no immediate value to us.

In those early days, our experimental protocols tested several possible methods for breaking the immune barrier. The most promising were as follows:

- Destroying the host's immune mechanism with total-body x-irradiation, followed by replacement marrow infusion.

- Paralyzing the immune process with multiple repeated skin allografts.

- Tricking the host by introducing the donor antigen prior to transplantation in the hopes that this antigen would act as a decoy for a subsequent allotransplant.

- Maintaining a transplant organ long enough to allow the host and graft to adapt to each other.

- Matching donor and recipient by cell types, using white-cell typing modeled on known red-cell typing techniques.

- Weakening the immune response by administering agents such as toluene blue and nitrogen mustard.

Temporary Success, Eventual Failure

But nothing worked. All our various laboratory protocols, while inventive and based on available scientific evidence, failed. However, Dr. John Mannick, then at the Mary Imogene Bassett Hospital in Cooperstown, New York, and Dr. Moore's successor as Surgeon-in-Chief at the Brigham & Women's Hospital, did report success with a dog kidney transplant following total-body x-irradiation and bone marrow replacement. He was working with a hematologist, E. Donnall Thomas, who had received training at the Brigham.

Thomas approached the problem as follows: First, some of the patient's bone marrow cells would be harvested and stored under conditions that would keep them alive, for a time. (Bone marrow cells give rise to both red and white blood cells, and the white cells are the cells of the immune system.) Total-body x-irradiation would then be used to wipe out the bone marrow cells that remained in the body, thus effectively destroying the body's immune capabilities. This defenselessness would give a transplanted organ time to "take" before the stored bone marrow cells were reinfused. Once back in the body, these cells would hopefully multiply and reconstitute a functioning immune system that would presumably attack the transplanted organ less vigorously; moreover, the transplanted organ, having been spared rejection for several weeks, would be better able to resist the attack with greater vigor.

We thought perhaps we were on the right track. Not only did this approach seem to be the most promising one, it was also the most practical. But even though we had some success with it in the use of skin grafts in mice and rabbits, we were less fortunate with the canine kidney transplants. Initial function was often excellent, but rejection was inexorable, and we began to doubt whether we were on the right track after all. Fortunately, every year or so we had the opportunity to perform an identical-twin transplant, and that would go a long way toward recharging our flagging spirits. Thomas Starzl, the renowned transplant surgeon at the University of Pittsburgh, describes this time in the history of transplantation as "a long list of tragic failures leavened only by occasional encouraging notations such as those in identical twins."

Testing the Radiation/ Bone Marrow Protocol in Man

In 1957, using a protocol of total-body irradiation followed by bone marrow transfusion, Dr. Merrill and I began a study of 12 kidney transplant patients who were not genetically identical. Even though I felt intuitively that this approach was overly complex, and our lab experience with dogs did not support the irradiation/marrow protocol, our experience with rabbits and mice was moderately encouraging, and this treatment seemed the most promising option for patients otherwise doomed to die. (At this time, chemical immune suppression had not yet been developed.)

Gladys Loman, a 31-year-old mother of two, was the first person in our study. She had only one kidney, which was unfortunately situated very close to her appendix. When this solitary kidney became infected, the surgeon in charge of the middle-of-the-night emergency operation understandably thought he was removing an infected appendiceal mass. Only after the "mass" had been removed did he realize that it was her kidney. Mindful of the Brigham transplant program from all the publicity surrounding the Herrick twins, he courageously referred Gladys to us.

In contrast to our twin transplant patients who conveniently came with a spare donor kidney, we did not have a kidney for Gladys. Fortunately, we were able to "make do" with one from a patient involved in a neurosurgical study being conducted by Dr. Don Matson. In his protocol, one healthy kidney was removed from patients requiring a shunt to drain fluid from the brain to the urinary bladder and thus prevent brain damage from excessive cerebral pressure. Previously, these "expendable" kidneys had been used (with family permission) by Drs. John Enders, Thomas Weller, and Fred Robbins as a possible culture medium for the poliomyelitis virus. Their ultimate success in culturing the polio virus (for which they received the Nobel Prize in 1954) led directly to the Salk and Sabin vaccines that eradicated the once dreaded disease. When I asked Don if one of these spare kidneys could be made available for Gladys, he jokingly commented that he had been involved in one Nobel Prize venture, now perhaps he'd become involved in another! How I wish he had lived to see his offhand prophesy realized.

We administered three hemodialysis treatments to Gladys, followed with high doses of total-body irradiation. At the time, some hospitals were beginning to build sterile rooms as part of their kidney transplant program, but since the Brigham did not yet have one,[22] we used an operating room as a next-best solution. Doctors, nurses, and visitors scrubbed before entering.

Gladys' transplant did not work immediately, but after two weeks the kidney began to excrete urine. We were hopeful, but after 30 days her white blood cell count plummeted in response to the x-ray treatment. The infused marrow did not function, and Gladys died of infection. In spite of the tragic outcome, this stalwart patient provided valuable information for our pursuit of a successful transplant.

Death of a patient is always a sad event, even when the outcome is clear. Many families, realizing that a transplant is their last hope and success uncertain, comment that even if the prospective transplant fails, they hope it will help other patients in the future. In those early kidney transplant years, patients, doctors, and nurses melded into a family. Naturally, we shared the family's sorrow at Gladys' death, but we had the encouraging knowledge that her final weeks were brightened by the improving function of her transplant. She and her family hold a special place in my heart. We came so close!

One Month in the "Big House"

I had been working almost around-the-clock caring for Gladys while, at the same time, trying to maintain my other numerous commitments. I was squeezing in private patients, attending committee meetings for the American College of Surgeons, and spending considerable time in the lab. I felt deeply committed to all of these pursuits, but they were beginning to take their toll. Dr. Moore pulled me aside one day and suggested, strongly, that I take a rest. Bobby emphatically agreed.

I was too tired to put up a fight, so two days later Meg and J. (Joseph) Link (our two middle children) and Bobby and I drove to Woods Hole on Cape Cod and got on the first ferry that came along. As a child I had summered in Newport, so I knew little about the Cape and Islands. I thought it would be a fun adventure to hop on whatever boat happened along and have faith that it would take us somewhere wonderful. It did. We found ourselves on Martha's Vineyard, and we loved it immediately.

We hadn't been in Edgartown for even one full day before we went to a real estate agent to inquire about summer rentals. The agent told us about the common practice of renting space in Edgartown and ferrying over to Chappaquiddick Island to swim. When I suggested the reverse would be preferable, the agent directed us to Vance Packard, an author who lived on Chappaquiddick and was going away for the summer. We boarded the little Chappy ferry and found the esteemed Mr. Packard struggling single-handedly to get a refrigerator into his house. The four of us pitched in and helped.

We must have done a good job, because he agreed to our renting what he referred to as his "big house" from mid-July to mid-August. Along with the house came a boat and a couple of horses, making for an idyllic summer. Days were spent flying kites, picnicking, sailing, playing tennis, and swimming until our skin puckered. Mid-August came much too fast; none of us wanted to leave. I think we sensed on some level that Martha's Vineyard would come to be deeply important in all of our lives.

A Tenuous Success

Fully rested and eager to get back to work, I returned to the Brigham to find a second

Bobby always looks this refreshed on the tennis court; I seldom do! This photo appeared in the December 1, 1958, issue of Sports Illustrated, *in the article "Scientists in Sports," edited by Vannevar Bush.*

patient enrolled in our x-ray/marrow study—a 12-year-old boy who, like Gladys, had lost his solitary kidney to infection. Although we treated him with total-body x-ray treatment and bone marrow from his mother, the potential kidney donor, plus fetal spleen and liver cells, he died 25 days after the x-ray treatment from hematologic and infectious complications. The kidney transplant was never done.

Our third patient, John Riteris (described in Chapter 11) was our only success using the x-ray/bone marrow protocol. The next patient, G.C., was not transplanted because her mother, the prospective donor, developed a urinary infection before the second x-ray treatment. While the mother was being treated for this infection, the patient herself died of uremia and infection with severe marrow depletion despite vigorous medical treatment.

Four of the remaining eight patients had perfect function of the transplanted kidney for 4 to 14 days, only to have the organs stop functioning suddenly. The transplant site was swollen and tender, and they died within a few days. At postmortem examination, the blood vessels and tubes leading from the kidney (ureters) were not obstructed. Death was due instead to acute rejection. One other patient had hyperacute rejection that occurred on the operating table within one hour after we released the vascular clamps.

Some have wondered why we continued in the face of so many failed attempts. With each failure, we learned a little bit more about preparing the patient, treating rejection, and timing the diagnostic tests. We were all focused on helping patients with end-stage renal disease. I was never discouraged. If we gave up, patients would have no hope at all. Where in the world could there be assembled a better team of clinicians and basic scientists than at the Brigham and Harvard Medical School?

I have been accused by many of being a "pathological optimist." I plead guilty. But it was not Pollyanna optimism. There were good solid grounds for hope. The identical twin experiences—by then about 18 in number—were bright beacons leading the way toward our goal. The group at Cooperstown, New York, with Drs. Joe Ferrebee, Don Thomas,[23] and John Mannick had already achieved success in a dog who survived with the combination of total-body x-ray and bone marrow infusion. In our own lab we had been successful in allografting skin in mice and rabbits following several x-ray/marrow protocols. So there was a real basis for optimism in the approach we were taking. Providentially, however, an even better approach to suppressing immune rejection—chemical immune suppressive drugs—soon arrived on the scene.

CHAPTER 11

JOHN RITERIS
First Allogeneic (Non-Identical-Twin) Kidney Transplant

> *Procedure:* Non-identical-twin kidney transplant using radiation for immune suppression
> *Date of Operation:* January 14, 1959
> *Institution:* Peter Bent Brigham Hospital, Boston, Massachusetts

The third patient in our transplant program, 24-year-old John Riteris, had a fraternal twin brother, Andrew, who wished to donate his healthy—but not genetically identical—kidney. Because the marrow replacement in the two previous patients had failed and both died from infection, we decided to use a sublethal dose of x-radiation for John's renal transplant.

The operation took place on January 24, 1959, and the graft functioned immediately. However, 11 days later, a massive perirenal infection developed, and we felt sure John would succumb in the same manner as the first two patients. Dr. J. Hartwell Harrison and I performed emergency surgery to remove both of John's own kidneys, leaving the donor kidney graft in place. John's blood counts slowly returned to normal, but only after 21 days of worrisome care. John then went on to make a complete recovery. He died 29 years later of congestive heart failure.

Andrew felt no hesitation in donating one of his kidneys to his brother John. In a letter he wrote to me years later, Andrew explained his point of view:

> John and I never conversed in a donor-donee context. We were brothers and each other's best friend, and there simply seemed no reason

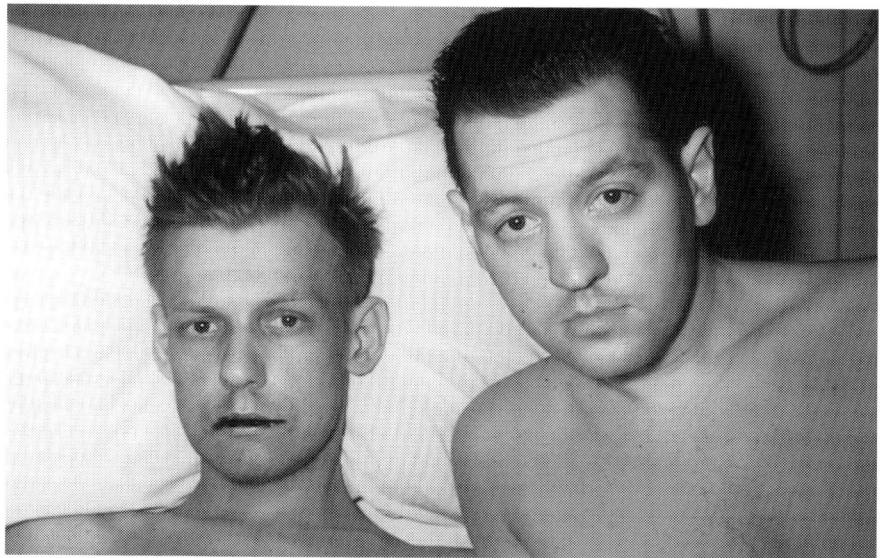

The Riteris brothers prior to the transplant operation. John (left), in the terminal phase of kidney failure, and his healthy brother, Andrew (right).

to discuss our personal contributions, if indeed they were such, to the history of kidney transplantation. I always believed, and still do, that the contribution of a donor is not an unusual one. It is nothing more than the rare chance, or fortune, to be a Good Samaritan to one's kin. John might have thought differently, but we never talked about it. The only reference he made to it was in an inscription in a book he gave me one week before his death, 27 years later. The inscription read: "To Andrew—Thanks for the second drink."

John Riteris was the first human being in whom the immunological barrier was broken. His survival gave us tremendous impetus to continue with the sublethal radiation protocol because we kept thinking we could duplicate the result. Although two French investigators— Jean Hamburger at Neckar Hospital and René Küss at Foch Hospital—had greater success than we did using the same protocol, neither group achieved consistent results.

Thomas Starzl[24] felt strongly that our success with John Riteris was the pivotal moment in transplantation:

This moved the field forward from the previously fixed position where only identical-twin cases of kidney transplantation had been successful. I have always thought that by breaking the genetic barrier, this became in principle the single most important case, psychologically and otherwise, in the history of the field of clinical transplantation.

(Journal of NIH Research, April, 1993, Vol. 5, p. 71)

While I was flattered by his comments, I disagreed with Tom. Had radiation turned out to be a consistently successful protocol, John's case would have been the turning point. But the truth is, we never knew why John went on to live for another 28 years. As a doctor, I now know that it is not necessary to know everything. If a patient—even just a single patient—survives with a good quality of life, that means a lot. As a scientist I may have been unhappy with the human x-ray protocol, but as the physician in charge of John's care, I was ecstatic. John himself

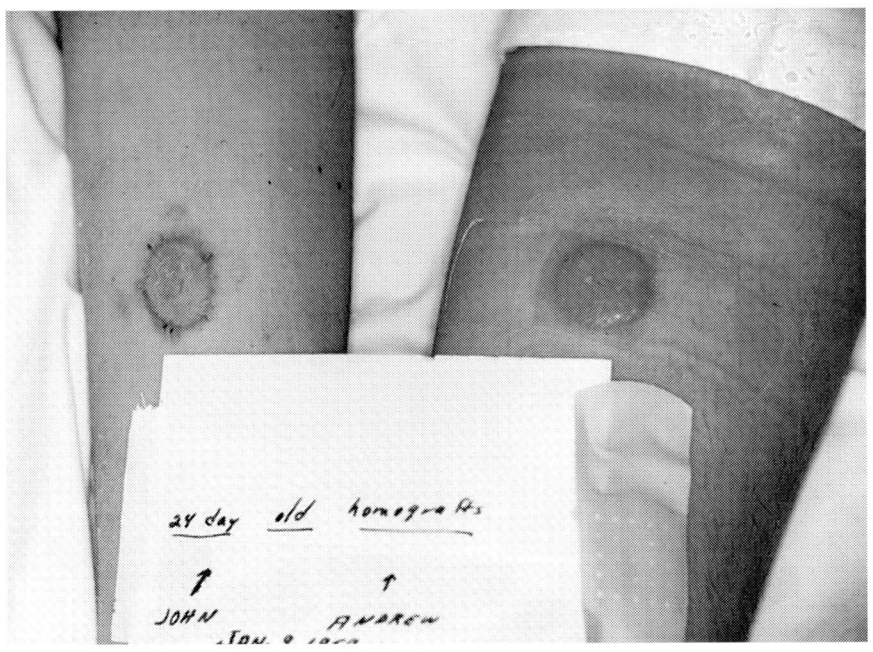

A skin graft on Andrew's arm (right) shows immunological rejection after 12 days—proof that the Riteris brothers were not identical twins.

John (left) and Andrew Riteris one year after the operation.

knew that every day was a gift and penned the following poem nine months after his surgery:

Ode to the Memory of a Moment

The sun that shines so bright today,
The sun, so full of life;
I'd stay a while, that's if I may
To stay with love and life.

But as the moons that come and go,
So life comes to a stop;
Like the river in a steady flow,
One simply can't catch up.

The setting sun, that sets and sets,
I call, and run, and shout!
But the sun from me just farther gets!
Why call, why run, why shout?

There is no catching up with her,
There is no change to fate;

JOHN RITERIS, *First Allogeneic (Non-Identical-Twin) Kidney Transplant*

My heart, it fills with tired air,
The day is getting late.

This beautiful last rose of years,
The last of all the light;
Soon it will die, but as if tears
Had made it look more bright?

And tenderness and love to me
Are but a memory;
And so is all that makes me "me"
Yes, just a memory.

John M. Riteris
November 11, 1959

CHAPTER 12

THE DAWN OF CHEMICAL IMMUNE SUPPRESSION

As it turned out, the "x-ray/bone marrow" method of suppressing the immune system was merely a journey down a side road toward success in the field of organ transplantation. Along the way, we had learned important details about patient care, and certainly John Riteris would say the trip had been worthwhile. But as a protocol for human immune suppression it was cumbersome and unpredictable. Fortunately, a new option—immunosuppressive drugs—appeared on the scene and offered a less complex approach to the problem.

In 1959, Dr. Robert Schwartz and Dr. William Dameshek, both hematologists at Tufts Medical School in Boston, reported in *Nature* (Vol. 183, p. 1682) on the immunosuppressive effects of an anticancer drug called 6-mercaptopurine (6-MP). This drug had been synthesized by biochemists Dr. George Hitchings and Dr. Gertrude Elion at Burroughs-Wellcome, Ltd., as part of their lifelong study of purines and pyrimidines, the building blocks of proteins.

The Schwartz and Dameshek experiments were simple and decisive. Rabbits were given 6-MP and a foreign protein (antigen) that normally would cause them to produce antibodies against it. When both the drug and the foreign protein were given simultaneously, the rabbits failed to produce antibodies against the antigen but were still able to make antibody against other proteins. In other words, they "tolerated" the introduced protein because co-administration of the 6-MP fooled their immune systems. The implication was that one could weaken the immune response in a specific fashion without weakening it more generally.

This "drug-induced immunological tolerance," specific only for the antigen introduced at the time the drug was given, was a striking finding. It demonstrated that these test rabbits were not "immunological cripples," unlike rabbits in which the immune system had been damaged or

| ADENINE | 6 MERCAPTOPURINE | B W 57-322 |

ACTIONS

1. Specific inhibition of antibody production when administered during the inductive phase of antibody synthesis.

2. Unspecific inhibition of rapidly dividing cells.

POSSIBLE MODE OF ACTION

Interfere competitively with the biological role of Adenine, thus impair synthesis of DNA, RNA and protein.

Chemical formulas of adenine, 6-mercaptopurine (6-MP), and BW57-322 (now called azathioprine, or Imuran), a refined form of 6-MP. Note how similar the synthetically made 6-MP is to the naturally occurring adenine, the only difference being the substitution of a sulfhydryl group (SH) for ammonia (NH_2). The five-sided elements in the upper right portion of the Imuran structure is a substitute for the single hydrogen element in 6-MP. Although it is a fraudulent substitute for adenine, the body is fooled.

eradicated by lethal or sublethal irradiation. Their immune systems still functioned normally; they simply did not attack a specific antigen. Such tolerance turned out to be just what the doctor ordered.

Even more heartening, Dr. Roy Calne in London (and later Dr. Charles Zukoski in Virginia) was using the drug in the canine kidney model with promising results. The transplanted kidney presented a whole group of foreign antigens. Encouraged, I could not wait to get started testing the drugs in our lab. At Peter Medawar's suggestion, Roy Calne came from London to work with us as a Research Fellow. On his way to Boston, he visited Drs. Hitchings and Elion at the Burroughs-Wellcome laboratory in Tuckahoe, New York, where they gave him several other experimental drugs to test as well.

Within a few weeks of Roy's arrival at the Brigham, we had a dog survive 35 days with a functioning allograft using 6-MP as the only immunosuppressive agent. To put this breakthrough in perspective, con-

The Dawn of Chemical Immune Suppression

sider our prior experience. For almost a decade, I had done renal transplants in hundreds of dogs using many different protocols. The longest survival time was 15 days. Yet that "survival," achieved using the x-ray/bone marrow protocol, was relative. The dogs barely subsisted and were sickly and lethargic. In contrast, the dogs treated with 6-MP were lively after their transplants. It was clear that chemical immunosuppression was vastly superior to x-irradiation.

I was a willing convert; I knew that drugs were the way to go. But Dr. John Merrill did not wholeheartedly agree. He had no "hands-on" connection with our lab and therefore did not witness (and, at first, was not particularly interested in) the outstanding results we were achieving. In a way, his skepticism was understandable. John had spent a year in Paris working closely with Dr. Jean Hamburger at Neckar Hospital, whose belief in x-irradiation had deeply influenced him. This belief was not unfounded, since both Hamburger and another French researcher, Dr. René Küss at Foch Hospital, were having sporadic success with the radiation protocol in patients. Just as my lab experiences

George Hitchings (left), the biochemist at Burroughs-Wellcome, with me at the dedication of the Hitchings-Murray Laboratory at Brigham & Women's Hospital in 1985. He and Gertrude Elion developed and synthesized the first immunosuppressive drugs.

were convincing to me, John felt equally sure that, in the clinical setting, we should continue with the x-ray/bone marrow approach.

We solved this difference of opinion by using only immunosuppressive drugs in one group of patients while simultaneously continuing the human radiation protocol study, which by then was about half completed. Our experiences with the radiation-treated transplant recipients were both tantalizing and frustrating, with periods of excellent function followed by the inevitable decline and finally death. The only exception was John Riteris (Chapter 11), who represented a living example of the "light at the end of the tunnel." While we seemed to be getting closer with each patient, the ultimate demise of all the others was heartbreaking for all those involved: the doctors, the patients, and their families.

Success in humans seemed possible, but elusive. In contrast, our increasing success using drug therapy in the lab was invigorating. Soon dogs were surviving and acting normally for over 100 days after having received kidney allografts, and their only treatment consisted of daily doses of immunosuppressive drugs. The most effective drug we used was azathioprine (Imuran). It seemed only a matter of time before we could translate these experimental results to the hospital patients.

Animal caretakers Heywood Wornum and Bill Barry at a party for "New Hampshire," our 1,000-day canine transplant survivor.

A Fruitful Collaboration

With great optimism, Roy Calne and I made numerous trips to visit Hitchings and Elion in Tuckahoe, New York, and they frequently visited us in Boston, to exchange progress notes directly. For meaningful communication, we had to learn some basic principles of immunology, microbiology, and biochemistry. They, in turn, learned about the basics of clinical care. Over a period of several months, armed only with a blackboard, some chalk, and our combined expertise, basic scientists and clinical scientists worked together to try to find a logical selection and sequencing of a variety of drugs that might knock out just enough antibodies to suppress the immune system without disabling it entirely. It was so exciting that we never thought of it as work. It was like one big family, including the dogs. Whenever Hitchings and Elion visited us, the dogs greeted them with tails wagging, and they called most of the dogs by their names.

In all, Roy and I tested over 20 different drugs, most of them derivatives of 6-MP. Our survival results continued to improve with each subtle alteration of the protocols. Ultimately, it was azathioprine (Imuran), a derivative of 6-MP, that provided the best therapeutic index (i.e., ratio of function/morbidity). The results we were achieving in the lab with Imuran were impressive. Not only were the dogs alive, but they were lively, healthy, and able to procreate and have normal offspring. We watched with satisfaction and gratification as increasing numbers of dogs survived for hundreds of days. When we had a 1,000-day survivor, named "New Hampshire," we tied a ribbon around the dog's neck and had a party.

Insights into Immunity

Along with our satisfying association with the scientists at Burroughs-Wellcome, we also had the privilege of working with a steady stream of talented research fellows attracted to our Brigham/Harvard program. Dr. Ken Porter, a pathologist from London's St. Mary's Hospital, had preceded Roy Calne and contributed immensely to our x-ray/bone marrow protocols in mice and rabbits. Dr. Guy Alexandre from Belgium, who followed Roy, expanded our immunosuppressive drug studies in dogs.[25]

The years from 1959 to 1964 were sparkling, bursting with insight into transplantation biology and suggesting new avenues to investigate.

What an antidote to the discouragement of the previous four years. It was "total immersion," as we all worked together to answer the myriad questions. As Peter Medawar said,

> The whole period was a golden age of immunology, an age abounding in synthetic discoveries all over the world, a time we all thought it was good to be alive. We, who were working on these problems, all knew each other and met as often as we could to exchange ideas and hot news from the laboratory.
>
> (From *Memoirs of a Thinking Radish—An Autobiography*, 1986, Oxford University Press, p. 135)

One of the most important of those questions was, "Do the drugs *completely* suppress the host immune response?" In other words, "Is the animal an 'immunological cripple,' unable to withstand ordinary everyday infection?" The answer proved to be "no." The transplanted dogs that were treated with these drugs and survived for as long as a year with normal kidney function could still reject skin allografts from other donors. In fact, they could still reject skin grafts from the original kidney donor! (We kept all donor dogs alive as part of the experimental design.) Interestingly, during the 10 to 15 days that elapsed while the test skin allograft was being rejected, kidney transplant function deteriorated somewhat; however, once the rejected skin was completely gone, renal function returned to normal.

Another indication that a drug-treated transplant had retained immunological function came when a dog accidentally cut its lip five months after the transplant. The cut progressed to an infection (osteomyelitis) of the jaw that I felt would surely prove fatal. However, after good wound care and antibiotic treatment, the dog healed normally with no impairment of renal function. This was a convincing, serendipitous demonstration that the animal's normal immune mechanisms were intact.

We also wondered whether the drugs could be discontinued after several months of normal function. The answer was equivocal. Some dogs were successfully weaned from their drugs, while others required restarting the drugs. In summary, it was too unpredictable to stop administering drugs for fear of losing the kidney.

Several other questions begged for answers:

- *Did the prolonged survival of the kidney in its new host allow it to "adapt" to the new environment (i.e., lose its immunological identity)?*

  We tested this theory by reimplanting the transplanted kidney back in its original donor and found that it could indeed function happily in its old environment. Living elsewhere had not added to its antigenicity.

- *Were the different survival times in individual animals determined by differences in the absorption or metabolism of the drugs?*

  We tried to answer this question by transplanting two kidneys at the same time, one each from a different donor, and found that the recipient could reject one kidney while retaining the other. This finding provided strong evidence that metabolism and adsorption of the drug were not critical factors in success. In some instances, long-surviving recipients were able to reject the second kidney *from the original donor*, while the first transplanted kidney continued to function without incident. Although this biological observation presented a challenge, we chose not to investigate it further for fear of being diverted from our immediate goals.

- *Would the drugs affect endocrine function? Would the dogs be sterile? If they were fertile, would their puppies be deformed?*

  Answers to these three questions also came serendipitously after two of our long-surviving transplanted drug-treated recipients got cozy on the runway, and the female produced a normal litter.

One interesting peripheral discovery that came from our transplant work was the existence of a "hierarchy" of tissue and organ rejection. Skin is the most difficult of all to transplant; in fact, we still cannot transplant skin allografts permanently, no matter what drug and dosages are used. The most likely explanation for this is that over the eons skin has evolved as our ultimate protective barrier against environmental foreign proteins, making its role in immunity a vital one.

Spring of 1961, outside the laboratory at Harvard Medical School. From left to right: Larry Ayers, animal caretaker; Roy Calne; Trudy Elion; George Hitchings; Dr. Donald Searle; Dr. Ted Hager (one of John Merrill's Research Fellows); and me. All four dogs are thriving on transplanted kidneys after removal of their native kidneys.

Where Ignorance is Bliss, 'Tis Folly to Be Wise

In those early days of transplantation, none of us realized that the rejection process was reversible. We had assumed that rejection was an "all-or-none" process—once started, loss of the graft was inevitable. But we discovered, first in animals and later in patients, that rejection could be reversed by adding drug dosages or employing certain intravenous infusion techniques.

At that time, most of the today's fundamentals of transplantation biology were still unknown: the presence of different kinds of lymphocytes (such as B and T cells) and their different roles, the existence of chemical messengers (called cytokines) by which the immune system directs its army, and the mechanisms by which the immune system recognizes any antigen as either "self" or "foreign." It was likely that the lymphocytes that all looked so much alike under the microscope actually fell into different groups and that they had ways of communicating with one another. Yet the details were completely unknown to us.

In science and medicine, however, substantial progress can occur even in the absence of total understanding. We simply tested every possible avenue to achieve our goal of helping patients. We did not proceed rashly or blindly; rather, we labored steadily, pursuing every potential lead. We established productive liaisons with basic scientists and were not influenced or intimidated by the pessimism of other clinicians or basic scientists. For our own studies, we demanded solid evidence that renal allografts could function normally under appropriate conditions in genetically unrelated populations of large animals.

Animal experimentation was absolutely essential to the success of human organ transplantation. Our experimental animals were maintained in dry, well-ventilated cages and were fed and exercised regularly. Some ultimately became pets of lab personnel. We treated our laboratory animals with care and compassion, had an "open-door" lab policy at all times, and shared our surgical expertise with interested veterinary students. When necessary, we took these experimental dogs to the nearby Angell Veterinary Hospital for special care.

A Glimmer of Light

With such solid evidence nipping at our heels and frolicking out in the courtyard, we felt sure the time had come to adapt the Imuran protocol to patients.

Donald Toby, a strapping 22-year-old, was the first patient to be treated with Imuran. In March of 1961, he received an unrelated infant's kidney from Dr. Matson's program (Chapter 10). However, we were not sure how much Imuran to give Donald. Extrapolating the drug dose from dog to man was difficult because each metabolizes the drug differently. Normal dogs metabolize, absorb, and excrete Imuran even more differently than terminal nephritic patients. Because Donald was so big, we chose to give him the same dosage of Imuran as we had given the dogs. For the first few weeks after the operation, it looked as though we'd hit a home run the first time at bat. Donald's tiny new kidney was pouring out gallons of urine. We had jugs of it and watched the accumulation with a certain glee. Four full weeks after the transplant, Donald was thriving. But by the 29th day, his white blood counts began to fall. The Imuran dose had been too high and had destroyed his bone marrow function. When he succumbed to infection, we were not totally discouraged, because he died from drug toxicity and *not* from organ rejection. As with Gladys Loman, we were saddened for

Donald and his family; however, we did feel we had moved a bit further along the road to success.

In December of that same year, we performed another transplant in a 38-year-old man using another infant kidney from Dr. Matson's service. This time we halved the Imuran dosage. For a week the patient's kidney function was good. When his white count began to fall, we temporarily stopped the drug but resumed therapy when the count started to return to normal. But it was too late. He died of kidney failure with convulsions 13 days after the transplant.[26]

For the third patient, a 20-year-old man, we again halved the dosage of Imuran and used the only available donor source—a cadaver. This transplanted kidney functioned poorly, and the patient died after 14 days.

In spite of these discouraging failures, success seemed close. We had actually been able to reverse the rejection process in our second patient—a previously unknown and totally unexpected phenomenon. Although aware of the need to consider such variables as drug dosage, extent of renal function, and genetic factors, we felt sure that it was only a matter of time before we would succeed. In fact, it took less than a year.

CHAPTER 13

MEL DOUCETTE
First Cadaveric Donor Kidney Transplant

> *Procedure:* Cadaveric kidney transplant
> *Date of Operation:* April 5, 1962
> *Institution:* Peter Bent Brigham Hospital, Boston, Massachusetts

On April 5, 1962, Mel Doucette, a 23-year-old accountant, happened to be at the Brigham for dialysis treatment when a 30-year-old man undergoing open-heart surgery died on the operating table. It was pure coincidence that this man's red cell blood type was compatible with Mel's. Since time was of the essence, we arranged to perform the cadaver transplant that evening. The operation went smoothly, and Mel's new kidney began to function on the fifth day.

Postoperative treatment is critical, and once again Dr. Merrill and I had an honest difference of opinion about what treatment would be best. I felt the Imuran dosage should be halved again and argued for a dose of 2 to 4 mg (compared with the 10 to 12 mg given to Donald Toby). Dr. Merrill disagreed. Reading our debate, as recorded in Mel's medical record starting on April 24, 1962, is akin to watching a fast-paced tennis match as Dr. Merrill and I volley the opinions:

MURRAY: "Treat him only with Imuran. Keep the dosage low and the protocol uncomplicated."

MERRILL: "Let's increase his dosage. If we are to give him maximum dosage it must be done at this time."

MURRAY: "Our chief aim is not to lose the patient to drug toxicity."

MERRILL: "Although we have no experience with it, it seems to me that small doses of whole body irradiation might perhaps impair the proliferation of drug-resistant clones of antibody-forming cells. . . . I wonder if it might not be possible to give him small doses of whole body irradiation in place of the Actinomycin. . . ."

MURRAY: "Dr. Merrill's idea of total body irradiation seems too hazardous in view of potential toxicity of drugs and X-ray. Moreover, the lack of any experimental data favoring such an approach argues for continuation of our present course of Actinomycin weekly and Imuran daily.

As much as this interchange reflects a friendly intellectual rivalry, it also illustrates the real anguish and uncertainty we had about how best to treat this patient. We had honest differences of opinion about the type and amount of drug to use and whether the drug should be supplemented by radiation. This was uncharted territory, and we knew all too well that the wrong decision could cost the patient his life.

Finally, we decided to continue the protocol I had specified. Mel Doucette survived. When he reached the one-year mark, we refrained from tying a ribbon around his neck, but we did deem the operation a

The earliest successful kidney transplant recipients (left to right): Bob Canada (donor = mother); Mel Doucette (donor = cadaver); Harold Rose (donor = brother); Don Messenger (donor = father).

success and the case worthy of publication. Our report in the *New England Journal of Medicine* in June of 1963[27] was a major impetus for worldwide organ transplantation.

In just eight years, beginning with the day the Herrick twins walked through the doors of the Brigham in 1954, we had reached our goal. The "holy grail"—the successful transplantation of an organ from a dead donor—was now firmly in our grasp.

The success of this operation ushered in the modern era of human organ transplantation. Our results with Mel Doucette were described by one observer as "a small glimmer of light in an otherwise gloomy picture." But with this triumph came some difficult issues.

From Experiment to Expectation

Soon after Mel's operation, transplants began to be performed with regularity at major hospitals around the world. By the mid-1960s there were so many surviving transplant recipients that special clinics had to be set up to monitor their status, and clinical fellows had to be specially trained to manage them. Dr. Merrill was instrumental in the organization of this renal evaluation program at the Brigham, and he and I assigned the medical and surgical personnel involved. I maintained daily contact with the laboratory and still managed to perform my regular plastic surgery operations on Mondays, Wednesdays, and Fridays. However, by 11:00 A.M. on Tuesdays and Thursdays, I felt compelled to be in the lab, where I remained often until midnight.

Dr. Charles B. Carpenter, who came to the Brigham in 1962 as a fellow because of the promising work we were doing in the field of transplantation, recently recalled the atmosphere at that time:

> My recollections of those days as a fellow are many, but the first things that come to mind are the extraordinary teamwork and sense of commitment among all the staff, and the personal and humane level of caring for the patients and their families. The atmosphere was fostered by Drs. Murray and Merrill, who, even when disagreeing about plans and policies outside the patient's room, would unite in warm personal support of the patient's interests.
>
> (*J Am Soc Nephrol* 12:203, 2001)

The major emphasis in my surgical life was changing from plastic surgery to transplant surgery. In addition, I had to tackle the administrative details of the clinical transplant program. Many issues needed to be resolved. The most pressing among them were defining "death," procuring and preserving donor organs, and determining ways to standardize and monitor patient care. But we also faced unique ethical and humanitarian questions. For example, when approaching a living donor, how could a clinician counsel the donor without appearing coercive? And when anticipating the availability of an organ from a critically ill patient, how could a doctor decide between trying to save one patient while another waited in the next room, desperately hoping for a donor? The advent of organ transplantation brought with it many such complex and perplexing issues. Overriding everything, however, was an element we could not control then and still cannot control today—the random occurrence of potential donors.

The International Conference on Human Kidney Transplants

As a way of resolving some of the issues that were within our power to resolve, the National Academy of Sciences/National Research Council jointly organized an international conference to be held in Washington, D.C., in 1963. The purpose of the conference was to pool and evaluate the data on *all* human kidney transplantations from many centers for the purpose of minimizing errors and identifying those factors in donor selection and patient care that contributed to success. Transplant groups came from France, Germany, England, Scotland, Denmark, and cities throughout the United States. As a member of the subcommittee on Tissue Transplantation, I chaired the meetings, and Peter Medawar attended in his well-deserved role as the premier leader in transplantation biology.

Some of the best minds in the field were present in that one room. Although organ transplantation was still in its infancy, there was a very real sense that it was burgeoning. It seemed everyone wanted a piece of the action, and the attendees—mostly young, aggressive, and ambitious doctors—jockeyed for prominent positions in the field.

Being concerned that in their eagerness to see results the participants might move ahead unfettered whatever the cost, I advocated slow and steady progress, and expressed the importance of long-term results.

I felt a bit like the mother hen at this meeting, trying patiently but consistently to maintain cautious optimism in the face of the almost entrepreneurial zeal for rapid progress.

One issue we all agreed upon was the need for implementing certain standards. Even though kidney transplants were being done with more frequency and with continually improving success rates, the procedure was by no means routine and the methods far from boilerplate. Everyone seemed to have a slightly different approach, and it soon became clear that if we could compare data from all the major transplant centers, we would have a yardstick against which our individual experiences could be measured. Although we all thought such a yardstick would be a very handy tool, the question then became how to create it.

Setting Up the National Kidney Registry

It was Peter Medawar who suggested that everyone document all past and future cases and send the material to me. This was like the Pope telling the Bishops what to do, and just about everyone complied. Once back at the Brigham, we designed wall charts detailing the findings for all our transplant patients. Martha Albro, a former patient who had been successfully treated for a malignant tumor of the neck, was employed as coordinator of the registry. She sent blank forms of these charts out to all the transplant centers, with strict instructions to return the carbon to us. At the end of every month, Martha would tally the results and provide a picture of the state of transplantation worldwide. At the end of each year, we published an international report on the findings.

From the very beginning of this kidney registry program, I knew it would be successful. At the time, I did a lot of traveling around the world on speaking engagements (and still do!), and everywhere I went these wall charts were being used. The system worked beautifully as a model of shared knowledge. We achieved almost 100 percent, worldwide cooperation even with the occasional jockeying for leadership positions in this exciting new field. The participants realized that they simply could not afford to be left out, and everyone eagerly participated in order to make it work. Renowned transplant centers were established by David Hume in Richmond, Virginia, by Tom Starzl in Denver, Colorado, and later by John Najarian in San Francisco and Minneapolis, and each cooperated fully.

Ultimately, 11 yearly reports were published. Although it was satisfying to be the hub of information for all the transplant teams around the world, in the early 1970s the program outgrew our ability to administer it from the Brigham. Responsibility was therefore transferred to the American College of Surgeons, where Dr. John Bergan of Chicago ran it for a few years until the government was willing to take over the program. Paul Terasaki at UCLA has expanded the program extensively and is currently running the program in conjunction with UNOS. It has been enormously rewarding to see how others have devised systems of organ procurement and distribution around the world. To think that it started with a suggestion from Peter Medawar and the cooperation of those few early transplant surgeons!

Defining "Death"

Even though cadavers had now become an acceptable source of kidneys for transplantation, the fact remained that the number of patients dying of kidney failure far outweighed the number of available donors. To increase the number of donors required putting in place some sort of procurement system, which in turn raised a more difficult issue. In transplantation, the time between death of the donor and revascularization of the organ in the recipient is critical, thus making the determination of exactly when death occurs of paramount importance.

Traditionally, "death" has been defined as the cessation of breathing and heartbeat, but these criteria had become obsolete as methods of resuscitation had improved. Across the country, the response to the seemingly simple question "When is a person dead?" varied widely. Most alarming was the position of certain doctors at the kidney conference who had stood up and said "I'm not going to wait for the medical examiner to declare the patient dead; I'm just going to take the organ."

Statements such as this, combined with passage of the Uniform Anatomical Gift Act in all 50 states in 1968, prompted the formation of the Harvard Committee on the Definition of Death, chaired by Dr. H. Beecher. I was on this committee, and our findings were reported in 1968 in a landmark paper, "A Definition of Irreversible Coma." This short paper, published over 30 years ago in the *Journal of the American Medical Association* (Vol. 205, pp. 337–340), advocated the determination of death based on permanent loss of brain function rather than on the cessation of breathing and heartbeat. This report, with a few modifications, remains the standard today.

THE BRIGHAM: A "UNIQUE WORLD RESOURCE"

Spending these years on the front lines of transplantation was unquestionably exhilarating. At no other time in my career had there been such an immediate, direct, and widespread application of work done in the lab to the patient setting. From an initial zero percent success rate, kidney transplantation could now be considered a consistently reliable option for patients with renal failure around the world. Today, the expected survival rates for cadaveric kidney transplants is about 85 percent, and those involving living donors are even higher. In 1997, doctors at the Brigham had performed 67 transplants, one-third of which came from living donors, and the success rate was 100 percent. In March of the following year, the Brigham held a celebration for all the kidney transplant recipients of the previous year.

How did the Brigham succeed in producing the first successful kidney transplants when there were several others groups working on the problem at the same time? In retrospect, I think it was because we were a multidisciplinary yet integrated group, working toward the same goal. We all met regularly, almost daily, to discuss progress and often shared research fellows, technicians, and lab facilities. John Merrill and his group in Nephrology were always ready to help us with renal function tests on our transplanted dogs, and we surgeons helped them with their tissue-typing experiments on humans and lab animals. Dr. Dammin and his fellows from Pathology also pitched in regularly. In fact, on any given day, we never knew which fellows from which department would be working in our lab.

Hindsight sometimes colors our recollection of events as they really happened and enables us to formulate the subliminal logic behind our investigation. Billingham described this phenomenon when he recounted Sir Peter Medawar's presentation of one of their joint papers:

> I was surprised that his account of our experiments bore no relation to their actual chronology . . . Some [experiments] we'd carried out had only serendipity as their justification. [But] in [his] lecture, "chance" received no credit . . . ; hindsight had enabled creditable reasons to be invented. . . .

As the story unfolded it had a beautiful, logical sequence, like the plot of a well-contrived detective story. It was obvious that the only things that were sacrosanct or inviolable were actual factual observations. Hypotheses could be invented or rejected at will, and the chronology of the experiments conducted and the reasons for embarking upon them were altered to make the best possible story.

> (From Terasaki PI [Ed.]: *History of Transplantation, Thirty-Five Recollections.* 1991, UCLA Tissue Typing Lab Report)

Recognizing this human trait, I have done my best to recount the events in the evolution of organ transplantation as they really did happen and in the order in which they happened, drawing extensively on my notes and records of the time. Nevertheless, the one thing I am absolutely certain of is the critical role the Brigham played in this story. As Dr. Tom Starzl so aptly put it, at the time of the 25th anniversary of the transplant:

> If gold medals were awarded to institutions instead of individuals, the Peter Bent Brigham Hospital ... would have qualified. The ruling board and administrative structure of that hospital did not falter in their support of their quixotic objective of treating end-stage renal disease.... The qualities of leadership, creativity, courage and unselfishness made the Peter Bent Brigham Hospital a unique world resource for that moment of history.

> (From *JAMA* 1984; 251: 2527–2573)

PART III

RECONSTRUCTIVE SURGERY

CHAPTER 14

JAY BALOUN, FRANK WINT, AND DAWN GERMASIAN
A Trilogy of Childhood Head and Neck Tumors

> **JAY BALOUN**
> *Procedure:* Recurrent orbital rhabdomyosarcoma
> *Dates of Operations:* September, 1957, through June, 1961
>
> **FRANK WINT**
> *Procedure:* Recurrent head and neck sarcoma
> *Dates of Operations:* June, 1970; February, 1980; and December, 1981
>
> **DAWN GERMASIAN**
> *Procedure:* Excision of facial and orbital tumor; reconstruction with vascularized composite graft from chest wall
> *Dates of Operations:* May 19 (excision) and May 29 (reconstruction), 1984
> *Institution:* All procedures performed at Children's Hospital, Boston, Massachusetts

Although my success with the Herrick transplant had been enormously gratifying, the recognition I received was in some respects a two-edged sword. Just what type of doctor was I, anyway? As my private practice began to grow, patients were referred to me for treatments ranging from general surgery to urologic and vascular surgery to plastic surgery.

Those who were referred for the surgical correction of cleft lip and palate, protruding ears, or hand and facial trauma were perplexed and wondered if I was a "real" plastic surgeon. Initial consultations with my patients would often begin with them an explanation of my background, which in a way made our doctor-patient relationship more personal. But to this day, some of my colleagues and patients are still confused about my true surgical identity. Was I a urologist? a vascular surgeon? a plastic surgeon?

My Own Office Space at Last

As my practice continued to grow, the office I shared with Dr. Cannon on Dartmouth Street began to feel too far removed from the hub of activity, being more than 2 miles away from the Harvard Medical School quadrangle. Longwood Avenue was where I really wanted to be. It was close to the Brigham and Children's Hospitals and the Surgical Research Laboratory, the geographic center of my medical life. Understandably, office space there was much in demand, and I had to wait three years before space became available.

When Dr. Jackson Thomas, a psychiatrist whom I had not known previously, offered to share his office with me at 319 Longwood Avenue, I felt I was home at last. Although the space was actually more of a cubbyhole than an office, it suited me fine. The only problem was that there was not enough room for both an examining table and a much-needed storage place for instruments and supplies. I couldn't have one without the other. The perfect solution proved to be a set of drawers specially made to fit *underneath* the examining table.

Money was tight, and I remember my excitement being mixed with a bit of anxiety as I spent $100 for that first table. It was leather-covered and had movable head- and foot-rests. Most of the furniture in our home had been inherited, and Bobby noted that the exam table cost more than we had spent for any of our home furnishings. But it was worth it. That examining table stayed with me throughout my career and went on to reign in a succession of considerably larger offices.

The Strong Influence of Dr. Farber

I first met Dr. Sidney Farber when he had lectured to us second-year medical students on the pathology of tumors. We called him the "silver-throated orator," an appellation that did not refer only to his lecturing style. Sidney had a remarkable gift for persuasion, and it was he who founded The Jimmy Fund, now the Dana-Farber Cancer Center, and convinced the world that childhood cancer could be cured.

In the late 1950s, a diagnosis of leukemia or a majority of the sarcomas was tantamount to a death sentence. In children and adolescents, these types of cancer were especially tragic. Dr. Farber, a pathologist by training, would often visit these terminally ill youngsters, who were typically tucked away in the farthest recesses of the hospital wards. One of his patients, a 16-year-old girl named Kathy Welch, crystallized for him the urgent necessity for cure.

A sarcoma is a tumor that arises in connective tissues such as tendons, muscles, and nerves. Kathy was being treated for a particularly aggressive sarcoma of the eye, specifically the orbit, the tissues that encase the eyeball. Despite three surgical excisions, the tumor kept recurring. Sidney watched helplessly as the mass grew first to the size of a tennis ball, then as large as a grapefruit. The mass created such a drag on the side of her face that he would often find Kathy with her head propped up in one hand, just to get some relief from the weight. The sarcoma was killing her in much the same way as would a parasite, and an efficient one at that. A mere 16 months after Kathy first noticed the small, painless mass on her left lower eyelid, she was dead. In every way, the weight of the sarcoma had become too heavy for her to bear.

This case was typical of the worldwide experience with recurrent orbital sarcomas. When Kathy's autopsy revealed that the tumor was confined to the local area around the orbit, and had not spread, Dr. Farber's dejection quickly progressed to determination. He vowed that when the next such case came along he would find surgeons capable of removing the tumor completely, at least offering the possibility of a cure.

Those surgeons turned out to be Dr. Don Matson and me. Always seeking better care for his patients, Dr. Farber had observed the two of us working together skillfully and cooperatively. Since Matson had extensive military and civilian experience with brain surgery, and I had similar experiences with orbital and maxillofacial problems, we often operated together on complex cases involving tumors, trauma, or congenital conditions. Therefore, when Dr. Farber's next patient with recurrent orbital rhabdomyosarcoma, Jay Baloun, came to him for help, it was natural that he would consult with us about treatment and, hopefully, cure.

Meeting Jay Baloun

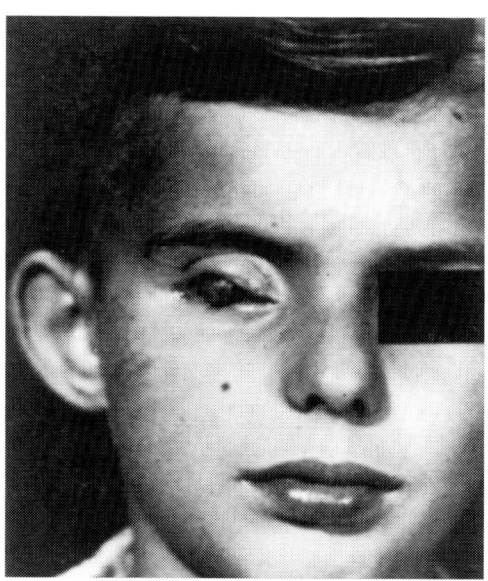

Jay as he appeared when I first met him. The walnut-sized mass was firmly fixed to the bony orbit.

Jay was a spunky 8-year-old boy from Cleveland, Ohio. He had first been seen at Children's Hospital in August of 1957 for a 13-millimeter nodule of recurrent rhabdomyosarcoma protruding from his right orbital cavity. He had already undergone three operations, x-ray treatment, and all the chemotherapy then available. As in Kathy's case, none of it had been effective. Each time the sarcoma recurred without mercy. Consultants at the Massachusetts Eye & Ear Infirmary told his mother, a nurse, that the tumor—a sarcoma that derived from skeletal muscle—was incurable. As she was preparing to take her son home to die, she decided to get yet one more opinion. She brought Jay to see Dr. Farber on a Saturday morning, squeezing in this one last appointment before she and Jay were to catch the afternoon plane home to Cleveland.

Never Enough Time

Noontime on a midsummer Saturday, Dr. Farber called me to consult on the case. I happened to be in my office, tidying up end-of-the-week details. I was anxious to get home to see Bobby and the four kids. This was an exceptionally busy time in my life—I was juggling my time between patients, laboratory work, national meetings, and residency teaching—and time with the family was at a premium.

In order to fit everything in, I routinely awoke before dawn. Since I often drove to work in the dark and returned home under the same conditions, I bought a second-hand Oldsmobile convertible just so I could get some fresh air. In New England, fresh air often means wet or very cold air, but that didn't stop me. I'd drive "topless" down the Worcester Pike (Route 9) in the dead of winter, wearing a thick wool hat and gripping the steering wheel with ski gloves. The other 6 A.M. commuters began to recognize me as a "fresh-air freak" and would honk and wave as I drove by. Every once in a while Wellesleyites still ask about that Olds convertible. I finally sold it after 10 years of service and 200,000 miles.

Saturday afternoons were the only daylight hours I had with family during those busy days. Our first four children's ages ranged from four to 9, and we enjoyed spending time bicycling, playing outside in the garden, or shopping for the inevitable household needs at the hardware store. Those afternoons were cherished by all of us, so when I answered the phone in my office that Saturday and heard Dr. Farber's plea for help, I was at first reluctant to listen. But Dr. Farber was characteristically persuasive, which is how I found myself, along with Dr. Matson, spending Saturday afternoon in Dr. Farber's office on the top floor of The Jimmy Fund building.

I was impressed with the strength of both Jay and his mother. This otherwise healthy 8-year-old boy was not going to let a little sarcoma get in his way. Despite his previous operations, x-ray treatment, and chemotherapy, he was in all other respects a normal kid, full of life. The sarcoma had recurred for the fourth time and was now the size of a walnut. But after examining him, it seemed that a curative surgical operation was within the realm of possibility. It was 1957, and I had never seen or heard of any such operation, but I was fascinated by the challenge and driven by a curiosity as to how we could accomplish it.

The orbital area between the forehead and the nose was, up until this point, a surgical "no man's land." Most surgeons avoided it. Dr. Matson and I analyzed Jay's situation and determined which essential anatomical structures had to be preserved. We decided to make no effort to save his vision of that eye. Instead, we

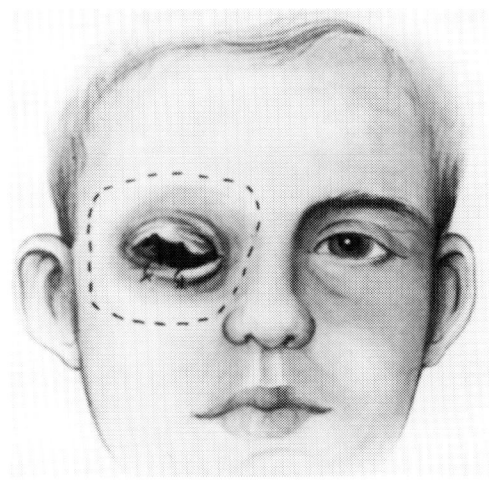

Dotted lines show the outline of the skin incisions to remove Jay's tumor.

would remove—in one block—the eye and all surrounding bone, muscles, and nerves between the brain above and the hard palate below. For the 1950s, this was radical surgery, but we knew a more conservative excision would ultimately prove to be fatal.

Back to the Anatomy Lab

Fortunately, I had access to the nearby Harvard Medical School Anatomy Lab where I could study and carefully plan the appropriate surgical operation. There I devised the most extensive resection possible that would still preserve brain function above and palate function below. Everything in between was expendable.

Dr. Matson and I explained the magnitude of the operation to Jay's mother and told her that we had never before done such a procedure. Knowing that this was Jay's only hope; she gave us the "go ahead." The alternative would have been to return home to Cleveland where Jay would die, most likely within a few months.

We operated a few days later. All went as planned, though the postoperative defect was large enough to hold a golf ball. We covered it with a split-thickness skin graft placed directly on the frontal lobe of the brain and right on top of the raw surfaces of Jay's nasal and oral cavities. This type of graft takes the topmost part of the skin—the soft epidermis and the top two-thirds of the underlying, tougher part (the dermis)—from one part of the body (the donor site) and moves it to where skin is needed. The lower third of the dermis at the donor site is left to heal: in 10 to 14 days,

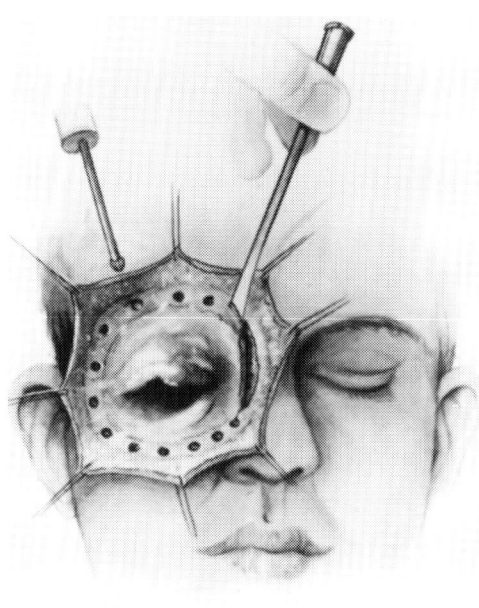

Beginning of removal of the bony orbit, from the frontal lobe of the brain above to the hard palate below.

it will grow back the missing two-thirds of the dermis, and all the epidermis. After the skin graft healed in place and there was no further need for dressings, Jay was able to go to school with a simple gauze pad as camouflage.

Contrary to my natural inclination to perform final reconstruction immediately following the excisional surgery, I felt in Jay's case that we needed the benefit of time for observation, to be sure his particularly aggressive tumor did not recur. In this I was in agreement with Dr. Hayes Martin's philosophy of delayed reconstruction.

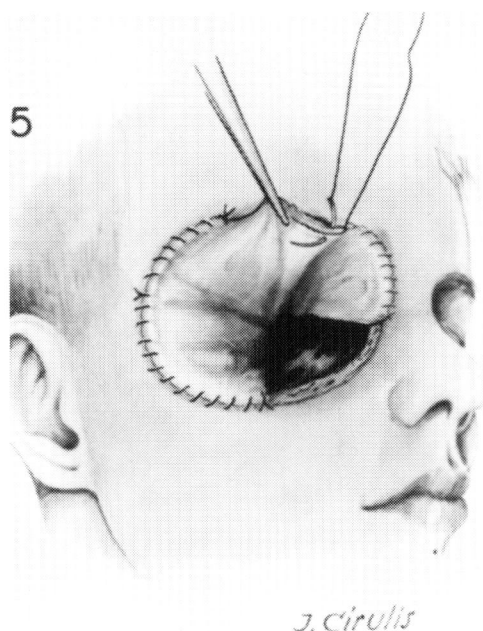

Skin graft from thigh is sutured in place to cover the operative defect.

Four years had elapsed without recurrence when we received word from Jay's family physician in Cleveland that Jay had begun to have convulsions. Our hearts sank, since this development implied that the sarcoma had recurred.

In 1961, Jay returned to Boston for examination, and we were thrilled to find our assumptions had not been correct. The sarcoma had not returned at all. Rather, infection had entered his brain through the crevices in the split-thickness skin graft and created an abscess in the frontal lobe. Split-thickness skin is not much thicker than cardboard and does not provide a foolproof barrier against the environment. Dr. Matson excised the brain abscess, but it was now clear that Jay required a more protective form of skin and soft tissue reconstruction.

The only reconstruction method available in those days was the multiple-stage transfer of tissue from one part of the body to another. Similar to the way we created Charles Woods' nose (see Chapter 1), we fashioned skin and fat from Jay's arm into a tube pedicle that resembled a suitcase handle and, in multiple stages, shifted it to the orbital area, leap-frog style. We thus created a sturdy covering for the

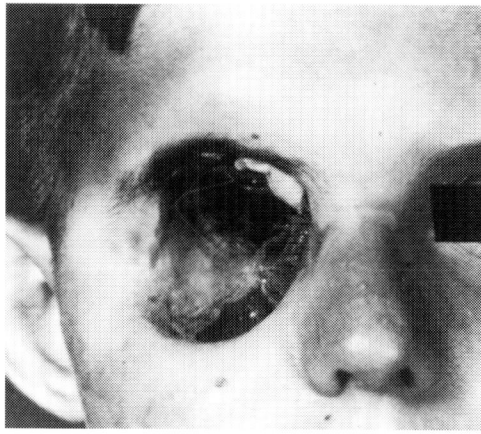

Jay 2 months after the operation, with skin graft in place.

brain, the paranasal sinuses, and the external skin surface that would offer protection against physical trauma and infection.

The reconstruction was successful and has served its purpose ever since. Jay has been content to use a frosted eyeglass lens as the only camouflage for his missing eye. Many years later, he stopped by my office to introduce me to his fiancée. Since then, he has married, has become a father, and leads a normal life, with no sign of recurrence of the tumor. Jay's was the first cure for childhood orbital rhabdomyosarcoma at Children's Hospital. Over the years, we published comprehensive reports (see Chronological Bibliography) on subsequent patients, two of whom will now be

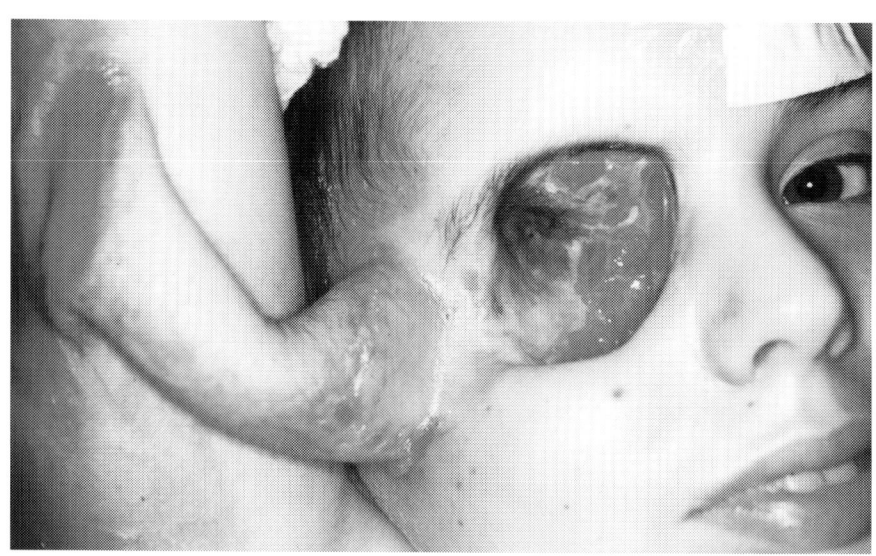

One stage in the six-stage transfer of a tube pedicle from Jay's arm to the orbit.

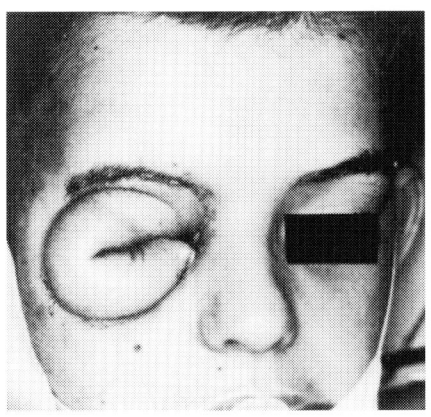 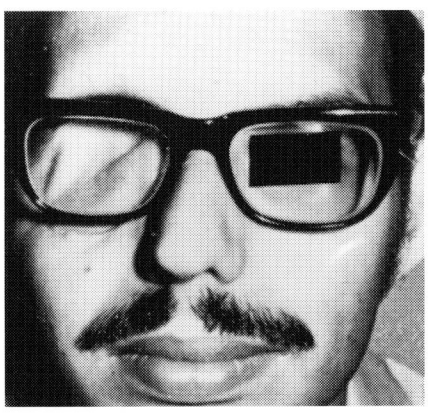

The next-to-final stage in the pedicle transfer. *Jay as an adult, 14 years after the resection.*

described briefly to illustrate the continuing refinements in surgical care over the next several decades.

Meeting Frank Wint

Frank Wint arrived at Children's Hospital 12 years after Jay's initial operation. His story demonstrates not only how far we had come during that interval but also that not every patient's death represents a failure.

In 1969, when Frank was five years old, he was diagnosed as having a peritonsillar abscess, an infection in or near the tonsils that is not at all uncommon in children. On further evaluation at a hospital in Lancaster, Pennsylvania, the "abscess" was found to be an orbital sarcoma. "We didn't even know there were such things as childhood tumors," recounted Frank's mother. "We were stunned. I actually fell into a chair when they told me."

Frank was referred to us at Children's Hospital because, fortuitously, one of the Lancaster doctors consulted on the case was a Harvard man who told them about a place in Boston called The Jimmy Fund. With no other alternatives, the Wints packed up and left the next day.

The Wint family had no idea what to expect when they arrived, having only the name of a doctor, Dr. Norman Jaffe, and the address of Children's Hospital. I later learned that they were worried about being just a number to us. They need not have worried. Dr. Jaffe arranged for them to be met at Logan by a police ambulance, and when they arrived at Children's, Dr. Jaffe was waiting for them outside. Mrs. Wint remembers: "Frank Jr. literally was carried out of the ambulance and straight into the arms of the best care he would ever have until he died. They held our beloved child and comforted and reassured him. And us in the process."

Frank underwent six weeks of radiation and chemotherapy. The tumor receded, and he went into a long remission. When Frank was 10 years old (in 1974), his parents felt comfortable telling him he'd had cancer as a child. Frank's response was characteristic of his good humor: "How about that," he said. "And I don't even smoke."

But in 1980, Frank discovered a small lump behind his ear. He and his parents were on a plane to Boston the next morning. Biopsy showed recurrence of the tumor. At this stage, the only treatment was extensive, radical surgery.

Although Frank's cancer was biologically similar to Jay Baloun's, it had spread over a larger area, invading part of his nose and palate. Accordingly, the excision needed to be more extensive. But because the tumor had invaded vital nerves and blood vessels, we could not remove as much tissue as we desired around the margins of the entire tumor. We were aware that the tumor might recur, but not necessarily. Regardless of the uncertainty, Frank's defect was too extensive for the "wait-and-see" approach we had taken with Jay.

We went ahead with the reconstruction, aided by the newly developed technique of microsurgery. Rather than the cumbersome and time-consuming pedicle method (in which the flap of tissue being transferred to cover the operative defect had to remain attached to its site of origin until the graft "took"), Dr. Joe Upton (whom I had recruited as a hand surgeon skilled in microsurgical techniques) and I were able to complete the reconstruction in a single operation. It took us 10 hours to transfer a block of skin, muscle, and subcutaneous fat from Frank's chest wall to the opposite side of his neck. (Jay's reconstruction more than a decade earlier had taken three months to complete.)

The Best Years of His Life

We knew we'd given Frank some time, but we weren't sure just how much. But each day counts, and Frank's parents describe the two-and-a-half years following this operation as the best part of Frank's life.

Frank began training for the marathon, and in November 1981, he ran the Marine Corps marathon in 3 hours, 43 minutes. He did it fast, which is how he did everything, and had never been in better shape. In early December of that same year, we saw Frank in Boston for his annual checkup. Everything looked wonderful.

Frank went home to prepare for the holidays. He was now 17 and had worked hard that fall filling out college applications and was looking forward to some rest and a much-anticipated family trip to San Francisco. But just a week after his checkup in Boston, his gum began to hurt. We all attributed this to irritation caused by the dental prosthesis covering the operative defect in the roof of his mouth. A few days later, while he was at school, the pain came back. Frank knew enough about his condition to check himself out of school and drive as fast as his VW bug would allow to his local doctor.

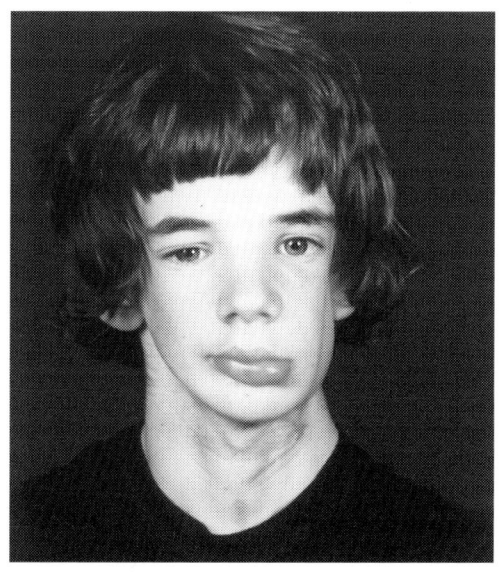

Frank Wint a few months after his second operation in 1980.

That same afternoon, Frank and his parents once again found themselves on an airplane, Boston-bound. I examined him right away and was distressed to see that the tumor had returned. And though I put my arm around Frank and told him we would do everything possible to help him, in truth the situation was grim. There was little we could do beyond keeping him comfortable and free from pain. We all knew Frank was going to die. I told the family to take their trip to San Francisco as planned.

The "End of a Happy Time"

Frank's mother described the best part of the trip: "The five of us went out for dinner in San Francisco, then Frank asked to be driven across the Golden Gate Bridge. We sat on the bank on the opposite side, all

Young Frank going the distance.

together. And that was the end of the happy time."

Frank was sick all that night. No one realized it was Christmas until someone happened to look at a watch the next morning and noticed the date. Frank's condition deteriorated hourly. Frank's dad carried him onto the plane home.

Dr. Mazzahari gave Frank a "honeymoon" drug, a short-acting medication that eased the symptoms sufficiently for Frank to go to the movies with friends on New Year's Eve. In spite of his condition, there was much to celebrate; he had recently been accepted to all four colleges of his choice. He had a wonderful last night out, then began a rapid decline the following day. Mrs. Wint called me in despair. I told her to bring Frank to Boston; we could at least try to give him radiation to reduce his pain. But it was too late. Frank slipped into a coma. He spent his last night on earth with the dog draped over his feet, and his sister, brother, mother, and father all taking turns lying beside him in bed, holding him close. Frank died early in the morning on January 5th, 1982.

Meeting Dawn Germasian

Dawn Germasian is the third patient in this trilogy of surgical advances in the treatment of orbital sarcoma. She came to us in 1984, 27 years after we first saw Jay Baloun and 15 years after we first saw Frank Wint. Dawn's case represents a later stage in our experience in the excision and reconstruction of facial and orbital sarcoma.

Dawn was a teenager with a sarcoma of the left cheek and upper jaw. For some reason, her parents' concern about maintaining her attractive appearance led them to deny the seriousness of her disease. They seemed to worry more about saving her looks than saving her life. Because of their misplaced concern, they were reluctant to accept the need for an operation, missing numerous appointments, delaying treatment decisions, and often harassing the doctors and nurses involved in their daughter's care. No amount of reasoning or explanation on our part seemed to be effective.

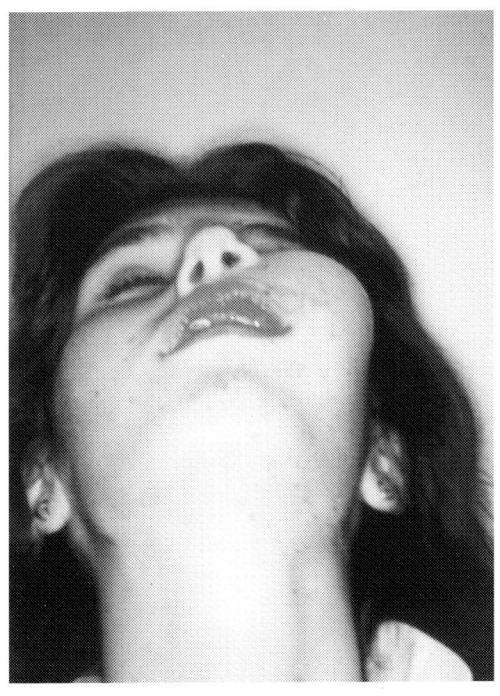

Dawn as we first saw her, with a prominent swelling in the left cheek. The tumor had extended into the oral cavity and had destroyed underlying jawbones.

Fortunately, by now our plastic surgery service at the Children's Hospital and Brigham & Women's Hospital (the new name for the old Peter Bent Brigham) had organized a well-functioning Craniofacial Center that offered a multidisciplinary, integrated approach to patient care. To provide maximum support for Dawn and her family during this difficult time, we mobilized an array of departments, including social services, nursing, anesthesia, psychiatry, hospital administration, and a legal team. I feared that without this special effort, Dawn's very survival was threatened.

During several consultations, both individually and as a group, we patiently explained that a massive surgical resection was required to offer the best chance for cure. Finally, her parents realized that we had Dawn's best interest at heart, and they reluctantly asked us to proceed. But once they made the decision to proceed, they wanted the operation to take place the very next day. Of course it was impossible to mobilize the surgical and nursing staff and operating room personnel overnight.

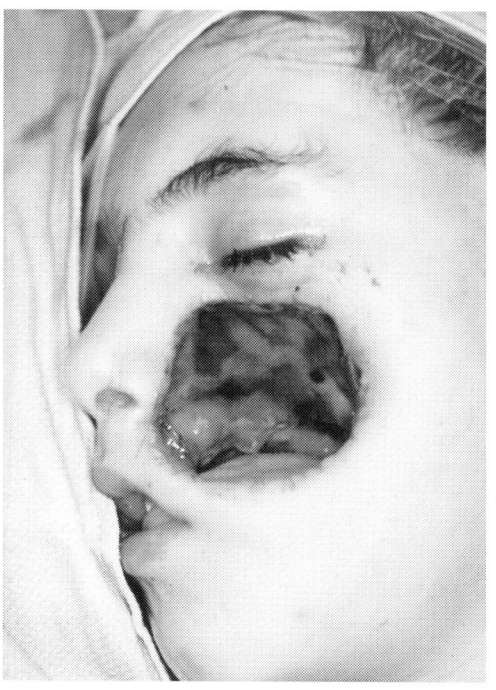

The postoperative defect, covered with a skin graft.

However, sympathetic to the mental turmoil of Dawn and her family, the Childrens' Hospital staff willingly came in on a Saturday—a day not normally used for operations—in order to expedite Dawn's procedure.

The operation went beautifully. We excised a golf-ball-sized mass of tissue that included the tumor, overlying skin, and underlying bone, nerves, and muscle. This left a huge cavity, with the oral and nasal cavities and pharynx exposed. We covered the defect with a split-thickness skin graft as a temporary measure to give us a few days to examine the specimen under the microscope to be sure the margins of the excision were sufficient. The final report from pathology showed that the tumor had been completely removed.

Five days later, Dr. Joe Upton and I filled the postoperative defect with a microvascular flap of skin and muscle taken from the left side of Dawn's chest. During an 8-hour operation, we repaired the raw surface of the mouth, the lining of the nose and the skin of the cheek, thus completing the excision and reconstruction in one hospitalization, with a most satisfactory result. Dawn was able to resume a normal life, with no recurrence of the tumor.

Although the reconstructive surgery for both Frank Wint and Dawn Germasian benefited from the use of microsurgery, Dawn's operation allowed us to refine the technique based on 10 additional years of experience. For Dawn, we were able to meet both the technical challenge of replacing the inner surfaces of the nose and pharynx and the esthetic challenge of providing an acceptable cosmetic result.

The sad irony of the respective surgical outcomes is that Frank was concerned only about survival and embraced life fully, even after an operation that left his face disfigured. Though he survived for only a few years longer, he and his family cherished the extra time together. Dawn, on the other hand, required time to adjust to her marred appearance and was slow to appreciate and acknowledge the combination of surgical skill and extreme good fortune that ultimately saved her life.

It is a long way from Jay Baloun to Frank Wint to Dawn Germasian. Dr. Sidney Farber would have been pleased. The multidisciplinary care Dawn received was a tribute to Children's Hospital and a fitting legacy for both Dr. Farber and Kathy Welch, the courageous 16-year-old girl who inspired him.

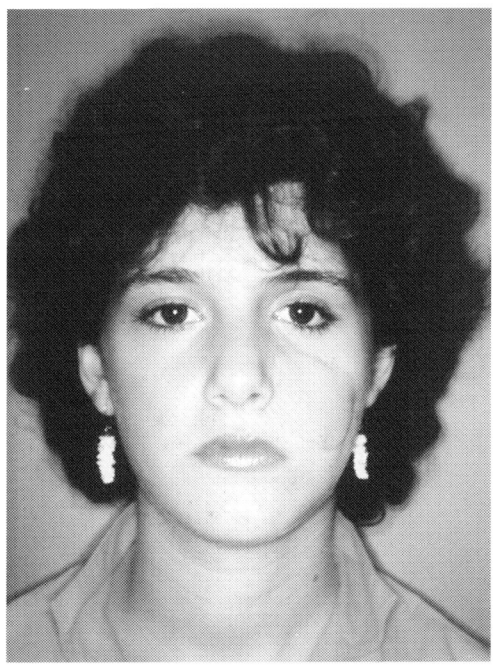

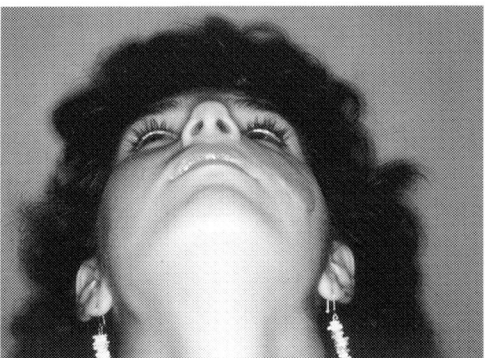

Dawn one year after the one-stage, microsurgical transfer of skin and muscle.

CHAPTER 15

Plastic Surgery at Home and Abroad

In 1962, at the invitation of Dr. Paul Brand, I spent two months working at the Christian Medical School in Vellore, India.[28] Paul was internationally known for his work in rehabilitating patients with leprosy. Using Dr. Sterling Bunnell's hand surgery textbook as his only guide, Paul operated while referring to the text, which was propped open next to the operating table. He developed novel procedures for restoring function. Then, so that these patients might have a real use for those hands, he set up cottage industries on the hospital grounds. The patients made rope, placemats, signs and ceramics, one of which now sits on my desk inscribed with the motto "Difficulties Are Opportunities."

I was delighted when asked to be one of a succession of 12 plastic surgeons who donated two months of our time training the surgeons at Christian Medical School. As I strolled through the streets of Vellore, I was struck by the number of people with uncorrected cleft lips and palates and other obvious facial deformities. This experience proved to be a defining time for me. I realized, in a very direct way, how privileged I was to be a plastic surgeon. As much as any other surgical specialty, ours enables us to give rapid and permanent help to persons so obviously in need. The two months I spent in India also reminded me just how much I had allowed my plastic surgery practice to take a backseat to the demands of the transplantation program. It was time for a reassessment.

When I left for India, Bobby, eternally understanding of my mission in surgery, elected to remain home with our children. Our fifth and youngest child, Tom, was age 4, and Rick was still only a gleam in our eyes. Bobby concentrated on family and friends and channeled any frustrations she may have had with me into improving her tennis skills at the Wellesley Country Club. When she entered competition, she sent

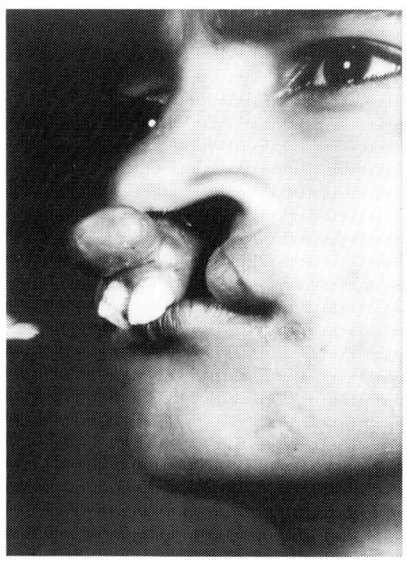 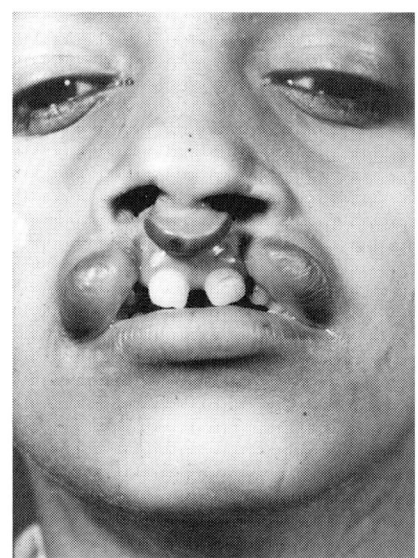

Examples of untreated clefts of lip and palate that were commonly seen in India in the early 1960s.

me weekly letters chronicling her progress. "Beat so-and-so in the first round," said the first letter, which was followed quickly by, "Won the second round." The next letter announced, "I am in the semi-finals."

I kept the Christian Medical School staff updated on Bobby's progress through the ranks, so by the time she reached the semi-finals, everyone was rooting for her. When the news finally came—"Won the finals, 6-2, 6-3"—we all cheered. I, in particular, was proud of her and couldn't help but take some of the credit. After all, it was I who first taught Bobby the game in the intense heat of our first summer at Valley Forge General Hospital, when she was pregnant with Ginny. The finals match must have seemed easy in comparison.

That victory was the first of many for Bobby. While I have won many mixed doubles and men's doubles tournaments, it is Bobby who has upheld the Murray family honor with a succession of singles titles over the years.

My True Surgical Identity

My presentations to the American Surgical Association on transplantation as well as subsequent papers on craniofacial surgery in 1975 and

1979 (see References 230 and 259) afforded me a worldwide and certainly unanticipated prominence. I seemed to have reached a pinnacle at an early age, and I could have spent the rest of my career basking in my good fortune in having become a leader in the field of transplant surgery. But even as I was immersed in my challenging work in transplantation biology, I never lost sight of what I considered my true calling—playing a leadership role in plastic surgery, especially in the area of facial reconstruction in children.

My responsibility as the plastic surgical representative on the American College of Surgeons Forum Committee helped keep me connected with this aspect of my career. But transplantation and its attendant issues were consuming a major portion of my time. As more transplant patients survived, they required more detailed postoperative care for longer periods of time. These demands, on top of those of my private practice, Chairmanship of the Division of Plastic Surgery in two major hospitals, and Directorship of the Surgical Research Lab at Harvard Medical School, made it impossible for me to continue to nurture the budding specialty of Craniofacial Surgery. In short, I simply had too much to do.

The time had come to make a decision: would I pursue transplant surgery or plastic surgery? It was no longer possible to do both well. My choice was instantaneous. In my heart of hearts, I knew that the one aspect of my surgical life I could never give up was reconstructive plastic surgery.

While some viewed my transition from transplantation surgery to reconstructive surgery as a radical change, it really was not. Both transplantation biology and craniofacial surgery are linked to the basic sciences—transplantation with immunology and pathology, and facial problems with genetics and embryology. Changing from one field to the other was as natural as changing from squash to tennis—both are racquet sports, just with a different racquet, ball, and court.

Dr. Moore urged me to consider my decision carefully. But I explained, "Franny, my heart is in reconstructive challenges, especially in children," and he understood. We spent the next two years transitioning two of our top research fellows, Alan Birtch and Dick Wilson, to take over my transplant responsibilities. My day-to-day coverage began to diminish, and my resignation as Chief of Transplant Surgery occurred in 1971. With that ending came a new beginning for me as a plastic surgeon without responsibility for transplantation.

A Joint Residency Program in Plastic Surgery—At Last!

Even during my heaviest involvement with transplantation, most of my work with patients involved plastic surgery issues. Plastic surgery was slowly taking hold as a recognized specialty, so it was a real milestone when, in 1964, I finally succeeded in creating a joint plastic surgery residency between the Brigham and Children's Hospital—the first such program in Boston.

This undertaking had been no easy matter. I knew I'd have problems because for a time I did not have operating privileges at Children's Hospital. Dr. Robert E. Gross was the Surgeon-in-Chief there, and under him as plastic surgeon was his close friend Dr. Donald MacCollum. MacCollum was the only pediatric surgeon at Children's to restrict himself to plastic surgery, and he jealously guarded his "territory." Although he referred many patients to me at the Brigham, Don made it clear that I was not to crowd him, and once told me straight out, "Joe, you're welcome to take over and operate at the Brigham but not at Children's."

My colleagues were upset that I couldn't get on the staff at Children's, but Dr. Cannon's advice to me prevailed, and I had the good sense to keep my mouth shut. Even when I attended Don's plastic surgical clinic, I would just sit and listen, even though I was frequently tempted to offer critical suggestions.

Finally, I was able to achieve entrée into Children's through a side door. Franc Ingraham, the Neurosurgeon-in-Chief, and Don Matson (Chapter 5), Franc's most active associate, invited me to admit cleft lip and palate patients on Children's neurosurgical service. Another major break came when I was introduced to Dr. Lennard T. Swanson, staff orthodontist and later Chief of Dental Services. Len was seeing many children with jaw and facial deformities, and the two of us began to collaborate on their care, concentrating first on the soft tissues around the nose and mouth and then on the upper and lower jaws (either individually or in combination). Even though Dr. Swanson and I were doing cutting-edge plastic surgery, Dr. MacCollum did not feel threatened, since he considered our efforts simple dentistry.

Surprisingly, it was Dr. Gross who ultimately accorded me full privileges at Children's Hospital. One day, out of the blue, he came to my office at the Brigham. He was ready to approve my long-standing request for a plastic surgery residency program to be jointly undertaken by the Brigham and Children's, adding that, in deference to MacCollum, he could not make me Chief. This didn't bother me in the least; I was delighted to have the privilege of uniting the two hospitals in a plastic surgery service following the model in neurosurgery established decades earlier by Dr. Harvey Cushing. I knew that a strong plastic surgery program required integration of a children's hospital and an adult hospital. This was obviously the best way to ensure a continuum of care as our young patients grew through puberty to adulthood.

The joint program proved to be a natural evolution. For one thing, the two hospitals were situated directly across the street from each other and were connected by overpasses. Furthermore, there was precedent for such a unifying program, because for years the two hospitals had shared neurosurgical and orthopedic departments. Gross, who had trained under Dr. Cutler at the Peter Bent Brigham Hospital, understood my thinking and ultimately gave me the go-ahead for what quickly became a thriving program.

CHAPTER 16

WALTER MURPHY
A Surgical No-Man's Land

> *Procedure:* Mid-face advancement using "keyhole" procedure
> *Date of Operation:* August 15, 1966
> *Institution:* Children's Hospital, Boston, Massachusetts

One of the first fruits of the joint plastic surgery program between the Brigham and Children's Hospital was our innovative treatment of Walter Murphy, a teenage boy with Crouzon's syndrome—a deformity of the face, orbit, and jaw that manifested as protruding eyes, sunken cheeks, and a pronounced underbite. Walter's case was rather severe.

In Len Swanson's words, "What we have been doing previously for these patients is not enough. Repositioning either the upper jaw or the lower jaw, or even both, will not be sufficient in this case. Somehow we've got to move his whole face forward." As simple as those words sounded, they led to a revolution in the field of craniofacial reconstruction. As far as I knew, such an operation had never before been done successfully, and I was excited by the challenge. All the "simple dentistry" Dr. Swanson and I had been doing at Children's had been the perfect warm-up for the operation we would perform on Walter.

A HEALTHY PERSPECTIVE

Walter's medical records note his appearance as "rather grotesque." With his peaked head and bulging eyes, it was a description with which not many would argue, and it would have been a fair assumption that

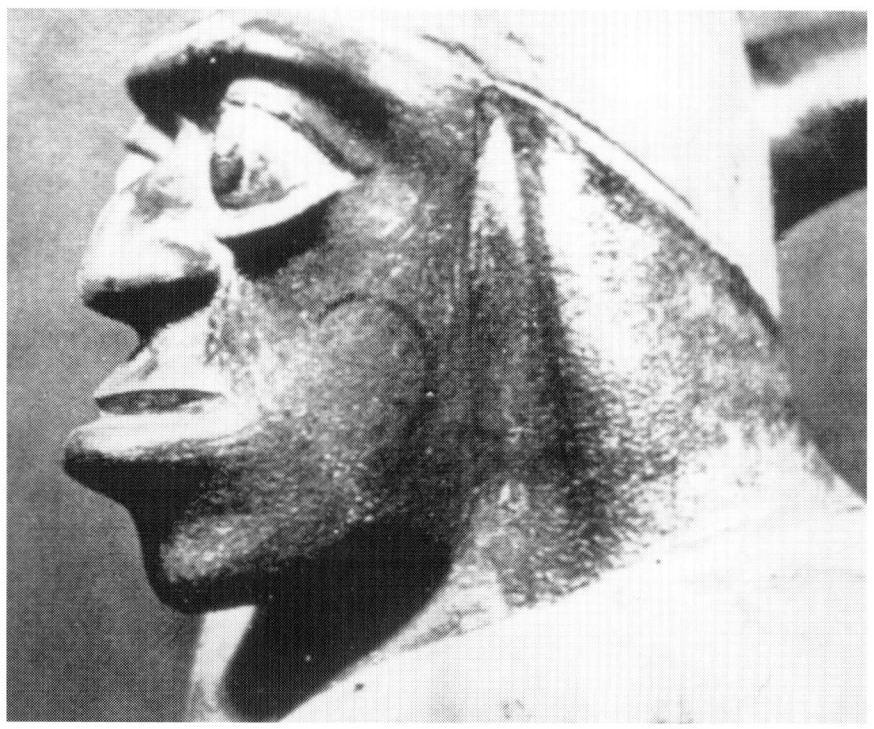

A typical pre-Columbian artifact demonstrating the facial characteristics of Crouzon's syndrome, including prominent eyes, sunken cheeks, and underdevelopment of the entire middle face. The seeming protrusion of the lower lip and jaw is only relative.

Walter had come to us looking for cosmetic improvement. That, however, was not the case. Walter never felt burdened by his appearance. The oldest of five, he described his childhood as happy and normal. He admitted to being chided about his appearance from time to time, but he never let it bother him. "Sure, I was aware I looked different. Aware of it, yes. Burdened by it, no."

But Walter had been dismayed when Dr. Swanson, whom he'd been seeing for treatment for years, told him he would not be able to have dentures later in life. Walter took pride in his beautiful teeth and agreed to the operation we were planning simply because it would correct his dental problem; any improvement in his appearance would be strictly a side benefit.

A Surgical "No-man's Land"

The operation Dr. Swanson and I were considering was revolutionary. Although increasingly complex maxillofacial surgery had been performed since World War II, no one had been able to gain complete access to the area around the eyes without destroying the patient's vision. This relatively unapproachable operative field was aptly termed a surgical "no-man's land." We considered a combination of surgical approaches—incisions above or below the eyes or across the bridge of the nose—but these would still afford only limited, piecemeal access, not the clear visualization of the entire area needed for extensive reconstruction.

A review of the literature showed that a similar operation had been tried only once before—by Sir Harold Gillies in England in the late 1940s. Sir Harold was a flamboyant surgeon, quite daring in his thinking, and his attempt proved to be a disaster. His paper reporting his experience was memorable owing to his stern admonition that the operation never be tried again.

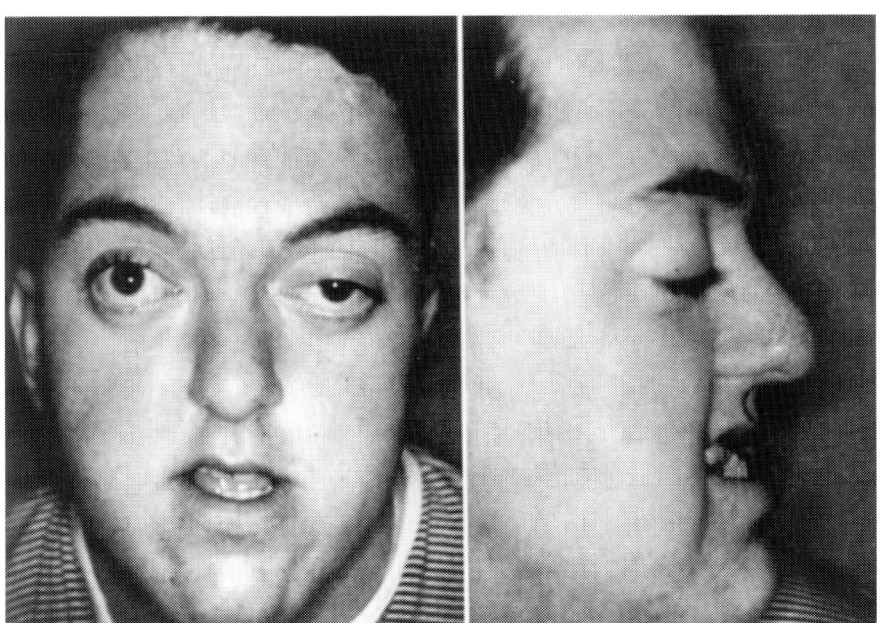

Front and side views of Walter Murphy when he was first seen in our clinic, showing the typical characteristics of Crouzon's syndrome: prominent eyes, flattened cheeks, and underdeveloped upper jaw, which makes the lower jaw seem to protrude.

Basic Anatomy to the Rescue (Again)

Determined not to repeat Gillies' errors, I retired to the anatomy lab, this time with Len Swanson, to work out the best way to mobilize the middle-third of the face while keeping the attached soft tissues in place. After diligently reviewing anatomy books, we came up with a possible solution. We would detach the facial bones from the skull and overlying soft tissue as a unit (a "monoblock") and pull everything forward to the desired position, much like opening a drawer. However, the problem of gaining sufficient access to sever the facial and cranial bones remained.

The operative technique Len and I devised for Walter was a "keyhole" approach. Using multiple incisions to gain access to the bones of the mid-face, we cut them free from their attachment to the cranial bones, thereby allowing us to advance the entire mid-face and upper jaw forward until the upper and lower teeth were in alignment. We then wired the upper teeth to the lower ones to achieve normal occlusion. After "opening the drawer" in this way, we filled in the gaps in the bone (the space behind the "drawer") with bone grafts from the hip area. The overlying skin remains intact, the eyes are protected during the operation by stitching the upper and lower lids together and using gentle retraction of the soft tissues. When all structures can be visualized and vital structures protected, we cut through the frontal bones at critically selected sites. To fill up the spaces resulting from advancement of the facial bones away from their attachments, we used iliac crest bone grafts.

 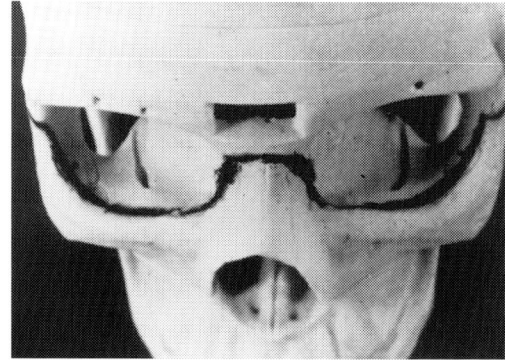

Left panel: Keyhole incisions (dotted lines) were made to reach the underlying bone structure to permit mid-face advancement.
Right panel: Black lines indicate where bone was incised. Other incision sites (not shown) were required within and behind the oral cavity.

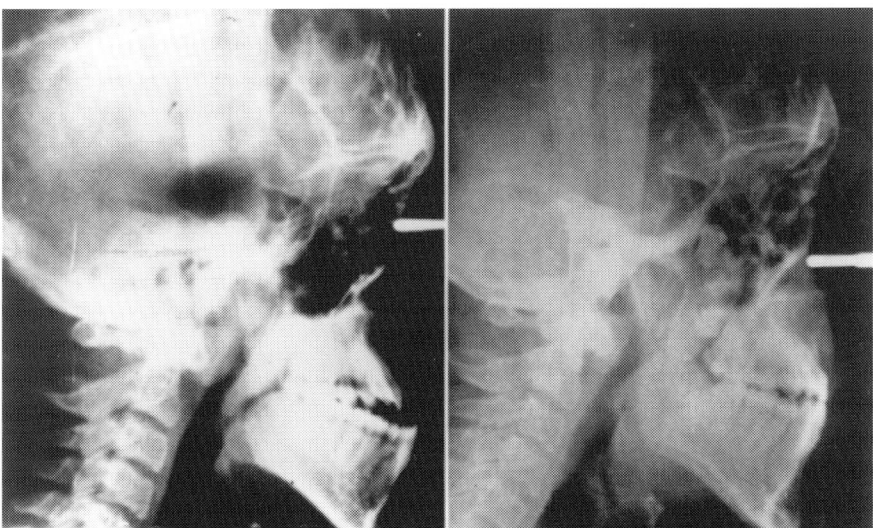

Left panel: Preoperative x-ray shows deficient relationship of mid-facial bones to lower jaw. Right panel: Postoperative x-ray shows how the advanced mid-face monoblock is now in a normal relationship to the lower jaw, which was not moved.

When the advancement was complete, the whole structure was stabilized by means of a large metal "halo" brace, kept in place with six screws set into Walter's skull. It was a rather dramatic-looking device, but entirely necessary to anchor the facial bones in their newly aligned position. Poor Walter wore that brace all day, every day, for eight weeks, but his discomfort and embarrassment were more than offset by the superb surgical result.

Len and I were delighted. Although Walter was pleased with the result as well he reserved his strongest expressions of joy for the day we removed that brace. "Stop the world, I want to get back on!" shouted Walter as the last screw was removed from his skull. And get back on he did. Walter graduated from Holy Cross College (my alma mater) and is now working in New York as a market analyst. He has three children and, coincidentally, his wife is a kidney transplant recipient.

Early Obsolescence

A far as we knew, our operation on Walter—the first total, one-stage correction of Crouzon's syndrome in the United States—was unprecedented. Since the insurance companies had no idea how to classify it,

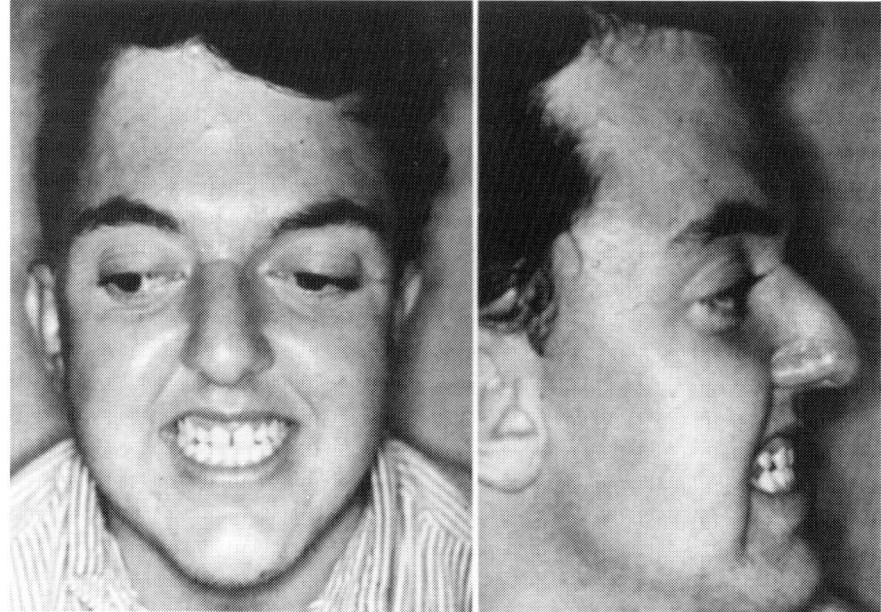

Walter Murphy 6 months after his operation.

they sent us a check for $125.00. It wasn't until I sent a detailed letter explaining the nature of the operation that they raised the amount to a whopping $450.00!

Dr. Swanson and I decided to describe our procedure in the journal *Plastic and Reconstructive Surgery* in an article entitled "Mid-Face Osteotomy and Advancement for Craniosynostosis" (1968, Vol. 41, pp. 299–306). The paper had already been accepted for publication, and all that remained was a final review of the galleys, which were sitting on my desk when Dr. Jack Penn fortuitously poked his head into my office. Jack was a friend and plastic surgical colleague who was on a visit to Boston from South Africa. As I listened with intense interest, he proceeded to tell me about the stunning presentation delivered by Dr. Paul Tessier at the recent International Plastic Surgical Conference in Rome in August of 1967. I had not attended that meeting because I had just returned from the International Transplantation Conference in Munich and had neither the energy nor the funds to turn around and head back to Europe. While I regretted not seeing Tessier's presentation, I was able to add the following footnote to our paper:

At the time this patient was treated, the authors had no knowledge of previous surgery for late manifestations of craniosynostosis . . . . Since then, we have been informed that Tessier has presented an exhibit of a series of treated patients at the IV International [Plastic Surgical Conference]. We have not had an opportunity to see Tessier's exhibit, and (therefore) cannot compare or contrast our plan and execution with his.

Craniofacial surgery is now routinely performed around the globe. Paul Tessier deserves all the credit, since his teaching had a world-wide influence (see Chapter 17).

CHAPTER 17

Marilyn Miele and Jimmy Hickey
The Tessier Legacy in Craniofacial Reconstruction

> *Procedure:* Correction of craniofacial deformities in two patients with variant forms of craniosynostoses
> *Date of Operations:* All in 1973
> *Institution:* Both patients treated at Children's Hospital, Boston, Massachusetts

I never again performed the "keyhole" operation that Len Swanson and I had devised for Walter Murphy (Chapter 16). Dr. Paul Tessier's more elegant technique for correcting craniofacial deformities immediately became the standard. I was delighted when, a few months after his ground-breaking presentation in Rome, Dr. Tessier attended a meeting of the American Association of Plastic Surgeons held in Williamsburg, Virginia (May 23–26, 1971), and we had a chance to discuss the matter. I saw him twice more in quick succession, so we really got to know each other.

In the spring of 1971, I spent a week in Paris to learn Paul's techniques first-hand. Each day he performed a major craniofacial operation while I watched from the sidelines and took notes furiously, much as I had done years earlier at Memorial Hospital in New York City (Chapter 6). Tessier's methods of exposing, moving, and stabilizing the craniofacial bones with minimal postoperative complications helped create the new specialty of craniofacial surgery. I came back to the States exhilarated and thoroughly prepared to follow Tessier's suit.

Meeting Marilyn Miele

Marilyn Miele, a 16-year-old Merit Scholar, was seen by Dr. Swanson in the Dental Clinic in January of 1973. By this time, the craniofacial program at Children's and the Brigham had grown considerably. Len referred Marilyn to the craniofacial clinic for possible correction of her dental malocclusion, flattened cheeks, and prominent eyes. Embryologically, her condition would be considered a variant of Crouzon's syndrome.

Tessier's Procedure à la Murray

Even though I had had the experience of treating Crouzon's syndrome successfully in the case of Walter Murphy, this would be my first time going solo" with Tessier's technique. Prior to the operation, Marilyn was evaluated by members of the departments of neurosurgery, ophthalmology, otolaryngology, radiology, psychiatry and psychology, nursing, and social services.

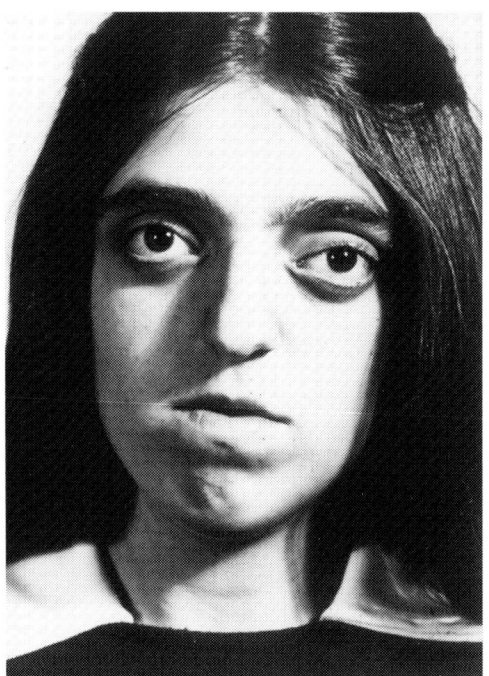

Preoperative view of Marilyn Miele, featuring the prominent eyes, flattened cheeks, and prominent lower lip and jaw characteristic of this variant of Crouzon's syndrome.

When the day of the operation arrived, I took extra precautions. I posted several "visual aids" on the wall of the operating room: full-face photos of Marilyn, her craniofacial x-rays, and a sequential list of the 78 steps that the surgical procedure would involve. With so much to remember, it would have been easy to overlook just one step and not realize it until it was too late. I placed asterisks next to those stages where I felt it would be safe

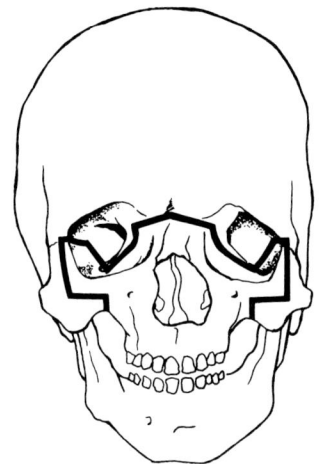 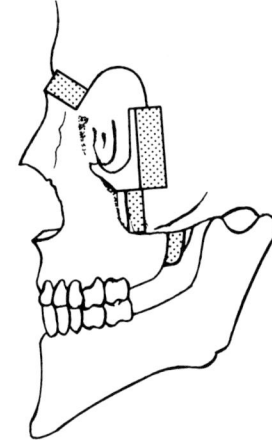

Left panel: Cuts in the bones (osteotomies) are shown by heavy black lines. Right panel: Stippled areas show bone graft sites, including blocks of bone at the nasofrontal junction, malar bones between the upper jaw (maxilla), and the pterygoid plates. Not shown are grafts placed in the floor of the orbits as well as additional onlay grafts placed for contouring.

to interrupt the operation should it be necessary because of excessive blood loss, an irregular heart beat, unstable blood pressure, difficulty in breathing, or an inordinate length of time on the operating table that might lead to vascular complications. Several times during my career I erred on the side of caution and did interrupt these craniofacial procedures, concluding them a few days later. But I have no regrets about this conservative policy because in all my years of performing these long and complex procedures there have been no operative deaths. Trying to be a "hero" can only increase the risk to the patient.

The operation took 12 hours, and our goals were met without undue hazard. In every way—physically, mentally, and emotionally—the operation was a success. Nine months after the surgery, Marilyn's grandmother sent us the following letter:

> Thank you for giving our granddaughter a new life. She is really lovely; she is radiant and happy. In all her young life we never heard her complain about her appearance, and she met the world with great courage, but now we know how much it did hurt.

Her words reveal how judicious correction of a physical deformity can also give a big boost to the soul.

Meeting Jimmy Hickey

Jimmy Hickey was born with multiple manifestations of craniosynostoses: an asymmetrical, enlarged, and flattened head, and eyes set far apart. His mother showed no interest in him. Fortunately, Jimmy's grandmother, Catherine, was able to see beyond his deformity and visited him often in the Wrentham State School (Chapter 10), a home for children diagnosed as mentally deficient, where Jimmy had been placed shortly after he was born. He had been there more than two years before one of the staff physicians finally recognized that he was psychologically and intellectually normal. Jimmy's grandmother became his legal guardian and brought Jimmy home, where he learned to walk, speak, and develop in a nurturing setting. For several years she tried to find medical help for his facial deformity. One day, in the summer of 1968, she happened to read an article in the newspaper about our work and called the craniofacial clinic for an appointment.

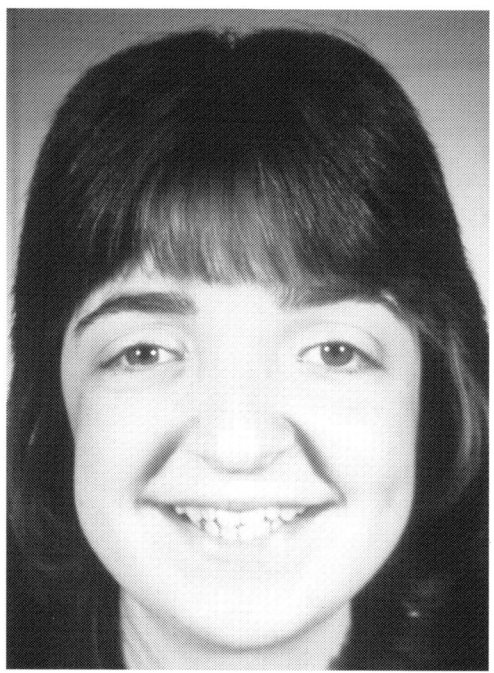

Postoperative view of Marilyn Miele 2 years after her surgery. The eyes are no longer prominent, although they are still slightly asymmetrical. Her cheeks are now convex rather than flat; her teeth have normal occlusion, and her chin is now properly aligned.

Even though I was becoming proficient in these massive craniofacial operations, Jimmy was only seven years old, and I thought he was just too young for the operation. I wrote in his medical record:

> The defect is a hypertelorism [abnormal distance between two paired organs] with widening of the eyes, depressed forehead, small nose.

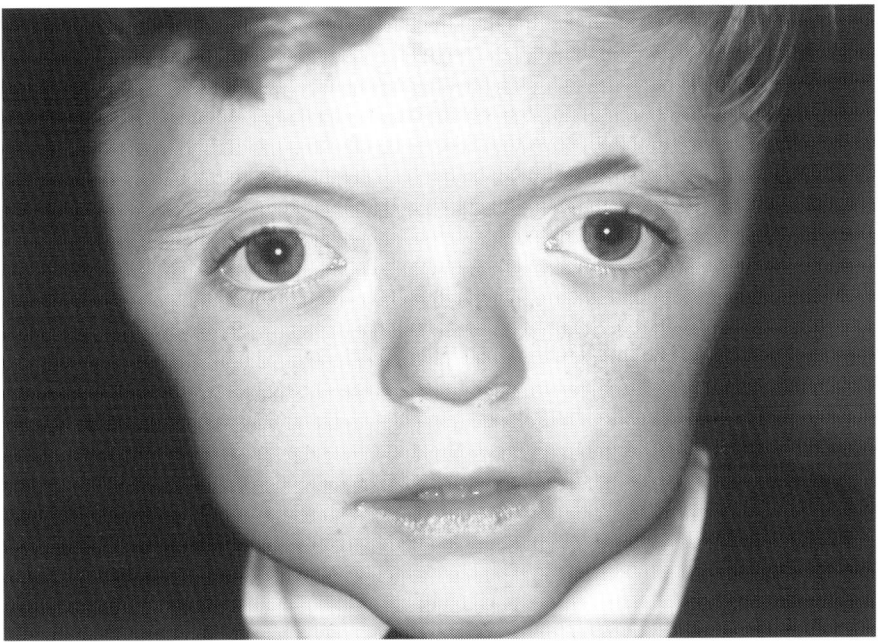

Jimmy Hickey prior to his operation. Note the widely separated eyes, bulging temples, flat face, and small nose. The break in the eyebrow is common in this condition.

The occlusion looks good. I would not consider doing anything on this boy at this time. However, he might want to have a Tessier operation done sometime to narrow the nose, but this would be a rather major job for a little boy who is really getting along quite well. Return on a yearly basis just for follow-up.

One year later I was still ambivalent about doing the operation and wrote in his record

Possibly we might do a hypertelorism operation on him when he is in his mid-teens, although it might be that a camouflage with just plain ordinary eyeglasses will be the best therapy.

By 1973, Jimmy was in sixth grade and was both physically and emotionally ready for the operation. He seemed to me to be an exceptionally fine boy despite his difficult start in life. A psychological evaluation

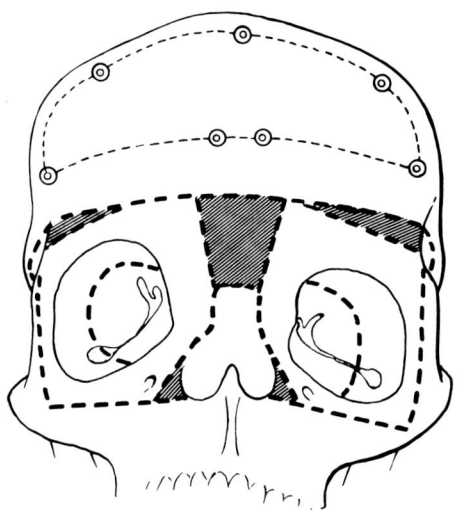

Bone excised

Seven burr holes made in Jimmy's forehead provided points of entry for a flexible wire saw used to cut through the forehead bone and expose the brain. Connecting these burr holes are dotted lines showing the path of the saw. The dotted lines surrounding the orbits, deep within the orbits, and along the nose and cheeks indicate the sites where the bone was severed to allow mobilization of the bony orbits. Shading represents those areas where bone has been excised.

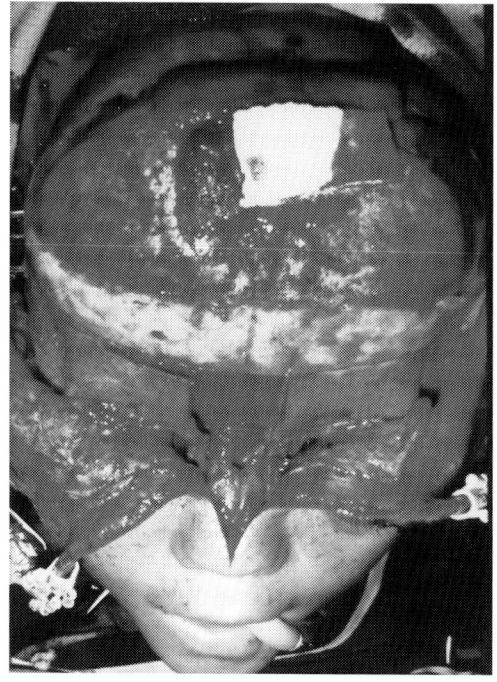

The brain has been exposed, and a cotton pad is being used to temporarily prevent bleeding. A solid bone strut has been preserved between the brain and both bony orbits. Note the gap between the orbits created when part of the forehead and nose was removed. Nasal cartilage is visible. The tube delivering anesthetic can be seen on the left corner of his mouth, firmly secured to the teeth with wires.

revealed a well-oriented, alert young man in good health who was eager to have the corrective surgery done.

Jimmy's procedure would be my second Tessier-style operation. I prepared for it in much the same way as I had for Marilyn Miele's surgery, although this time the list of operative steps was even longer. I studied photographs of Jimmy's face and then cut them into puzzle-like pieces so we could re-arrange them and have some idea of what we were striving for as an end result. I smile to myself now to think that we approached such a complex operation using such simple tools as a pair of scissors and tape. Today, computed tomographic (CT) scans and magnetic resonance imaging (MRI) are more rapid, efficient, and effective means of assessing such cases and projecting outcomes, but these technological advances do not necessarily lead to a better final surgical result.

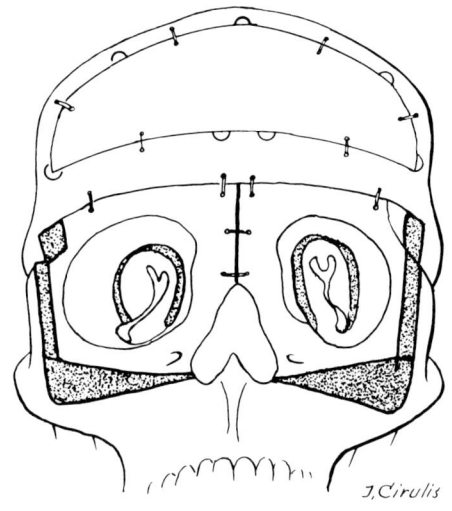

GRAFTED Bone graft

Forehead bone has been replaced, and both bony orbits have been moved to the midline, wired together, and stabilized by wires connected to the stable strut above the orbits. Shading represents areas where additional bone has been grafted for stabilization.

In terms of exposure of the operative site, the surgical approach was the same as that for Marilyn Miele but required more extensive exposure of the brain. In Marilyn's case we had cut, separated, and mobilized the mid-facial bones that were attached to her skull. Only a minimal area of her brain was exposed and for only a brief time. Jimmy's operation was riskier because a greater portion of the brain was exposed for a longer period of time. We actually had to retract the brain with surgical instruments as we cut the full 360 degrees around each bony orbit. The portion of the forehead and nose between his eyes was then removed as a single unit, creating a gap between the two orbits. This space we then closed up by shifting the orbital bones to the

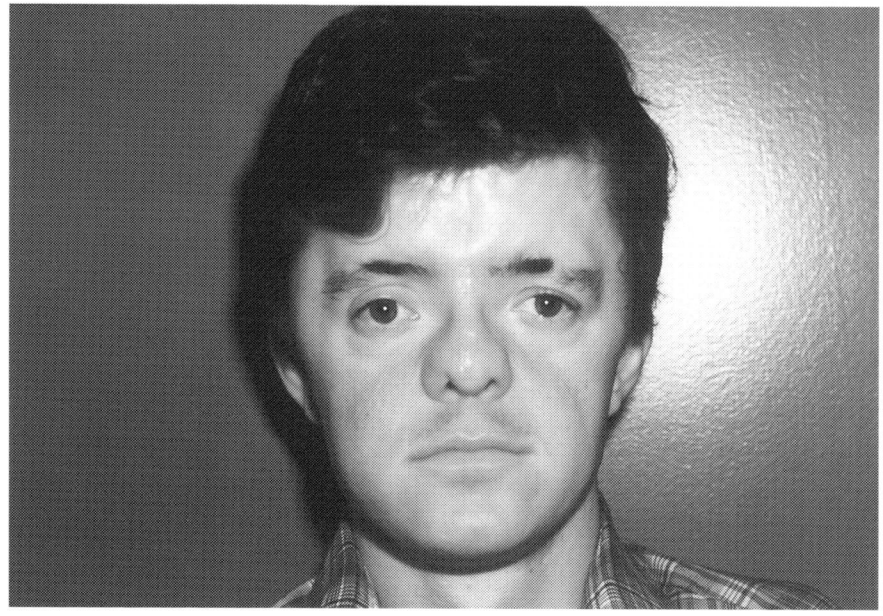

Jimmy Hickey 12 years after the operation.

midline of Jimmy's face and wiring them together—all the while keeping eyeballs, nerves, and muscles intact as they too were moved to the midline. Supplemental bones grafts obtained from Jimmy's ribs and hip were used to fill in the gaps in the forehead and cheeks and to stabilize the nasal-orbital-facial unit.

The operation went well, with no surprises or complications. Jimmy was hospitalized for 12 days and then released. He is currently employed at a utility company in Massachusetts and is married with children.

THE TESSIER LEGACY

The success of Marilyn's and Jimmy's craniofacial operations, in addition to all those that followed, can be directly credited to Dr. Paul Tessier. It was he who single-handedly created an entirely new field of surgery that revolutionized the care of patients with congenital, neoplastic, and traumatic cranio-maxillo-facial problems. But not only did he create the field, he nursed it through its early difficult and often discouraging years. Once he had achieved predictable, beneficial results, he unselfishly shared his experience and techniques with the world, breaking onto the international medical scene at the Rome conference attended by my colleague Jack Penn (Chapter 16). Practitioners then beat a path to Foch Hospital in Paris where, at his own expense, Paul organized outstanding teaching clinics for surgeons from all over the world. Later, he established liaisons with selected hospitals throughout the world, which he still visits regularly to help train the surgical and nursing staffs. His work changed forever the thinking about the correction of facial differences. This towering figure raised the specialty of plastic surgery to new heights, and patients and plastic surgeons alike continue to reap the benefits from his contributions to modern surgery.

Dr. Paul Tessier and I outside the Plastic Surgery Department of Children's Hospital. Paul became an active member of the Brigham/Children's plastic surgical staff and remained so until my retirement. In 1975, he received an Honorary Fellowship in the American College of Surgeons.

CHAPTER 18

TRAVELS WITH FAMILY AND COLLEAGUES

Throughout the 1960s my life became increasingly busy. Since the earliest days of my career I had been an active participant in the American College of Surgeons (ACS). I had attended my first meeting in New York City as a guest of Dr. Bradford Cannon back in 1947, when I was still stationed at Valley Forge General Hospital, and I recall riding the train from Pennsylvania into Manhattan.

In the early 1950s, Dr. Cannon had represented the field of plastic surgery on the Forum Committee of the ACS Program Committee. In this capacity he was responsible for selecting research papers to be presented at the annual meeting, a task for which he was well suited. When his 5-year appointment came to an end, I was invited to succeed him. My own appointment lasted from 1958 to 1964 and overlapped my membership in the National Institutes of Health (NIH) Surgical Studies Section, where I evaluated grant applications. Serving on these two committees exposed me to the full range of innovations in plastic surgery that occurred after World War II.

When both these assignments were completed, I had some time to catch my breath and become reacquainted with my family (by then six children strong). But the respite didn't last long. In 1967, I was chosen to be President of the Boston Surgical Society in addition to being asked to serve as one of two surgeons (the other being the cardiac transplant surgeon Dr. Richard Lower) on the Immunobiology Studies Section of the NIH. The latter opportunity helped me keep abreast of worldwide developments in the field of immunology over the four-year term (ending in 1971), which overlapped yet another ACS appointment, that of Regent of the ACS—a 9-year term!

Looking back, I'm amazed that I had any time at all to see patients. Yet somehow I managed to meet all my obligations in addition to maintaining a satisfying caseload. The pressure of those years was relieved by judicious use of the limited free time I did have.

Mixing Business and Pleasure

Another chance for me to stay informed about the cutting edge of plastic surgery was my participation in the Plastic Surgical Travel Club. Dr. Milt Edgerton, then Head of Plastic Surgery at Johns Hopkins, asked nine of us post-war plastic surgeons to join in an informal travel club that would meet for a few days each year at a host hospital. The idea was to observe surgical operations, visit research labs, meet other staff members, and look at organizational structures, all the while visiting interesting places and having some fun in the process. Perhaps it was no accident that all nine members of our travel club later became presidents of one of the two major plastic surgical organizations.

Originally the travel club was intended to be males only. It was in 1958 at our Boston meeting that I, as host, insisted that we invite our wives to join us on these forays. I felt that since we each spent so much time away from home in pursuit of our professional careers, it seemed only fair that our wives share in our professional lives whenever possible. This gesture was a first for the club, and the suggestion rankled a few of the male members, although it certainly made me happy and spread a lot of good will among the wives of our group.

Our Island Refuge

Because of my hectic schedule, time with Bobby and the children was at a premium. One rule was held inviolate: we would take a family vacation for a full month every year. The first year I worked with Brad Cannon, he insisted that I take one month off every year. So, heeding his advice as always, I chose the month of July. Right after Christmas, Bobby, the children, and I would begin planning how to spend our sacred time together. Over the years, we have spent every July camping, hiking, and backpacking across a good portion of the globe.

No matter how much we traveled, Martha's Vineyard continued to beckon, and we returned to the island as often as we could. Bobby and I were constantly on the lookout for any land we could afford to purchase there. Meanwhile, we pitched our tents at campsites on the main island (which we Chappyites considered the "decadent" one) and

Left panel: The Matterhorn, with the village of Zermatt in the foreground. Right panel: Twenty feet from the summit, led by my guide, at 9:00 A.M. on September 21, 1971.

took the little ferry over to Chappy for our real fun. These wonderful times with family and friends provided the perfect complement to the exhilarating but often hectic routine of hospital work and committee meetings.

Martha's Vineyard never failed to provide welcome rest and relaxation from my ever-growing workload. Even though I had stepped down as head of the Brigham transplant program, my commitments continued in the form of service on local and national committees, speaking engagements, and meeting deadlines for ongoing publications and grant applications. But each spring, come daffodils and pussy willows, my heart began to turn with anticipation to our annual July vacation.

Time and again we were told that we'd never find any land on the Vineyard that was even close to affordable. Our children gave up all hope. But in the fall of 1970, we learned that several acres in the middle of Chappaquiddick had been sold to a developer who just happened to live near us in Wellesley. Bobby and I immediately paid him a visit. Suddenly, owning property seemed possible. We borrowed on our life insurance to make a small down payment and, in December of 1970, became the overjoyed owners of eight acres of inland property.

Never ones to waste time, we set up camp on our property on a January weekend in 1971. Bobby and I, along with our sons Tom and Rick, and our youngest daughter Kathy, then a freshman at Wellesley College, reveled in being on our *own* land, rather than at a public campsite. We were in heaven, even if "heaven" was a bit chilly at that time of year. We gathered wood for a fire, and for many years the ashes remaining in the makeshift fireplace kept the memory of that special weekend alive. Unfortunately, poison ivy, undetected on the barren firewood, also kept the memory of that weekend alive for several itchy days afterward.

Come summer, Bobby, Rick, Tom, and I spent our time at our own campsite working the land. With the help of Foster Silva, a Chappy native and friend, we used sledgehammers to drive a well point for a hand pump, cleared areas of poison ivy, and blazed trails through the woods. We did this for two years running, and these were among the most wonderful, carefree summers we ever had. With no house yet to care for, there was ample time to swim or to read while resting against a favorite tree. Pots and pans hung from the stumps of tree branches, and we scattered our sleeping bags and tents among the pine groves. It was open-air living, 24 hours-a-day, and we all loved it. Since I was routinely the first one up in the morning, I'd often go down to the beach by myself. Some might call this loafing, but it turned out to be astute business planning. Over time, a few persons on the island noticed my love and appreciation of nature.

That fall, at an ACS meeting in San Francisco, Dr. Ed Self, a Chappy friend and an esteemed surgeon from Columbia Presbyterian Hospital, mentioned to me that 40 acres of land on Cape Poge might be coming up for sale. Cape Poge is the northeastern-most point of Martha's Vineyard. Surrounded by water and loaded with land birds and shore birds, and boasting some of the best fishing in the northeastern U.S., this was prime, unspoiled land. I was ecstatic at the opportunity and urged Bobby to come look at the property with me. As the voice of reason, she told me to calm down and quietly reminded me that we couldn't even afford to build a house on the piece of Chappy land we already owned. Of course she was right, but I knew the Cape Poge property was a once-in-a-lifetime opportunity.

It didn't take much to convince Bobby to indulge my wishes, and she came with me to hike the land. It was beautiful, wild, unspoiled beach adjacent to the Cape Poge Lighthouse. We couldn't help but fall in love with it. Fortunately, the owner, Dr. Dick Parmenter, cared more about the stewardship of the land than money. And thanks to my now well-established reputation as a "nature freak," we were able to arrange a three-way transaction among Dr. Parmenter, The Trustees of Reservations (a Massachusetts Conservation Society), and me. By December 31, 1972, we owned another piece of heaven—40 acres of it!

Tent City

Situated on the Cape Poge property was an old, one-room shack that had served as the boat house for the Coast Guard lifeboat. The antique square nails used in its construction revealed its true age. The shack came with a kerosene stove, lanterns, a hand pump, and an outhouse. Foster Silva advised us to push the house over and start from scratch. But for us Murrays, accustomed to tents and sleeping bags, this shack was a veritable castle.

The Murray mansion, as we first saw it, on Cape Poge, Martha's Vineyard.

We spent our first summer on this property in 1973. The kids pitched tents beside the house, while the grown-ups "camped" inside. Over the years, we made the roof, walls, and floor of the house watertight and added a deck, porch, and bedroom. By 1977, thanks to a wind generator, we had enough electricity to run a ⅓ horsepower water pump. That meant hot running water *inside* the house. We still keep the outhouse for security (and sentimental reasons). Today, the house is snug, lovingly livable, but still simple.

As for the inland property on Chappy, Bobby no longer needs to hang our pots and pans on tree branches. In 1980, we finally built our winterized "Treehouse" there, later adding a tennis court and, installing a lap pool after my stroke in 1986. Today, Bobby and I like to stay at this house, while the children and their families use the Cape Poge property.

The Monks Lectureship

I continued to be dismayed over the fact that I had been unable to engender universal respect for plastic surgery as a specialty, even at my own institution. Although the Brigham surgical and medical staffs readily acknowledged my own personal ability and skill, only reluctantly did they allow me to present my work at Grand Rounds. Plastic surgery was still considered by many a frivolous undertaking and was, sadly, closely identified with cosmetic surgery.

Dr. Robert M. Goldwyn was the first general surgical resident at the Brigham after me to opt for a career in plastic surgery. After completing his plastic surgery residency in Pittsburgh, Bob returned to Boston to join the Brigham surgical staff. Together, we were determined to improve the stature of our specialty at Harvard Medical School. We decided to start with a trial lecture and invited Dr. Reed Dingman, Chief of Plastic Surgery at the University of Michigan and a member of my Travel Club, to deliver the first talk. Reed was both an M.D. and a D.M.D. as well as the internationally respected author of the book *Treatment of Facial Fractures*. Bob and I thought he would be a "safe" choice and his topic would be of interest to general, plastic, and dental surgeons alike.

As it turned out, Dr. Dingman's lecture was so well received that we decided to establish an annual plastic surgery lecture, which we named after Dr. George Monks. Dr. Monks had been a professor of anatomy, dentistry, and surgery at both Harvard Dental School and Harvard Medical School. He was the ideal namesake for the lectureship because, in addition to being the founder and first president of the Boston Surgical Society, he was also a noted sculptor. His technical, creative, and artistic abilities in those two overlapping disciplines neatly encapsulated what plastic surgery is all about.

The first official Monks Lecturer was, appropriately, Dr. Paul Tessier. He spoke on advances in craniofacial surgery, the field he had pioneered. His presentation was a spectacular start for this ongoing lectureship, which now enjoys national and international prestige.

CHAPTER 19

IYLENE BECKER
A Dilemma—Life or Speech?

> *Procedure:* Creation of a tracheo-epiglottic flap (barrier between the mouth and lung) to prevent aspiration pneumonia
> *Dates of Operations:* May 2 and 16, 1969
> *Institution:* Children's Hospital, Boston, Massachusetts

Iylene Becker's chances for survival greatly improved the moment a hot-water bottle fell on her head. Chance often plays a role in medicine, and had it not been for the scalding burn Iylene suffered that day, I might never have become involved in her care. That minor accident set in motion a string of events that culminated in the creation of a surgical operation for an unusual medical condition—aspiration pneumonia.

Iylene Becker was nine years old in 1969 when she arrived at Children's Hospital in Boston. In attempts to determine a cause for her cyclic vomiting and weight loss (15 pounds), her parents had spent several months seeking answers at hospitals in her hometown in Maryland, where the diagnoses had ranged from stomach ulcers to ear infections to psychosis. Finally, a neurosurgeon detected a brainstem tumor and referred Iylene to Children's for treatment.

Examination and biopsy revealed an extensive tumor of the brainstem that was neither malignant nor life-endangering. Nevertheless, a curative surgical excision would require manipulation of specific nerves in the brainstem that govern the muscles used in swallowing. Dr. John Shillito, the neurosurgeon, pointed out that swallowing might be temporarily impaired after the operation, but function should return to normal within a few weeks or months. What he didn't foresee was how close to death Iylene would come in that interim period.

A Harrowing Interval

The weeks following excision of the brainstem tumor were touch-and-go. Whenever Iylene tried to eat, saliva, liquids, and solid food entered her windpipe (trachea) and lungs instead of her esophagus and, with each swallow, her respiratory tract became more inflamed. The presence of such foreign material in the lungs inevitably leads to a condition called "aspiration pneumonia," and on four separate occasions, it almost caused Iylene's death.

In recorded history, aspiration pneumonia was the cause of death of the Greek poet Anacreon, who in the fifth century B.C. inhaled a grape seed. In 400 B.C., the great physician Hippocrates warned against "forced swallowing." And in 1781, John Hunter, the renowned Scottish surgeon, anatomist, pathologist, and physiologist, stated in a court of law, "Everyone claims that a little brandy will kill a cat. I have made an experiment. In all of those cases where it kills a cat, it kills by going into the lungs rather than into the stomach." With the development of anesthesia in the 1800s, the early use of chloroform and ether occasionally led to fatal complications from aspiration pneumonia.

As a stopgap measure for Iylene, nurses passed soft tubes (catheters) down her throat several times a day to suction the debris from her lungs. Even so, Iylene ran a constant fever and, unable to ingest food, became weaker and thinner with each passing day. Nursing care, no matter how skillfully performed, was obviously not a long-term solution. She desperately needed a more effective *interim* treatment to tide her over until the damaged nerves healed and normal swallowing was restored.

A variety of specialists were called in: ear, nose, and throat doctors, plastic surgeons, thoracic surgeons, and general surgeons. Even a group of premier neurosurgeons who were visiting Boston for a convention were consulted. No one could come up with a solution.

Time was running out. As Iylene's mother recalled, "We knew Iylene was continuing to aspirate, and were told the pneumonia would kill her if something wasn't done. But it didn't seem like anything could be done. We waited and hoped."

This was when, during one of her physical therapy sessions, a full hot-water bottle fell off a file cabinet and hit Iylene squarely on the head, leaking scalding water on her scalp. One of my plastic surgery residents was consulted about whether Iylene might require a skin graft, so he brought the case to my attention. Since the scalp burn was not too severe, it healed within days with judicious cleansing and dressings. But it was Iylene's medical condition that intrigued me; it presented an unusual challenge.

Speech or Life?

While at Memorial Hospital in New York City, I had seen cases of postoperative aspiration pneumonia in adult patients who had been treated for advanced cancer of the head and neck area. When the condition became severe enough to be life-threatening, we would remove the patient's voice box (larynx). Although a laryngectomy was a surefire way to prevent aspiration, and thus pneumonia, it also caused permanent loss of speech. In older patients with extensive cancer, this loss did not seem too high a price to pay for a cure. But for Iylene, an eight-year-old girl, whose underlying condition was completely curable, laryngectomy would be a drastic step. Surely there had to be a way to curtail spillage of food and liquids into her lungs without destroying her ability to speak.

At this time, my plastic surgery resident was Mutaz Habal, an indefatigable, fast-moving surgeon who worked every night for two years covering plastic surgery at both the Brigham and Children's Hospitals. (Incidentally, he followed John Woods as my second career plastic surgery resident.[29]) Having the company of a surgical resident for almost 24 hours a day is a great privilege, akin to having a surrogate son or daughter with whom to share the thrill of patient care and scientific innovation. Freshness, curiosity, and enthusiasm emerge from this pairing of youth and experience, and everyone benefits—especially the patients!

Mutaz and I felt intuitively that some surgical solution must be possible, and we bounced ideas back and forth throughout the day—on our early morning and evening rounds, and even late at night, as we walked the almost half a mile between the emergency wards of Children's Hospital and the Brigham. Yet our brainstorming and searches of the surgical literature for hints or clues were in vain.

Finally, I posted a notice in the pathology department asking that I be called whenever a suitable cadaver became available for study. Mutaz and I wanted to examine the complex anatomy in that small area at the back of the throat where the tongue, pharynx, esophagus, and trachea merge in our ongoing search for a *reversible* way to block the entrance to the lungs without disturbing speech and swallowing.

Eureka! A "Permanent" Temporary Solution

Mutaz and I finally settled on what we believed would be a workable solution. The part of the voice box that sticks up at the top is called the epiglottis. If we sewed this small piece of tissue over the entrance to the larynx (much like putting a lid on a trash can), any food or air that entered her mouth would necessarily be directed to her stomach. That would solve the aspiration problem. Meanwhile, air could reach her

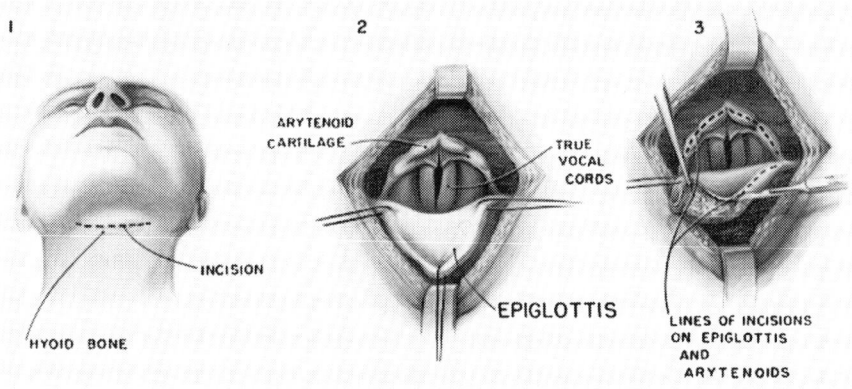

Left panel: Site of incision just above the hyoid bone, to which most of the muscles used in swallowing are attached.
Middle panel: Three traction sutures have been placed in the epiglottis (the "lid" to be put over the trash barrel). Behind is the entrance to the larynx and lungs. The vocal cords are situated immediately below the arytenoid cartilage, another attachment site for the delicate muscles involved in swallowing and speech.
Right panel: Dotted lines on arytenoid cartilage and epiglottis show where incisions are made to create raw surfaces for sewing the "lid" over the entrance to the trachea and lungs.

lungs by means of a tracheotomy, a surgically created opening in her throat (tracheostomy). With the tracheotomy tube in place, she would be able to breathe but not to speak. But at least she would still be alive. Once her damaged nerves had a chance to heal, the tracheostomy could be closed, and Iylene would in all likelihood be able to breathe and speak normally again.

The operation went as planned. We blocked the entrance to the larynx by using the epiglottis as a trap-door flap. After waiting five days, we conducted a simple experiment. We gave Iylene a glass of water to drink to test whether the water would travel to her stomach, as it should, or would be diverted into her lungs. Upon drinking the water, Iylene began choking and coughing violently; the water had gone straight into her lungs.

After a few more days, we tried again. The doctors and nurses assembled in anticipation. This time we gave Iylene a small cup of purple grape juice. She drank it easily, and one of the nurses inserted a catheter into the tracheostomy, below the level of the trap-door flap, to test the effectiveness of the operation by suctioning the contents of the trachea. The aspirate came back clear, proof that we had successfully blocked the entrance to her lungs. Everyone in the room was overjoyed.

Still, there was no yardstick by which to measure Iylene's daily progress. After a kidney transplant, one can measure urine output. After a skin graft, one can assess its viability just by looking at it. But in this case, we did not know how to judge success. Looking down her throat with a laryngoscope was not wise because it might do harm, cause pain, and delay healing. Fortunately, her temperature chart telegraphed the good news. After six months of continuously spiking fevers, Iylene's daily temperature readings fell to normal within three days after the operation and remained so permanently.

Iylene started to eat and drink without gagging, and within two weeks she had regained 18 pounds. Patient, family, nurses, and doctors were delighted! Now we could safely await the return of her nerve function. Iylene was then sent home to be cared for by her original physician. We kept in touch and saw her at regular intervals, planning to restore the entrance to her larynx when we felt it was safe to do so. Since we could not predict when that would be, we decided arbitrarily to wait six months before deciding when to release the trap-door flap.

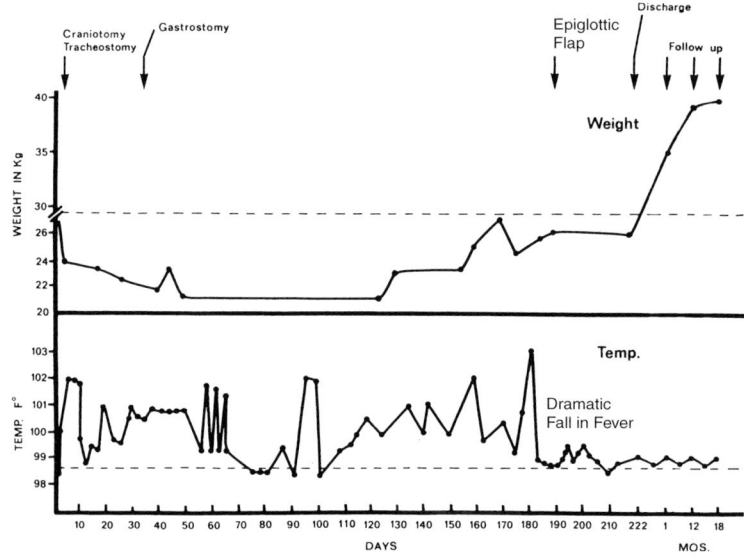

The multiple temperature elevations, which ranged from 102° to 104°F over the 6 months prior to the operation, indicate the severity of Iylene's condition. Note how her temperature rapidly dropped to normal only 48 hours after the operation.

Speech After All

Our plan seemed reasonable at first. But just try and take normal speech away from *any* young girl. About five months after her operation, Iylene waltzed into my office at Children's Hospital and said, in a soft voice, "Hi, Dr. Murray." I nearly fell off my chair! I couldn't imagine how she was managing to speak with her larynx closed off. An examination of the operative site with a mirror and laryngoscope right then and there showed a pinpoint opening in the suture line. The passageway between her mouth and lungs had not been completely blocked after all. Somehow the Good Lord had created a one-way valve just large enough to allow air to pass up from her lungs and over her vocal cords, and just small enough to prevent saliva and food from getting down into her lungs.

We obviously were delighted to accept this unexpected gift of selective wound healing. Iylene continued to progress well, and after 12 months we had another decision to make. The pinpoint opening, while allowing a whispering speech, was not large enough to carry her through a lifetime.

Iylene 33 years after the operation.

Iylene and her parents were concerned. "We didn't want to mess with a good thing," recalls Iylene. "I was alive, and was able to speak. What more could I want? We didn't want to push our luck." But it was not all luck had brought us this far. We never would have undone the operation if we were not confident that its benefit would outweigh its danger.

Even though this was unexplored territory and I had some misgivings, my expectations were high and we proceeded to reverse the operation. Doing so required reopening the original incision in the neck and releasing the trap-door flap. Iylene healed uneventfully from this second operation and her phonation continued to improve over the next several months. It has now been 33 years since Iylene's operation, and she is leading a normal life. I received a letter from her recently in which she said she is doing well.

Mutaz Habal and his successor, Tom Vecchione, coauthored two papers about Iylene and several similar patients who followed her. Mutaz was the primary author of the first paper (*Reconstructive Surgery* 1972, Vol. 49, pp. 305–311), while Tom was the primary author of the second one.

Iylene was a unique thread in the tapestry of my life as a surgeon. Although the solution we devised for her medical problem was not a major stepping stone in surgical advancement, nor a beacon for surgical research, it did save her life. The conscientious surgeon directs 100 percent of his or her attention to the patient at hand, be the condition rare or commonplace. As for the nurses and residents who worked tirelessly on Iylene's case, they have the immense satisfaction of having restored essential functions to a fine young woman. What more can anyone ask?

CHAPTER 20

THE IRAN EXPERIENCE
Teaching at Queen's Hospital in Tehran

Late in 1974, I received another invitation to teach abroad, this time in Iran. Dr. Cyrus Ossanlou, the head of Queen's Hospital for Burns and Reconstructive Surgery in Tehran, asked if I would spend a month there caring for patients and helping to train Iranian surgeons and nurses. My colleagues Paul Tessier from France, Fernando Ortiz-Monasterio from Mexico, Bengt Johansson from Sweden, and George Crikelaire from New York City were also invited. We taught in succession, amounting to a full five months of intensive training and patient care.

I left Boston the evening of November 14, 1974, after a hectic day of preparation. My escorts to the airport that evening were enthusiastic ones. Bobby and our oldest daughter Ginny, along with her six-month-old daughter Hannah (the first of 15 grandchildren), seemed even more excited than I was. Bobby and our sons Tom and Rick would join me later in Tehran, but it was a bit wrenching to realize I wouldn't see them for an entire month. I had mixed feelings about this trip and was worried that I might be shirking my responsibilities, not only to family but to the Children's and Brigham Hospitals as well.

When I arrived at the Tehran airport, an associate of Dr. Ossanlou whisked me through customs. After a few hours of rest in my suite at the Sheraton Hotel, I began my first day of work.

GETTING DOWN TO BUSINESS

Queen's Hospital was devoted entirely to burns and reconstructive surgery. Being a new hospital, it was modern and well equipped, although much of the equipment was still wrapped in its original packaging. I could see that over the next four weeks I would be serving as chief technician as well as chief surgeon.

Dr. Ossanlou, a prominent plastic surgeon, had used his rapport with the Shah and Shahrin to convince them of the need for a hospital of this type. I learned later that he had recently been demoted from a university position, and his appointment as head of this new hospital had created a professional schism between Queen's Hospital and surgeons at more established hospitals. Understanding that this type of rivalry is just part of human nature, I cooperated with everyone who invited me to speak or teach, while maintaining my primary commitment to Queen's Hospital. Some surgeons tried to refer private patients to me, but having been warned about this possibility, I politely refused. I wanted no diversions from my primary goal: teaching. Any doubts I might have had as to why I sometimes accepted these assignments abroad vanished during my first hospital rounds. Being exposed to patients with such stark, pressing needs was an eye-opening experience. One of the first patients I saw was a shepherd whose nose had been torn off by a wolf attacking his flock. I felt that my lifetime of training had prepared me to come to this place. Aware that good fortune had bestowed on me a certain talent and superb education, I felt obliged to contribute my best to these patients. In so doing, I received far more than I gave. This was doctoring at its best!

Each visiting doctor brings his or her own style to a hospital. Tessier, for example, brought along his own scrub nurse and instruments and spent the entire month demonstrating highly technical operations. My approach was different. I used the equipment at hand and operated *alongside* the staff nurses and surgeons in order to help them become more confident and self-sufficient. The doctors were sponge-like in their eagerness to learn, and they saved their most challenging patients for "the Professor," as they called me. By the end of my first week we had an effective schedule of operations, patient conferences, and teaching seminars. Enthusiasm grew daily, and I glowed when they performed straightforward reconstructive operations and started to become creative problem-solvers.

A Startling Array of Anomalies

At times, Queen's Hospital seemed like a United Nations in microcosm. I saw Kurds from Iran, Turkey, and Iraq; Turks from both Turkey and Iran; and Afghans, Baluchis, Azerbaijanis, and many other nomadic groups. Patients usually arrived accompanied by their extended families. When parents, siblings, aunts, uncles, and cousins were not filling the rooms or crowding the hallways, they could be found gathered on the hospital lawn, cooking the patients' meals over small, makeshift stoves. Most of the nomads wore bright-colored tribal clothing, which created an almost festive air that belied the severity of the patients' problems.

Of all the patients I saw, the babies and children with facial tumors and vascular anomalies particularly fascinated me. In addition, there were children with burn contractures of the trunk and extremities that occurred when children fell into the open-floor ovens. Such injuries

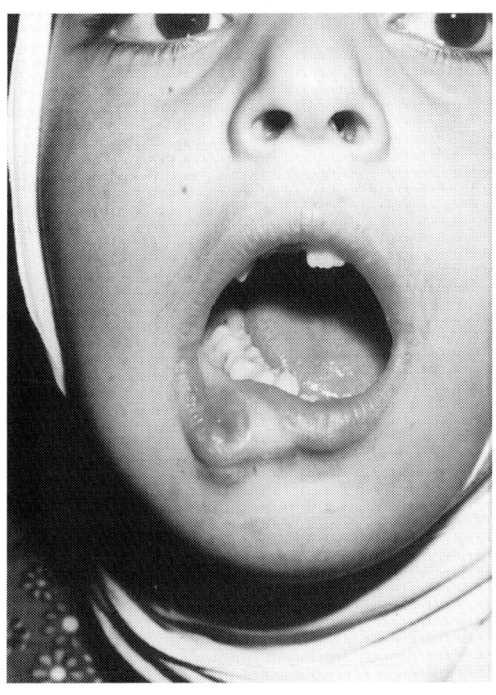

A young patient with a "double mouth"—one of the intriguing anomalies I witnessed at Queen's Hospital.

were common and were some of the most severe I'd ever seen. As a result of the scarring and contraction of the skin, thumbs had shifted to a fixed position halfway up the forearm; in other cases, knees had become jack-knifed and were almost cemented against the belly. Dreadful scars and gaping cavities around the mouth, nose, and eyes were also a common sight, because facial infections spread rapidly in these often malnourished patients.

Certain patients can pique our curiosity and stimulate research. One morning on rounds at the Queen's Hospital, the doctors excitedly showed me a teenage girl with a "double mouth." This duplicate oral cavity was adjacent to her normal mouth and contained identifiable lips, mucous membranes, and teeth. Although I vaguely remembered reading about this bizarre condition, I had never seen it. While the situation was readily correctable, I was curious about how it could have developed embryologically. Most congenital abnormalities mimic a stage of embryological development, but this one baffled me completely.

The puzzle of the double mouth almost surely had a genetic explanation. On a flight to Japan 25 years after I encountered this patient, I read a revelatory article in the journal *Science* (Vol. 267, pp. 1788–1792, 1995) in which the authors summarized research showing that mice and humans possess similar "growth" genes. In 1978, in the journal *Nature*, Edward B. Lewis had summarized his 30 years of research on how fruit flies develop. With remarkable intuition, Lewis predicted that fruit flies have a series of linked master genes that control the development of the fruit fly embryo. In a beautifully orchestrated hierarchy, each gene turned on the next gene, leading to a fly that had a head, a middle, and a tail, with certain organs being single and others being paired. Subsequently, it became clear that Lewis was right not only about the role of these genes in the fruit fly but also about the role of similar genes in higher animals, including humans. For this work, Lewis was awarded the Nobel Prize in Physiology or Medicine for 1995, along with Christiane Nüsslein-Volhard and Eric F. Wieschaus.

Regarding our young patient, one of these genes (or a secondary gene that it triggered) must have been abnormal. Who knows? Perhaps this finding will prove to be the basis of generating new organs for old—a revolutionary idea, certainly, but no more so than Gregor Mendel's observations on the genetics of garden peas in the mid-1800s. Ironically, Mendel's theories lay fallow for several decades, but ultimately they led to the era of modern genetics.

A "Kept" Surgeon

During my stay in Iran, my hosts certainly took good care of me. I was well fed, well sheltered, and pampered in every way. Each day breakfast was delivered to my suite at the Sheraton, along with the Tehran daily newspaper, and a car was at my disposal at all times. After two weeks in this city, I had spent the equivalent of about $15.00 of my personal funds.

A tennis court situated on the hospital grounds perfected the scenario. The Shah's personal tennis pro was at my beck and call, and I played tennis almost daily—before, after, or instead of lunch. My first "formal" tennis game bordered on the surreal. The tennis balls we used had worn, smooth surfaces. Our ball-boy was crippled by burn contractures of his hands and face, but that did not stop him from randomly bombarding us with balls, even while we were serving. My opponent, though a poor player, was intent on winning. He called out erroneous scores and misjudged the lines with abandon. When not dodging balls or arguing over a lost point, he chatted with friends on the sidelines. Guards from the adjacent army hospital glared at us from behind a wire fence, gripping their Tommy guns. As background for this most unusual of tennis matches stood the massive, 18,000-foot Elburz mountain range, its peaks sparkling with early snow.

Getting Assimilated

It is amazing how much can be accomplished in the absence of outside responsibilities. My days at the hospital were full, but I still had time left to take advantage of the strange and beautiful country. I found my own private niche in the University of Tehran Library, where I studied the Persian alphabet and read to my heart's content. Persian and Islamic history came alive. At the American and British embassies, I read journal entries of earlier travelers and learned enough of the Farsi language to understand billboards and newspaper headlines. Medical students and residents escorted me to concerts in the city and joined me on weekend hikes up nearby mountains. I became friendly with several families and often dined with them in their homes, developing a real respect for Islamic culture in the process. In terms of the political scene, it was common knowledge that every hospital—in fact every institution— sheltered a member of the Savak (the secret police). Understandably, conversation was apolitical and bland. Only when hiking with colleagues in the mountains on a one-on-one basis did I learn who the "spy" was and which of the hospital staff had family members imprisoned or missing.

In spite of all this new and stimulating activity, life seemed unreal. My daily walk to and from the hospital felt like a walk through a movie set. What was quite real, however, was how much I missed my family. I was delighted when Bobby, Tom, and Rick arrived in mid-December. It was strange to see them in the Tehran Airport, the same terminal where the roof had collapsed only one week before under the weight of a sudden snowfall. My "unreal" world suddenly became quite real again as the kids took over my well-ordered Sheraton suite and claimed it as their own. But I enjoyed the mess because it felt like home away from home.

The family and I spent an unforgettable holiday traveling around Iran. We visited Isfahan, the jewel-like city that Bobby knew about from studying Faure's chanson "The Roses of Isfahan." Our tour also included Shiraz, home of the new medical school where English was spoken,[30] and Abadan, site of the mammoth oil-processing plant on the Persian Gulf, across from Iraq. (One day I saw in our local paper a photo of an Iraqi bomb dropped on Iran, reminding me that the political climate was still volatile!)

On the day we left Tehran, we stopped at the hospital for our final goodbyes. I had to hold back tears as I struggled to say words of thanks to the gracious staff for welcoming me totally into their world. The staff, in turn, overwhelmed us with their gratitude and presented Bobby and me with a beautiful silk Isfahan rug. We keep that rug in our home in Wellesley and in summer roll it up and take it with us to Chappy—a constant reminder of those wondrous Persian days.

I sometimes wonder why I undertook some of these foreign ventures. Did these experiences make me a better or worse surgeon, a better or worse parent? I do know that they gave me a new perspective about myself. In a sense it was liberating to become a solo individual again. For a brief period, I was no longer the responsible director of a plastic surgery service in a highly competitive environment; I was not the conscientious devoted father trying to set standards; I was not responsible for household bills or medical manuscripts. I had nothing to think about apart from this little Persian world. For one month I was complete ruler of the hospital, with none of the administrative headaches normally associated with that role. But when I returned to Boston, I felt rejuvenated, ready to take on the ever-growing demands of our now flourishing craniofacial program.

CHAPTER 21

LISA FEDERICO AND NATALIE KAPPER
Expansion of the Craniofacial Clinic

> **LISA FEDERICO**
> *Procedure:* Correction of hemifacial microsomia
> *Date of Operation:* October 1, 1981
> *Institution:* Craniofacial Clinic, Children's Hospital, Boston, Massachusetts
>
> **NATALIE KAPPER**
> *Procedure:* Correction of hemifacial microsomia
> *Date of Procedure:* March 17, 1981
> *Institution:* Craniofacial Clinic, Children's Hospital, Boston, Massachusetts

The Craniofacial Clinic had evolved logically and steadily. As a member of the Children's Hospital surgical staff, I had worked harmoniously for over 20 years with Dr. Lennard T. Swanson, Chief of Dental Services, treating increasing numbers of patients who benefited from our combined plastic surgical and orthodontic skills. Because of this long-time association, organization of a Craniofacial Clinic seemed just a seamless continuation of our earlier work together.

Originally, in the 1950s and 1960s, the bulk of patients we saw had cleft lips and palates and had formerly been treated by Drs. Ladd, Gross, and MacCollum. When patients became too old to be treated at Children's, it was an easy transition to care for them at the Brigham. At first, Len and I saw patients randomly, but soon we established the Cleft Palate Clinic to cluster the more complex cases. As we began to integrate Dr. Paul Tessier's teachings on craniofacial reconstruction, the "Craniofacial Clinic" evolved.

Gathering a Professional Team

As one of only three or four craniofacial centers in the United States, our clinic attracted patients from all over the world. With the increasing referrals, it became clear that we needed additional help. In 1974, I recruited two new staff members, both from the Massachusetts General Hospital: Dr. John Mulliken, a young plastic surgeon who had been recommended by Dr. Bradford Cannon, and Dr. Leonard B. Kaban, M.D., D.M.D., an oral surgeon. In 1977, Dr. Joe Upton joined the team. Joe hailed from Yale, Houston, and New York's Roosevelt Hospital and was a plastic surgeon by training, with a special interest in hand surgery and microsurgery.

Recognizing the importance of the psychological and social backgrounds of our patients and their families, I invited two psychiatrists, Dr. Myron Belfer and Dr. Alexandra Murray Harrison, and a psychologist, Dr. Francine Cohen Pillemer, to join us. The addition of Ms. Dottie

Dr. Tessier (left), Dr. Lennard Swanson (right), and I consulting on a craniofacial patient in 1972.

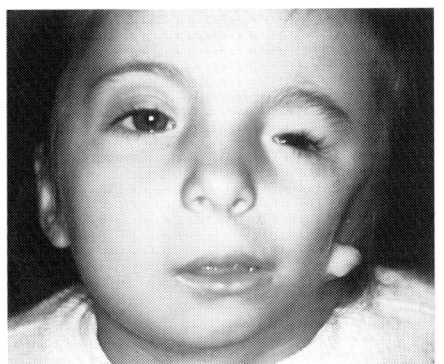
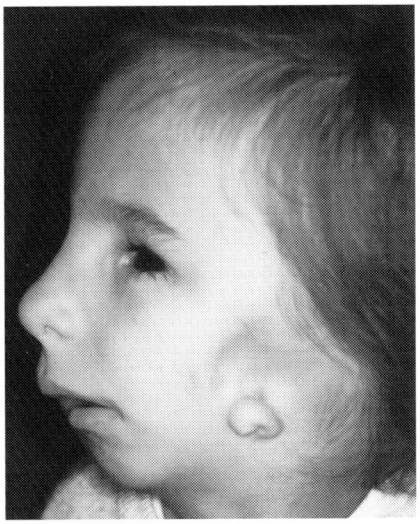

Severe form of hemifacial microsomia in a 5-year-old girl seen at the Massachusetts Crippled Children's Clinic at Mt. Auburn Hospital in 1952. Note the abnormal development of her ear, orbit of the eye, the upper and lower jaws, the part of the skull under the ear (the zygomatic bone), and the skin and subcutaneous tissues on the right side of her face.

MacDonald from Nursing and Ms. Joan Leahy from Social Services completed the craniofacial team.

While each of the team members was impressive in his or her own right, together we constituted a force greater than the sum of our individual talents. John Mulliken taught me about vascular malformations, Joe Upton gave me insight into congenital hand disorders, and Len Kaban instructed me about oral surgery. Sharing my daily work with eager residents and students added frosting to this already rich cake.

Through the years Bobby has wisely cautioned me not to try to mold each new staff member into a "Joe Murray." Her insight helped me recognize that each person has his or her own unique ideals and vision. Not everyone can be a team player or wishes to do laboratory research or publish clinical papers. Now, in the twilight of my career, I also recognize the inestimable value of the team effort. Throughout my career, my learning about and enjoyment of life have been elevated and enriched by working with others, and I can't resist encouraging future generations to share their knowledge generously and work selflessly with one another.

Hemifacial Microsomia

A common facial anomaly, second only to cleft lip and palate, is a congenital condition known as hemifacial microsomia. Usually the facial features of these children are asymmetrical, with the asymmetry involving mostly the ears and jaws; however, the eyes, nose, and facial muscles and nerves as well as subcutaneous tissues may also be affected. Variations of the condition are practically limitless: some patients appear almost normal, while in others the features are severely distorted. Very likely, these conditions also stem from abnormalities of the genes that Edward Lewis discovered, those controlling development of the body during development of the embryo. Invariably, these children have normal intelligence.

I saw my first patient with hemifacial microsomia in 1952 while working with Dr. Cannon at Mt. Auburn Hospital in the Massachusetts Crippled Children's Clinic.

A Three-dimensional Solution to an Old Problem

In the early days, planning treatment for individuals with hemifacial microsomia was fragmented and depended on the specialty of the physician who saw the patient first. Plastic surgeons concentrated on correction of the external ear, otolaryngologists worked on the middle ear, and orthodontists focused on aligning the teeth.

Dr. Cannon and I were no different. During the early years of our collaboration, we considered the ear and jaw as separate problems; it never occurred to us to think otherwise. We struggled to elongate the lower jawbone in a one-dimensional plane, deferring ear reconstruction until puberty. Years later, we progressed to a two-dimensional concept and finally adopted a three-dimensional view.

Today, it is embarrassing to realize how long it took us to devise a logical plan of treatment. It seems so obvious now. But in fairness to ourselves, we lacked the surgical and anesthetic expertise at that time to perform these operations safely. By the time we saw Lisa Federico in our Craniofacial Clinic 25 years later, in the mid-1970s, we had evolved an integrated analysis and systematic plan for treating this complex condition. Lisa's operation would represent a synthesis of all the previously distinct surgical techniques and the culmination of all that we had learned.

Meeting Lisa Federico

From the time Lisa was born, her parents began making the rounds, consulting with a host of dentists, pediatricians, orthopedists, and otolaryngologists concerning what could be done to correct her facial anomaly. Each specialist they visited proposed a different solution. We first saw Lisa in 1976, when she was 10 years old. Although we outlined a tentative treatment program and were prepared to proceed, the family was reluctant to accept our plan. We heard nothing further from them as they continued to seek advice from other sources. Finally, four years later, they returned to Children's Hospital.

I was the one to evaluate Lisa on this return visit, and in doing so I learned a valuable lesson. In my enthusiasm about the potential treatment, I explained to her and her family why she was an excellent candidate for surgery and began to enumerate the various features requiring correction. Suddenly, to my astonishment, Lisa burst into tears. Perhaps I had catalogued her facial defects too graphically, or perhaps this was the first time she truly realized that she needed treatment. Whatever the reason, I realized that I should have been more sensitive and spent more time getting to know her better. After all, she was still a young teenager and, like most teens, was probably intensely concerned with appearance and body image.

In any case, a week later Lisa and her parents decided to go ahead with the surgical correction. However, her father and mother firmly requested that we minimize the preoperative workup and omit the standard interviews with the psychiatrist, surgical nurse, and social worker. Such consultations had been expressly designed to prepare both patient and family for the emotional ramifications of surgery, but Lisa's parents felt she had had enough evaluations at other clinics to last a lifetime. Sympathetic to their wishes, we chose to forgo these meetings. It was a decision I would soon regret.

By this time, the bones of Lisa's face had achieved their maximal growth, so, in planning her reconstruction, we could not take advantage of any additional changes in their size and configuration. We would have to manipulate her features as they were. After studying dental models and special facial x-rays, we formulated an operative plan. To our delight, the eight-hour operation went flawlessly.

A few days afterward, however, I received an urgent call from Lisa's parents. They were distressed because they no longer recognized their

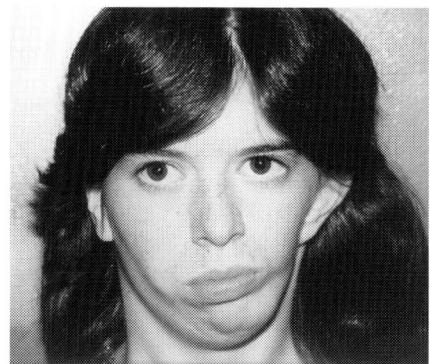
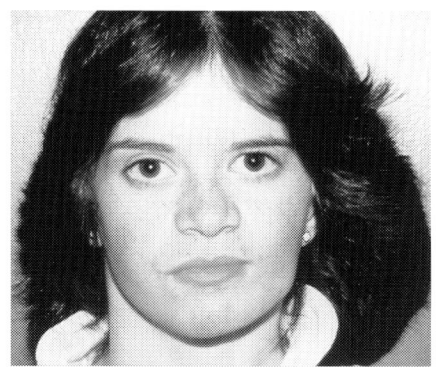
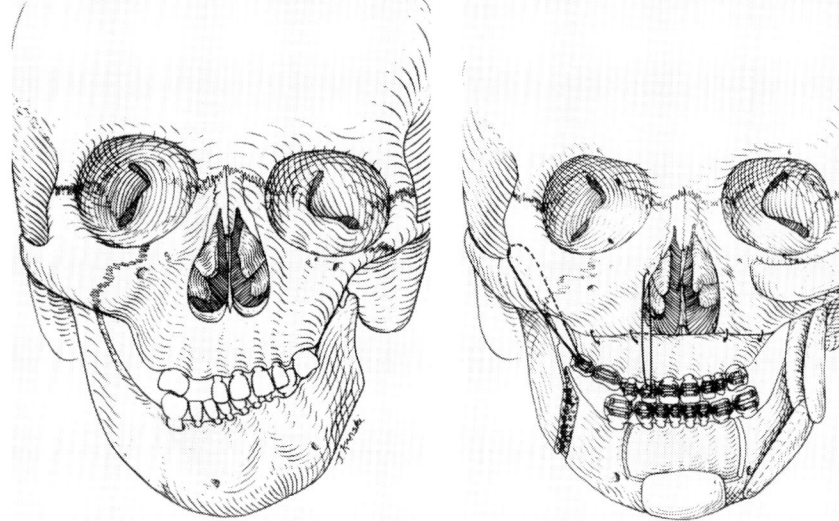

Lisa Federico before and after bony repair of left hemifacial microsomia.
Upper left: At age 14, Lisa's entire lower facial region, including her chin, has shifted to her left. The lower jaw is asymmetrical, and the left cheek is depressed from the midpoint of the chin to her right earlobe (causing a "ridge-and-valley" appearance). Her ears are not symmetrically positioned, and the floor of her left nostril is elevated. The left orbit and left cheekbone are underdeveloped.
Upper right: At 18 months after Lisa's surgery, facial symmetry is improved as a result of the skeletal correction, although some slight soft-tissue deficiency remains.
Lower left: Preoperative sketch showing asymmetry of underlying bony structures.
Lower right: During the 6-hour operation, normal dental occlusion and facial symmetry were achieved through multiple osteotomies and onlay bone grafts.
(From Murray J.E.: Four-dimensional approach to the analysis and treatment of hemifacial microsomia. In Brent B. (Ed.): The Artistry of Reconstructive Surgery. 1987, C.V. Mosby, St. Louis, pages 575–585.)

own child and asked me to "undo" the operation. I did what I could to assuage their anxiety and encouraged them to wait a bit longer, explaining that once the swelling subsided they would most likely feel differently.

They agreed to give the treatment a chance, and though it took a few months, both Lisa and her parents ultimately accepted and were even pleased with the results. Their initial reaction, however, illustrates that surgical preparation is not enough. As Myron Belfer, the psychiatrist on our team, had emphasized so strongly, patients and their families need to avail themselves of medical, dental, psychological, sociological, and personal support services to help them understand and accept the complex and sometimes drastic changes in appearance that come about after such surgical manipulation.

Meeting Natalie Kapper

Another young girl, Natalie Kapper, had also been referred to us through the dental clinic. Compared with Lisa, Natalie had a less severe form of hemifacial microsomia, but she had some paralysis of the nerve involving

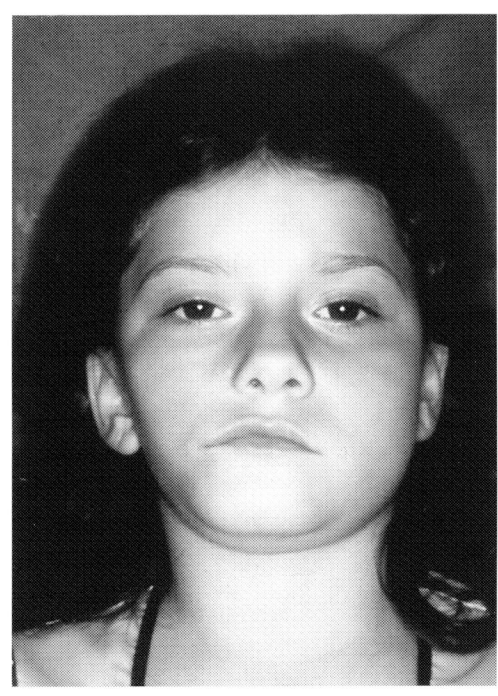

Natalie at age 11. Although she looks almost normal, her right ear is lower, her right cheek is less full, and her chin deviates to the right.

the right side of her forehead and her right lower lip. In addition, insufficient soft tissue over the right body of the lower jawbone and right cheek caused her right ear to be lower than her left. We had been following Natalie since she was five years old. By age seven, she was beginning to exhibit some negative psychological effects of the deformity.

Unlike Lisa, whose facial bones had matured by the time of treatment, Natalie's still had the potential to grow more. We took advantage of this growth potential and began orthodontia to realign the teeth of both jaws. This intervention was not intended to cure the problem but merely to position the lower jaw (the mandible) so that it would ultimately meet the upper jaw (the maxilla), which would continue to grow, and result in the proper occlusion. This preoperative orthodontia set the stage for the later operation that would be far less extensive, but more effective, than Lisa's.

By age 11, Natalie's face had become more asymmetrical. The chin was drifting to the right, and the lack of soft tissue on the right side of her face had become more obvious. This was typical for this disease; as one side of the face grows faster than the other, the asymmetry increases. It was clear to all of us that the time had come for the operation. Naturally, Natalie was extremely nervous. I spent considerable time with her and her parents, explaining in detail all that they could expect before, during, and after the surgery.

Incorporating a Fourth Dimension

The surgical correction involved moving the lower jawbone forward (anteriorly), downward (inferiorly), and a leftward rotation toward the midline—a three-dimensional shift. But expanding our scope since we treated Lisa Federico, we took advantage of a fourth dimension—time—to allow the upper jaw to grow downward into proper occlusion with the lower.

Natalie benefited from the "four-dimensional approach" to treatment. By utilizing the growth potential, we were able to achieve a better outcome with a less extensive operation. This concept of "inductive" surgery, which is distinct from excisional, reconstructive, and transplant surgery, is a far cry from the early days when Dr. Cannon and I struggled with the problem piecemeal. By the time Natalie came along, we had realized that the astute application of time (and patience) would ultimately yield a superior result. However, we then faced another

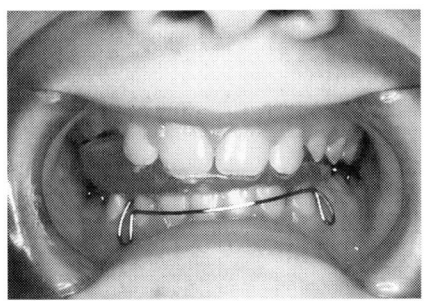 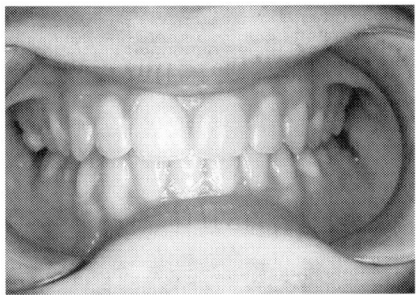

Left panel: Elongating Natalie's right lower jaw created a space for the upper jaw to grow down to meet it. Over time, the plastic prosthesis, placed between the upper and lower teeth to maintain the open space and keep the lower jaw in a horizontal plane, could be shaved proportionately to accommodate growth of the upper jaw.
Right panel: Results after 2 years. With the lower jaw in a horizontal plane, the upper jawbone has grown downward and filled the surgically created space between the upper and lower teeth, normalizing Natalie's occlusion.

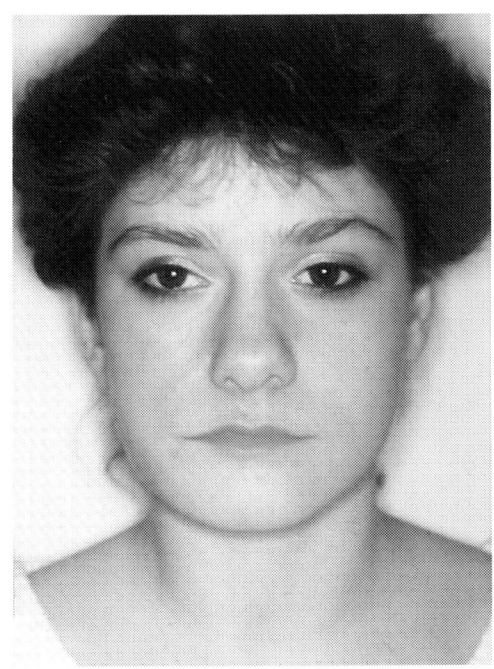

Natalie several years after her treatment. Note that the chin point, nose, lips, and jaws are now symmetrical.

challenge: determining the appropriate time to intervene. If we operated too soon, when the patient was too young, we might destroy the growth potential; if we could predict the growth patterns, however, we could optimally guide subsequent growth.

The Evolution of Body Image

Psychiatry and psychology play important roles in the final assessment of a surgical result. A fine aesthetic or improved functional result does not guarantee patient (or family) satisfaction. Much depends on their expectations and understanding prior to the operation. Dr. Myron Belfer describes the formation and changes of a person's body image as occurring in four distinct phases: infancy, school age, adolescence, and adulthood. Deformed persons and persons of normal appearance experience markedly different pathways of body image development.

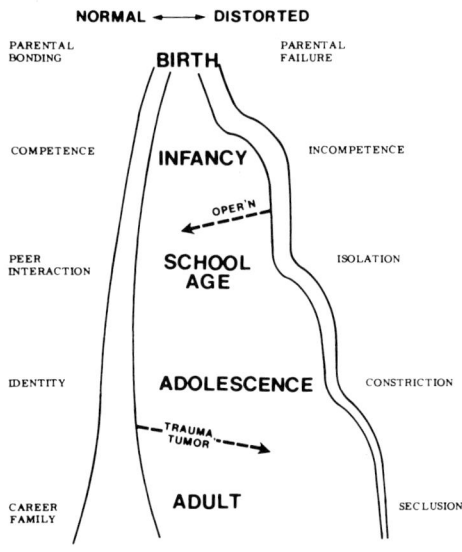

Two markedly different pathways of body image development. The pathway of normal body image development (left) broadens from birth, through infancy and adolescence, to adulthood. In direct contrast, the pathway of abnormal body image development (right) begins to narrow at infancy and becomes increasingly constricted into adulthood.

The psychological impact of a deformity is manifest differently at each stage in body image development. For example, a deformed infant, when rejected by parents because of the deformity, may drift further and further from the "mainstream." When the child has a congenital deformity, the normal pattern of an increasing sense of competence derived from sensory input from hands, mouth, eyes, ears, and nose may be stunted.

At school age, a handicap thwarts peer interaction, cognitive growth, and mastery of skills. Peer isolation begins. Diminished mental

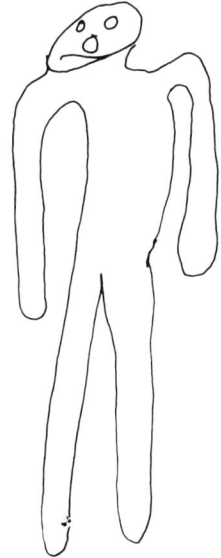

Left panel: Preoperative sketch of a "man" drawn by an 11-year-old boy during the standard "Draw-A-Person" test.
Right panel: The same test repeated 6 weeks postoperatively reveals a striking change in body image perception.

performance and a failed sense of mastery become a subconscious part of the psyche.

During adolescence, the deformed youngster becomes further separated from his or her peers. An uncertain sense of identity, diminished career goals, and a feeling of seclusion and failure often envelop the patient. These feelings are exacerbated in adulthood, when the deformed adult can have a sense of isolation, diminished achievement, and feelings of anger and conflict.

Surgical intervention at any phase tends to shift the deformed patient toward the normal pathway. The reverse is also true. If a person with normal appearance acquires a defect, whether through trauma or tumor, the path of body image development veers away from the "mainstream" toward the progressively constricted pathway of isolation and seclusion.

Today, we advocate correction of facial differences as early as possible, so the patient may embark on the ever-widening pathway of normal development.

CHAPTER 22

COSMETIC SURGERY
Not Just A Pretty Face

> *Procedures:* Rhinoplasty, cleft lip repair, and otoplasty
> *Dates of Operations:* 1953–1985
> *Institutions:* Brigham and Children's Hospitals, Boston, Massachusetts

The general public commonly—often intuitively—identifies plastic surgery with cosmetic surgery. It is almost as if "the physician is morphed into a cosmetician." Because professional advertising is no longer proscribed, and any physician can self-qualify as a plastic surgeon, the responsibility to offer realistic guidance to the public about the limitations and expectations of cosmetic surgery falls more and more to plastic and reconstructive surgeons. The common bond for all surgeons dealing with the physical appearance of their patients is an appreciation of the aesthetic elements of living.

I first became aware of the complex reciprocal interaction between appearance and function while at Valley Forge General Hospital in Pennsylvania during World War II. There my colleagues and I cared for hundreds of men who had sustained mutilating injuries of the face and extremities. For injured hands, we improvised all sorts of reconstructive operations to obtain maximum function from whatever bones, tendons, and skin remained intact. When unable to restore acceptable appearance (which unfortunately was common), we offered lifelike plastic prostheses to be employed when they attended social gatherings. But the soldiers seldom used them. They ended up on shelves, gathering dust.

It became clear that what these men really wanted was functional improvement. Even the toughest, most hardened young men were pleased by the smallest functional improvement. Paradoxically, an improvement in function increased their acceptance of their deformity. Possibly the soldiers who had lived through the dangers of war realized that function was more important than appearance.

It could be that their deformity represented a kind of "badge of courage"—evidence that they were moving on with their lives. Whatever the reason, at an early point in my professional life, I became sensitized to patients' responses and adjustments to physical deformities.

I have noted a similar relationship between function and appearance in civilian patients as well. The patient who has lost a nose or an ear as a result of cancer or traumatic injury prefers a replacement made from living flesh rather than a more normal-looking prosthesis.

Moreover, from my plastic surgical experiences in India, Iran, and Mexico, I noted that social function can be as important as physical function. In Vellore, India, at the Christian Medical School with Paul Brand (Chapter 15), I repaired an incomplete bilateral cleft lip in a teen-age girl. This birth defect did not impair any essential physical function. She could eat without difficulty and could speak clearly. Although she was a healthy girl with a caring family, she happened to live in a society where unmarried women were shunned. For her, "cosmetic" surgery was critical simply because it made her eligible for an acceptable marriage. No surgeon would refute the value of performing corrective surgery on this girl, although the indication for such a procedure was purely societal.

In our western society as well, social survival is a critical factor. Consider the child with an incomplete cleft lip. As far as his general health and physical condition were concerned, he would unquestionably be able to function normally all his life. Yet no one would begrudge or deny this child surgical correction.

COSMETIC SURGERY, *Not Just A Pretty Face*

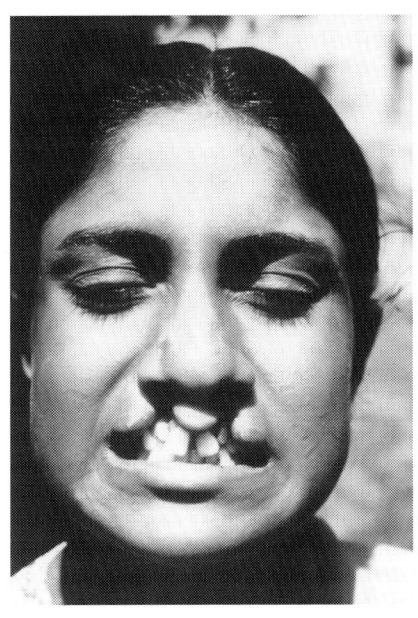

Left panel: A bilateral incomplete cleft lip made this teenage girl ineligible for marriage within her Indian culture.
Bottom panel: The patient, with her mother, a few months after the cleft lip repair.

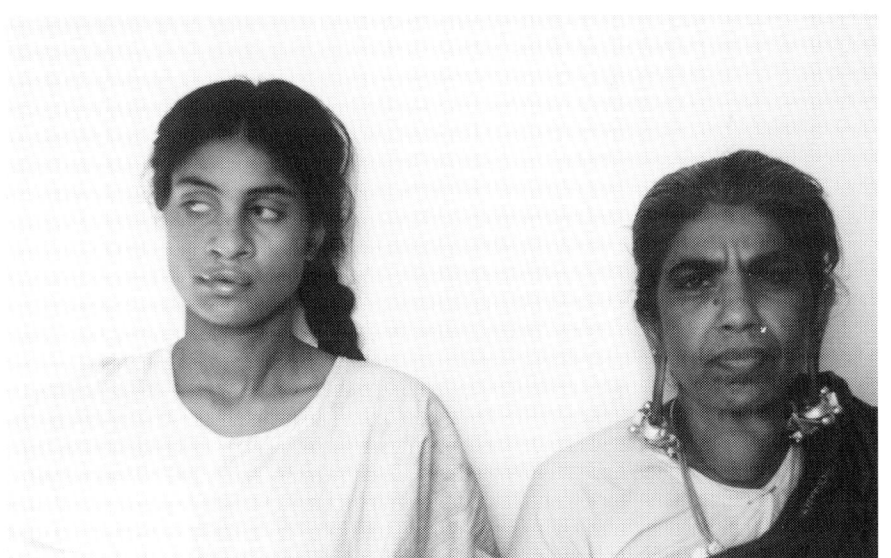

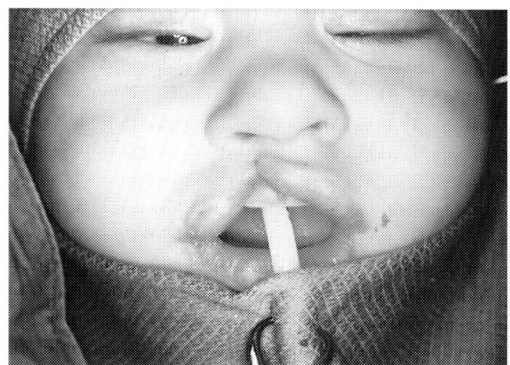 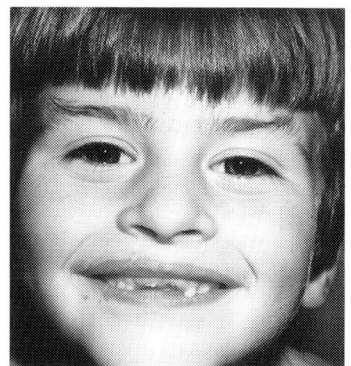

Repair of this incomplete cleft lip was purely cosmetic yet no one would deem it "frivolous."

The Complexity of "Simple" Cosmetic Surgery

"Social function" is also an indication for cosmetic surgery. The question is, how "abnormal" does a patient's appearance have to be to justify surgery? And who should make that judgment—the patient or the doctor?

Those of us who are blessed with so-called normal facial features are seldom aware of the full impact that even minor facial differences can make in a person's daily life. We may get a hint of this when others respond to a temporary change in our appearance, such as a black eye or a prominent bandage. "What happened? Cut yourself shaving? Didn't duck in time?" Although said casually and in jest, these comments do sink in. Imagine the cumulative effects over a lifetime!

Let us consider the case of Mrs. X, a tall, well-dressed woman in her mid-40s. Early in my career, Mrs. X came to my office and said she wanted a "nose job" (rhinoplasty). Her husband was by her side, encouraging and supportive, and I wondered why such a seemingly successful, well-adjusted woman would want a cosmetic operation at this stage in her life. When I expressed my concern about her motives, Mrs. X's answer was simple and to the point: "I have never liked my nose. I've finally decided to have it changed."

Perhaps because I was just starting out in practice and did not yet fully trust my instincts, I asked if she would consent to a psychiatric review before I proceeded with the rhinoplasty. She readily agreed to the evaluation but reiterated that all she wanted was to have a different nose.

Once the psychiatrist reported that he considered her perfectly normal, I was willing to operate. I told her what I could and could not do to restructure her nose, and as I did with all my cosmetic surgery patients, I emphasized that there was no guarantee of success. With her clear understanding of what she could realistically expect, I proceeded with the routine operation.

"The operation was a turning point in my life," Mrs. X later mused. The result was superior physically and even more successful psychically. Her husband cited an immediate change in her behavior. "She no longer seeks corner tables in restaurants to avoid showing her profile," he told me.

Even though some lay persons and physicians, especially "blood and guts" surgeons, might consider Mrs. X's problem minimal and her wishes frivolous, she felt differently. While others may have looked at her and asked what was wrong with her appearance, the fact was that she had looked at herself in the mirror every day since childhood, and she did not like what she saw. It embarrassed her, and that embarrassment affected her behavior and her sense of self-worth. Her nose presented a real impediment to her sense of well-being. Removal of that impediment, however minor, greatly improved her feelings about herself and affected her daily living.

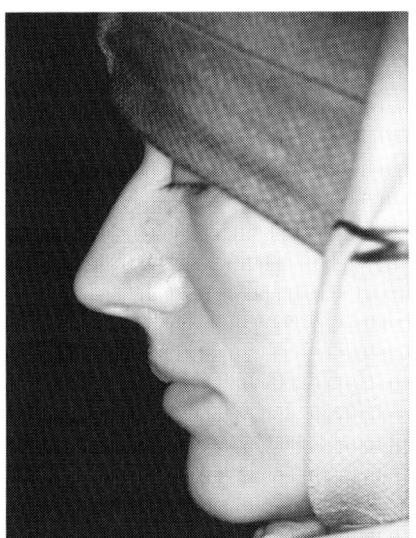 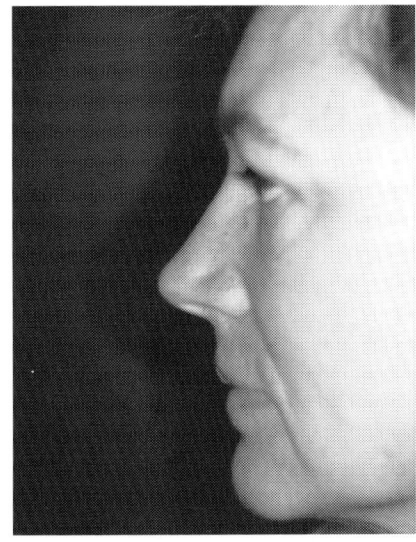

Mrs. X before and after her rhinoplasty.

A Divine Right

How does cosmetic surgery fit into the overall discipline of plastic surgery? In surprising contrast, it is both the least important and the most important subspecialty. In 1597, Gasparo Tagliacozzi, the father of plastic surgery, wrote:

> We restore, repair, and make whole those parts which nature has given but fortune has taken away, not so much that they delight the eye, but that they buoy our spirit and help the mind of the afflicted.

Three hundred and fifty years later, Will Mayo, founder of the Mayo Clinic, expressed this idea more succinctly: "It is the divine right of man to look human."

For me, the lure of cosmetic surgery has always been that it involves the psyche far more than other types of plastic surgery. Cosmetic (or "aesthetic," if you will) operations have a nonphysical, almost spiritual element. Although some observers have labeled plastic surgeons "psychiatrists with scalpels," I prefer to think of our work as *operating on the soul*. Of course, the plastic surgeon must be skilled technically. But more than surgical expertise is required. Professional judgment is critical; caring is essential.

When consulting with cosmetic patients, the surgeon must balance the attempt to help against the risk of doing harm. After all, these patients are rarely, if ever, suffering from some life-threatening condition. Unlike Mrs. X, who suffered from a lifetime of embarrassment because of a particular facial feature she never liked, some patients make up their minds that they will not be satisfied until they look like the models in advertisements that promote a certain "desirable" look. These patients might arrive for a consultation clutching images from a magazine that show the "perfect" nose or face. Because they are anxious to pursue these fantasies, the plastic surgeon is obligated to offer judicious advice and take care not to encourage unrealistic expectations. Leisurely preoperative discussions with such patients are essential.

My empathy for these patients has led me to follow a self-imposed rule: I would not on the first visit refuse to treat anyone seeking cosmetic surgery no matter how unreasonable his or her expectations. (Saying "no" to a patient's request for an operation is always more time-consuming than saying "yes.") Yet we have an obligation to explain the risks, the possible benefits, and especially the limitations of the cosmetic surgery being requested. I then suggest that the person give the matter more thought and return in one month if they wish to have a second consultation.

The Differing Motives For Cosmetic Surgery

Years ago a law student came to see me about correcting his prominent ears. Often termed "jug-handle" or "loving-cup" ears, the condition gives the face an almost cartoonish look, as though one were looking head-on at an automobile with its doors wide open. After I had examined him, explaining as I did so the pros and cons of a corrective otoplasty, the young man decided to go ahead with the operation without hesitation. He seemed well adjusted and confident, but before he left, I asked him one more question: why did he want to undergo such an operation at this stage in his life? He responded that he had never been unduly bothered by the usual taunts and jests during his childhood and puberty. Having enjoyed college and ranked well in law school, he felt he had achieved most of his life goals to date. Although he knew that he did not need the operation, he wanted it now for his own satisfaction. I was satisfied with his answer and immediately agreed to perform the operation.

A cosmetic operation of this type may be tricky, but it is not demanding. Results of bilateral otoplasty (reconstructive surgery of both ears) are fairly predictable and complications minimal. Even though this particular patient had made it through childhood unscathed, it is usually advisable to surgically correct prominent ears before a child reaches school age to avoid needless psychological trauma.

Many patients seek elective surgery to improve their appearance and self-image. One of the most common cosmetic surgical operations is the facelift, which offers temporary improvement for sagging facial skin—temporary, because the result depends more on stretching of the overlying skin than on rearranging the solid underlying structures of bone and cartilage. Thus, the results are never permanent. Nevertheless, combining a surgical facelift with surface treatments, such as chemicals, abrasives, or lasers, can provide satisfactory short-term results, producing the psychological and aesthetic benefits in patients whose expectations are realistic. For them, the time, discomfort, and expense involved are worth the discomfort. On the other hand, cosmetic surgery for redundant eyelid skin or fat (lid plasties) usually provides satisfactory results that are often long-lasting.

Certain types of cosmetic surgery do not appeal to me. For example, endoscopic liposuction—so-called "body sculpting"—seems unnecessarily life-endangering for conditions that can either be minimized by dietary discipline or treated more safely under direct surgical vision. Most plastic surgeons who limit their practice to cosmetic surgery do maintain the strict standards of professionalism. However, a surgical practice devoted entirely to non-emergency and highly lucrative cosmetic surgery can blunt the fact that they are professionals trained to advise and care for patients.

Cosmetic surgeons must remember that they are physicians and, as such, are not engaged in "business," nor are our patients "clients" or "customers." The medical profession exists primarily to serve society. Although personal advertising by physicians is no longer proscribed, we should not crassly peddle our wares. Patients are not purchasing a dress or a jacket that can be put aside later if it proves unsuitable. Rather, they are voluntarily subjecting a part of their body to a surgical procedure, with its attendant—albeit minimal—risk for unexpected complications in terms of scarring or poor healing.

To a surgeon, the most reassuring motive for a patient seeking cosmetic surgery is a desire to blend into rather than stand out from the crowd. An operation is a success when the patient is pleased. In other words, a successful operation depends upon the patient's reaction to it. Some of my patients have been exceedingly happy with what I considered a less than optimal anatomical result. Others have been dissatisfied with a superb physical result. The preoperative consultation sets the stage for determining the final outcome. During that consultation, you do what you can to effect a positive psychological result.

Personally, I have enjoyed caring for patients seeking cosmetic surgery. They can be helped by well-planned and well-executed surgical operations. A major challenge has been in the selection of patients—neither encouraging those seeking unrealistic results, nor discouraging those who are hesitant to occupy the time of a busy surgeon. Cosmetic surgery can serve society well.

CHAPTER 23

RAYMOND MCMILLAN
Surgery of the Soul

> *Procedure:* Congenital cardiac and facial differences; restoration of body and soul
> *Dates of Operations:* 1962 through 1977
> *Institution:* Peter Bent Brigham Hospital, Boston, Massachusetts

The full benefits from plastic surgery are epitomized by one extraordinary human being, Raymond Francis McMillan. Ray was born with a severe facial deformity known as Moebius syndrome. With no control of his facial muscles, he drooled constantly, and his tongue hung out. His lips were blue (cyanotic), and his ears consisted of small blobs of tissue. This relatively common congenital disorder often included a heart defect.

Despite the physical and emotional hardships he had endured as a child, Ray had an exceptional spirit. After spending the first five years of his life with his mother, he was sent to live at the Wrentham State School, the same mental institution where Jimmy Hickey had been admitted (Chapter 17).[31] Ray stayed there for 16 years and was released at the age of 21. One year later, he was referred to us at the Brigham by a local newspaper editor and clergyman.

Ray's problems were so extensive that it was difficult for us to know where to begin. After careful deliberation, we decided to tackle his facial deformities first—not only because it was his most visible and compelling problem, but because it was the easiest to repair. Also, it was the late 1950s, and operations on the heart were not yet possible; the heart-lung pump, necessary for such surgery, was still being developed. By the next decade, however, the field of cardiac surgery had progressed remarkably, and. Drs. John Collins and Larry Cohn were able to repair Ray's heart defect, which gave him considerably more strength and stamina.

We started our reconstruction by cutting his lower jawbone into two sections and repositioning each section so that he could close his mouth and control his saliva. A few months later, we detached portions of those facial muscles that could be controlled and reattached them to the corners of his mouth. This gave Ray the ability to smile, albeit in a limited way, for the first time. Subsequently, we operated on his hard palate to help improve his speech and revised the shape of his nose. These slight improvements increased Ray's self-esteem.

Ray lived alone and was self-sufficient. I helped him get a job in one of the labs at the Dana-Farber Cancer Institute and Children's Hospital and, on his way to or from work, he frequently dropped by my office. I enjoyed these casual visits and, on one occasion I suggested that he study for his high school equivalency diploma. A few years later, he bounded into my office, waving his diploma. I was deeply touched when he gave it to me to keep, saying he had no one else with which to share it.

Later, I suggested he do some writing. Apparently he acted on my suggestion. Excerpts from his unfinished memoir, uncovered after his death in 1997, were written as Ray sat on a park bench in the Boston Common.

> It is a beautiful day. I have a wonderful free, serene feeling just watching the people go by. I am writing this in the hope that it might help someone today.
>
> This story begins with despair and ends with hope. My name is Raymond Francis McMillan and I was born in Malden, Massachusetts, on January 15, 1943. I spent my first five years with my mother, whom I never really got to know.
>
> Because of my deafness, malformed heart and facial deformity, my mother and two social agents admitted me to the Wrentham State School. The School is situated in the New England countryside thirty miles from Boston. The oppressive Victorian buildings of a state hospital still stand, symbol of a time when people abandoned those with whom they could or would not deal. Historically, the hospital was the home of the unloved, the indigent, the handicapped and the insane. It was the total world and experience to thousands of emotionally

bereft people. The corridors echo with neglect suffered and cruelties done. And the institution was more like a prison, instead of a mental hospital. It was the antithesis of a nurturing environment; it was an unlikely place for me with my handicaps and I did indeed survive! I survived because I was blessed with a beautiful intelligence, humor and courage. Today I enjoy a normal life and a bright future.

While I was a resident at Wrentham State School, it took some time to get used to because I was very young and I was scared, lost, lonely and confused. My 16 years were a total nightmare and I wonder how I ever survived under those conditions and still was able to keep my head on straight. I was no longer wanted and I found it very difficult to live with the idea of being rejected by my own mother and family because of heart, hearing, and facial malformation. My family only visited me twice during my ordeal. My father came to visit me when I was 12; my stepfather came to visit me five years later and I saw my mother for the first time then. But that was the last time I saw either of them!

I got about four years of good education between 1959 and 1963. Of course living at the School was an education in itself. Under the circumstances I did my very best but I did not graduate nor did anyone else. There was no such thing as a high school diploma at a mental institution.

The people who were in charge at Wrentham State School did not think or feel that I could make it on my own in the outside world because of my handicaps and poor health. The longer I stayed at the institution the more angry I got and I can't count how many times I ran away from the place. When I got caught I knew I was in trouble and after so many beatings it became an everyday thing.

I was paroled (that's the word they used in those days) in April, 1964, at the age of 21. Boy was I glad to see that day come! I knew I had a long hill to climb and it wasn't easy at first but I was so happy to get out of the place they call Wrentham State School that I never looked back! I was not in the best of health but I was so excited to get out on my own for the first time. It felt so good to be free!

> "... to preserve freedom, we must begin with peace within ourselves and then spread it to others. Freedom is not a store-bought commodity. There are many ways freedom can be preserved, but with every freedom there is a responsibility and with every right there is an obligation . . . ."

—Vida Ivanouskas

On my first day on my own in the outside world, the weather was beautiful. It was a Friday. My first stop was at the White Swan Motel where I was to share a room with three other former residents of the Wrentham State School. The next day I went out looking for an apartment because I wanted total independence and wanted to be alone to prove to myself that I could make it on my own and in the community. I became a dishwasher and salad bar helper at the Lafayette House Restaurant.

My first year, 1964, was a very difficult year. I had trouble making the transition and I didn't know to whom, where or how to go for help. I didn't speak English very well since I had very defective speech. It made it very difficult to talk. As Abraham Lincoln said,

> "Most folks are about as happy as they make up their minds to be."

You know, he was right! The following year, 1965, I promised myself to be so strong that nothing could disturb my peace of mind. To talk health and make all my friends feel that there is something in them. To look on the sunny side of everything and make my optimism come true. To forget the mistakes of the past and press on to the greater achievements of the future. To wear a cheerful countenance at all times and to have a smile ready for every living creature I meet. To give so much time to the improvement of myself that I have no time to criticize others. To be too large for worry, too noble for anger, too strong for fear and too happy to permit the presence of trouble. To think well of myself and to proclaim this fact to the world—not in loud words but in great deeds. To live in the faith that the world is on my side so long as I am true to the best that is in me.

That same year I had an appointment with Dr. Joseph E. Murray, a plastic surgeon at the Peter Bent Brigham Hospital. He told me that he could help me and make my life a lot easier to handle. As the years went by I continued to see Dr. Murray even until this day. Throughout 1965 I spent a great deal of time as an outpatient. Four to six months was spent getting my jaw ready and strengthened for my first operation in 1966. I didn't know what to expect of the outcome but I knew there was a lot of work to be done and that I would have to be strong and have a lot of heart and to be brave and courageous and to do what is right and to take responsibility for my own actions. I expect nothing from the world but I realize that as I give to the world, the world will give to me.

I had my first operation in 1966, and additional operations in 1967, 1968 and 1969. They could only do a little at a time because I had a weak heart. Then in 1970 I went and had the open heart surgery and I was in the hospital for about seven weeks. I can honestly say they did a wonderful job. The surgery was performed by Dr. John Collins and Dr. Lawrence Cohn. I had my last operation in 1977. In the meantime, I did a lot of reading as part of my self education. I couldn't read well or understand all that I was reading. I kept on reading anyway!

Ray McMillan after corrective surgery for his facial deformity and cardiac defect.

Many people have severe facial deformities, either congenitally or as a result of injury or disease. They do not look like other people and because they are different, they are treated differently. They may even come to think of themselves as less than human. But beauty is not determined by a perfect figure and features. It is determined by the way you respect and honor yourself.

I had a very difficult time with my handicap and sometimes I had to fight with my fists. I had to fight to survive. Handicapped people are a part of our society that are beaten down time and time again. But we are a strong-willed and extremely proud people who desire no handouts, no charity and want nothing more than the simple chance to support ourselves through our own abilities. There are ups and downs and you can never be a quitter. There is a reason for living! There is a reason for being here. And there is always a way. No matter what you are going through, there is always a way."

—*Raymond Francis McMillan*

Ray died suddenly in 1997, seated in a car beside his best friend, on the way to lunch at a favorite restaurant. At his funeral, a circle of people far beyond his hometown of Wrentham came to mourn his passing. Many described Ray as a beloved friend. Jack Collins, Larry Cohn, and I agree that Ray was one of the most remarkable patients we have ever had the privilege to care for. We feel fortunate to have known him.

The impact the hospital staff and I had on Ray's life only partially involved scalpels and sutures. Simply because we cared for him and showed him compassion and basic human kindness, we gave him a feeling of worth and helped heal his spirit. The greatest benefit we gave Ray was not so much the freedom to control his facial muscles, but rather the freedom for his inner self to grow and glow. The external cosmetic improvements we made simply removed what had been a constant impediment to his daily living. Surely this was a case of true "surgery of the soul."

With Ray as the benchmark for the highest form of cosmetic surgery, it becomes apparent that the specialty is too precious to trivialize. Ray's life reinforces the principles of the Hippocratic Oath. All life is precious. His words remind us that our talents and skills can serve in unexpected ways. The memory of Ray continues to enrich my life daily by reminding me that, as someone put it, "Service to society is the rent we pay for living on this planet."

PART IV

THE LATER YEARS

CHAPTER 24

DR. JOSEPH E. MURRAY
Stroke Patient

> *Procedure:* Thrombosis of the internal capsule of the brainstem
> *Date of Operation:* March 20, 1986
> *Institution:* Brigham & Women's Hospital, Boston, Massachusetts

I was nearing retirement and had just three months to go until the new chief of plastic surgery would arrive. After a year-long search, the Harvard Medical School committee selected Dr. Elof Eriksson from the University of Southern Illinois. Because he was young and relatively unknown, some were openly critical of the choice, and staff morale suffered.

When the going gets tough, leaders must lead. I took on extra work and accepted unappealing assignments in my zeal to sustain the morale of the service and demonstrate the need and value of teamwork. I did not know the new chief either, but I'd learned early while playing sports that teamwork was the only thing that would bring the service through this transition. At all costs, we had to support our leader-to-be.

I took some comfort in the fact that Dr. John Mannick, Surgeon-in-Chief at the Brigham, and Dr. Aldo Castaneda, Surgeon-in-Chief at Children's, felt that finding my successor warranted a full medical school search committee. This indicated to me that plastic surgery at Harvard Medical School had finally come of age. Previously, all plastic surgical chiefs in Harvard hospitals had been selected by the incumbent Surgeon-in-Chief of the individual Harvard hospitals (e.g., Brigham & Women's, Children's, Mass General, New England Deaconess, Beth Israel).

I was working harder than ever at a time when I was supposed to be tapering off. In spite of my best intentions, my surgical responsibilities remained formidable. In addition to a crowded schedule of patients, I was involved in fund-raising at Harvard Medical School, developing the Craniofacial Center at the Children's and Brigham & Women's Hospitals, and mobilizing Chappaquiddick residents to fight against the use of private helicopters on our unique little island. This last responsibility was my duty as Chairman of the local committee for The Trustees of Reservations, the world's oldest conservation group, founded in 1891. Its mission is to preserve "natural landscapes as a museum for future generations," just as an art museum preserves works of art. (Interestingly, the equivalent British National Trust conservation group adopted TTOR's constitution five years later.) With all this activity and responsibility, I was looking forward eagerly to summer on the Vineyard.

STROKE

At 6:00 A.M. on Thursday morning, March 20, 1986, I was up early to prepare for a full day of activities. Though I had stayed up late the night before, I still had not completed my latest manuscript. I knew I had to get it done before hospital rounds, because after that I would be on an airplane to the University of Alabama Medical School, where I was to be Visiting Professor for a few days.

In the shower, mulling over details in preparation for the days ahead, I suddenly experienced a dull ache and strange weakness in my left leg. Seconds later, I had the same feeling in my left arm. It would be too much of a coincidence to have muscle spasms in both left extremities simultaneously. Thinking the sudden weakness was most likely cerebral in origin, I hoped it would go away. But it got worse with every second that passed.

I clumsily stepped out of the shower and managed to get myself dressed. But by now there was no denying that something serious was going on. The left side of my face began to tingle, and the little finger on my left hand was numb. At my request Bobby phoned Dr. Rick Tyler, Chief of Neurology at the Brigham, and she drove me straight to the hospital.

I was admitted immediately. Rapid-CT scanning revealed nothing catastrophic. An intravenous heparin drip was started, but my condition continued to deteriorate. By 4:00 P.M., the entire left side of my face was numb, and I could not move my left arm, hand, or fingers. My entire left leg and toes were paralyzed. However, my mind remained alert. In spite of the numbness, my facial movements continued to be normal, and I could spell and articulate the most complicated tongue-twisters the speech therapists could throw at me.

As I lay in the hospital bed, I realized I had suffered a serious stroke. That night, taking stock of my situation after all family and visitors had left, I vowed that even if there would be no more hiking, tennis, mountain climbing, or other outdoor activities, I would use whatever function I had remaining to the best of my ability. I took a mental inventory. All six children had been educated; the house was mortgage-free. Since I was due to retire anyway, the idea of no longer operating did not bother me. After a 42-year career in surgery, another few months or years would make little overall difference. The prospect of canceling other scheduled activities was pleasant. At least I had a good excuse.

The repeat CT scan the next morning ruled out intracranial hemorrhage; the tentative diagnosis was cerebral thrombosis or embolism of the internal capsule. By noon, I was able to move my left little finger ever so slightly. Hourly, I could identify minuscule areas of improvement. By Sunday, I was able to stand and take a few tentative steps. By Monday, I was walking. By Wednesday, all numbness had disappeared completely and practically all motion had started to return. Dr. Tyler advised that if I retired from medicine completely for six months and was diligent about my physical therapy, the chances of a good recovery were favorable.

Beginning Again

I spent the next several months relearning how to do the most basic things. Walking was a real struggle, but after several weeks I could maneuver comfortably with a cane. My 10-year-old grandson, Jody, taught me how to throw a ball and walk up stairs. He later cheered me on as I learned to ride a bicycle with "no hands." Walter St. Goar, a compassionate doctor-friend and a superb tennis partner, enticed me onto the tennis court as soon as I could stand unaided. He watched patiently because I couldn't even make contact with the ball. The irony was not lost on me that construction was just about to begin on the tennis court we had planned for our property on Chappaquiddick. I remember traveling down to Chappy with Bobby later that spring to check on its progress and realizing that we were building a court I might never be able to use.

I had long been aware that roadblocks along life's path can become stepping stones. I learned this firsthand during my tenure with Paul Brand in India when I performed plastic and reconstructive surgery on hundreds of patients with leprosy. The ceramic paperweight made for me by one of those patients still sat on my desk and was a constant daily support to me during my recovery. If "difficulties are opportunities," as the inscription said, then I could be sure of having a wealth of opportunities before me.

My 58th birthday celebration with Bobby in 1977.

The cause of my stroke has never been completely defined. But I have wondered if my sense of overcommitment and the nagging mental awareness of so many unfinished projects might have thrown the complex systems of my brain out of balance and caused the overtaxed organ to shout "STOP!" Whatever the physiological reason for my stroke, I interpreted the event as a message from our Creator that humans do indeed have limits, and that we can turn episodes like these into what my colleague, Dr. John B. Mulliken, describes as "creative illnesses." I felt fortunate and blessed to be alive and able to face the future with a clean slate. My current and future obligation would be to use the rest of my life with consideration to Bobby first, the family second, and my profession third.[32]

A Brief Retirement

Our grandchildren were arriving in a steady stream at this time, and Bobby and I kept busy traveling around the country welcoming them.

I maintained my professional commitment as Chairman of the Harvard Medical School Alumni Fund, but otherwise I retired completely from patient care, lecturing, and administrative responsibilities. The research in my laboratory continued under the leadership of my colleague, Dr. Nicholas Tilney, who had co-authored several important scientific reports with me. Dr. Tilney went on to make important discoveries about the biology of chronic immunological rejection, and served as President of the American Society of Transplant Surgeons. Although stepping down was a relief, it also meant a radical lifestyle change. I had no regrets and was well aware that what I was experiencing was simply a matter of life going forward.

But as I was puttering around on the Vineyard one August day, cutting wood and making trails named after each of our 15 grandchildren, I reviewed my life and began to think that the world had passed me by, that my contributions to surgery had already been forgotten. I wrote as much to my youngest son, Rick, in August of 1990. Two months later, I was informed I had won the Nobel Prize in medicine. Another radical lifestyle change was about to begin.

CHAPTER 25

NOBEL LAUREATE

"Dr. Joseph Murray, please come forward to receive the Nobel Prize in Physiology or Medicine from the hands of His Majesty, the King."

With these words Dr. Gosten Garton concluded his summary of the work that led to my receiving the Nobel Prize in Physiology or Medicine, the full and formal name of what most people call simply the "Nobel Prize in Medicine." He delivered it first in Swedish and then in English. I was seated with the other nine Nobel Laureates on one side of the stage of the Stockholm Symphony Hall. The King and Queen of Sweden sat directly opposite us, flanked by Princess Lillian and Prince Bertil, on blue-and-gilt thrones. Huge bouquets flanked the curtained entrance at center stage, and red and gold zinnias and carnations were arranged along the footlights and stage balcony. A bright blue carpet bore the gold Nobel insignia. The overall effect was breathtaking.

As I walked across the stage to meet King Gustav IV as he approached me from the opposite side, the whole experience seemed like a fairy tale. Here I was—a clinical doctor, a surgeon whose professional life was devoted primarily to taking care of patients—receiving the world's most prestigious scientific prize. I happily extended my hand to receive the gold Nobel Medal and the accompanying Nobel Certificate, enclosed in elegant red leather covers. I then correctly made the three customary bows: first to the King, then to the nominating members of the Karolinska Institute who were seated behind me, and finally to the audience of 1,700 invited guests.

I took my seat as the King then presented the Nobel Medal to Dr. E. Donnall Thomas, co-recipient of the prize for his work on the transplantation of dissociated (bone marrow) cells and Harvard Medical School alumnus, Class of '48. The portion of the ceremony dedicated to the awards in Medicine concluded with a fanfare by the Stockholm Symphony Orchestra. My mind was filled with images and memories of all those who made this moment possible—my parents who gave me

Accepting the award from King Gustav IV of Sweden.

Bobby and our six children at the award ceremony in Stockholm.

such a solid foundation, my wife Bobby for her constant support, and the several hundred patients whose lives had become intertwined with mine.

Old News Travels Fast

When I first heard that I would be receiving the award, Bobby and I were in Lafayette, California, visiting our daughter Meg before I attended a meeting in nearby San Francisco. It was October of 1990. Since it is many hours later in Sweden than on the West Coast of the U.S., the announcement was made at about 4:30 A.M., Pacific time. Traditionally, the Nobel Committee announces the names of the prize winners to the media before officially informing the recipients. In this case, because I was away from home, it took two days for them to catch up with us, faxing us the citation from the Nobel Committee. Until then we were not quite sure exactly how the award read.

Nor did I hear about the prize from the news media, though not for their lack of trying. One overeager reporter, hoping to be the one to break the good news, called several area hotels in search of "Dr. Murray." He found a "Dr. Murray" registered at one hotel, awakened him, and told him that he had just won the Nobel Prize. Unfortunately, he had found the wrong Dr. Murray.

So I found out about winning the Nobel Prize in the best possible way: from my family. Our son J. Link, in Marion, Massachusetts, got a call from his brother-in-law in North Carolina, a physician who had heard it on the radio en route to early hospital rounds. J. Link, not being sure where Bobby and I were, called our daughter Ginny, who lives near us in Wellesley. Ginny, knowing we were in San Francisco, then called our daughter Meg at 4:40 a.m., who woke us with the wonderful news. Thus, by the time Bobby and I finally got the word, it was 5:00 a.m. on the West Coast and already old news back home on the East Coast!

We had to leave Meg's home shortly, because months earlier I had agreed to be the guest speaker at the American College of Surgeons (ACS) Presidential Dinner at The Fairmont Hotel in San Francisco. In typical fashion I had neglected to obtain a hotel reservation and had had to phone ACS headquarters from Chappy at the last minute, begging for *any* space still available at The Fairmont—a cubby hole or broom closet would do.

En route from Meg's home to The Fairmont Hotel, we stopped at St. Mary's Church for prayer, thanksgiving, and reflection. Bobby and

I needed a moment to catch our breath before attending the formal press and TV conference set up nearby. Reality hit home when we arrived at The Fairmont a few minutes later and the manager rushed to greet us with the news that we were being upgraded from the "broom closet" to the Regency Suite.

I turned to Bobby and said, "Now I know it must be true." Bobby rolled her eyes at my characteristic good luck and said, "Joe Murray, you always luck out of the holes you dig for yourself!" The Regency Suite had four phone lines, and we needed every one of them as phone calls came in from all over the world. My children were pinch-hitting as press secretaries. Meg helped field calls in the hotel room, while Ginny did the same in Wellesley. Rick took time away from his graduate classes at UC Berkeley to drive us hither and yon, and Tom, who happened to be in San Francisco on a business trip, pitched in as well. It was a breathtaking, whirlwind day, and, frankly, I can't say the pace has slowed down much since.

Post Nobel

The three questions I am most often asked about winning the Nobel Prize are the following:

- *Did I expect it?*

    I knew that I had been nominated several times over the years by a wide variety of people and groups. In 1988, The Nobel Committee had awarded the prize to my colleagues, biochemists George Hitchings and Trudy Elion (Chapter 12), for their "discoveries of important principles for drug treatment," one of which was Imuran. I interpreted this gesture as the Committee's way of acknowledging the field of transplantation and assumed that they considered my transplant work too oriented toward patient care. So I really was surprised (and elated) when I was notified two years later that I had been selected.

- *Did the prize change my life?*

    It certainly did. For one thing, it soon became impossible for me to slip unnoticed into any medical or scientific meeting, and even more impossible to leave early. More seriously, I felt an increased responsibility to the many other surgeons who have made excellent scientific advances while at the same time taking superb care of their patients. So many of them are equally deserving of the prize.

- *What did I do with the money?*

    No one person is responsible for progress in any field, especially in present-day medicine. Were it not for Harvard Medical School, the Brigham & Women's Hospital, and the Children's Hospital, and the persons who founded and maintained them, I would never have been able to accomplish what I did. It was only proper that the prize money be donated to help these institutions continue their medical missions.

A Clinician Scientist

Although I had only the slimmest scientific background in high school and college, in medical school I found it natural and logical to integrate my knowledge of basic science with its applications to clinical practice. Patient care has always been the bedrock of my professional life. But when it came to Nobel Laureates, I was a rarity in this regard. The first Nobel Prizes in Physiology or Medicine were awarded in 1901. Since that time, only three other "clinical" surgeons—that is, those who were directly involved in treating patients—have been recognized: Emil T. Kocher of Switzerland in 1909 for his work on the physiology, pathology, and surgery of the thyroid gland; Alexis Carrel of France and The Rockefeller Institute in New York in 1912 in recognition of his development of techniques for performing surgery on blood vessels; and Charles B. Huggins from the University of Chicago (and Harvard Medical School Class of '24) in 1966 for his discoveries concerning the hormonal treatment of cancer. Indeed, many winners of the Nobel Prize in Medicine are not M.D.'s, and therefore have never practiced medicine; rather, they are Ph.D.'s in the biological sciences.

The work for which most of my fellow Laureates have been honored was of a basic scientific nature, such as insights into immunological defense mechanisms, the discovery of viruses that cause human diseases, genetic control of intercellular communication, and insights into how the brain works. Without question, those discoveries by researchers who concentrate their efforts in the laboratory rather than in the clinic have had a direct and far-reaching impact on patient care worldwide.

Incidentally, since I received the prize, my "hands-on" clinical experience has served me in good stead at various Nobel functions. At one such event, the wife of a Laureate fell and hurt her ankle rather severely. Although there were at least 200 medical professionals in attendance, not one of them could do anything to help her. Finally somebody said, "Let's get Dr. Murray. He's the only one of us who takes care of patients for a living." Everyone laughed, but it was true. On another occasion, on a boat trip with a group of Laureates and their families, a young girl became ill with abdominal pains. I was the only one on board who recognized that she was suffering from acute appendicitis. We radioed ashore and were met at the dock by an ambulance. I then accompanied her to a nearby hospital where her appendix was removed before it ruptured.

A Life in Science

I have never felt a conflict between basic and applied science. In fact, Louis Pasteur settled the issue 150 years ago when he wrote:

> No category of science exists to which one could give the name of applied science. Science and the application of science are linked together as a fruit to the tree that has borne it.

Medical students and residents often ask me whether a Ph.D. is essential for a person with an M.D. to do research. My answer is always "No." Basic scientific research and clinical research are made stronger by their association because both disciplines are in pursuit of truth. For me, it was the rigors of laboratory research combined with the humanism of patient care that enriched my daily living. A doctorate in one of the basic sciences—or any discipline—will always increase one's background understanding, but it is not what I consider one of the three essential ingredients for a medical doctor.

- **Curiosity.** It was curiosity that led me to wonder as a child about the ants making trails on the paths I walked in the woods. (Was it the same leader every time?) That same curiosity is what captured my interest when observing the strange behavior of skin allografts and autografts being used on patients at Valley Forge General Hospital. *Curiosity selects the problem.*

- **Imagination** is needed to make the mental leap and bridge the hidden connections between seemingly unrelated observations.
- **Persistence** allows one to keep going during the inevitable periods of discouragement and despair.

Of these three essential ingredients, curiosity is key, because selection of the problem takes precedence over everything. This is why I advise students to choose a problem to solve that truly motivates them. Only thus will they find the energy to persevere through periods of discouragement and surmount any roadblocks they may encounter in seeking the answer.

My life has been an incredibly fortuitous amalgam of events. Many seemingly random assignments, apparent setbacks, and events occurred along the way. It was the combination of curiosity, imagination, and persistence that opened wide the doors to a medical Wonderland I'd never even dreamed of. The fact that a fellow who entered medical school with no overt interest in research could somehow parlay this admixture of nature's gifts into a career as fulfilling as mine is truly "curious." As Alice said as she marveled at the astonishing sights of her own Wonderland, "It just gets curiouser and curiouser."

A Life of Service

Although my life as a scientist has been immensely rewarding, for me, the greatest satisfaction has come from having spent a life in the practice of medicine, as a surgeon. The practice of medicine is a life of service. Working hard to help someone else is a reward in and of itself. Moreover, you have to solve plenty of puzzles in the daily practice of surgery. Although the solutions may not be important enough to society as a whole to win you a scientific prize, they are all-important to the person who has asked for your help. Furthermore, solving some of these "little" problems can be every bit as intellectually challenging as solving a "big" problem.

Finally, there is something about the practice of surgery that has meant the most to me—more than the intellectual challenge of solving a puzzle, more than the rewards of trying to help others, and more than the gratitude of those you have tried to help. In our patients, we witness human nature in the raw—fear, despair, courage, understanding, hope, resignation, heroism. Our patients teach us about life. In particular, they teach us how to deal with adversity.

If I had been Charles Woods (Chapter 1), would I have had the will to survive for six weeks with 70 percent of my body burned, and the ability to endure two years of unimaginable pain? Would I have had the dignity and confidence to walk out into the world with a disfigurement that would cause people to stare at me for the rest of my life? I honestly don't know. I know only that Charles taught me what a human being can achieve, and should strive for, in dealing with adversity.

And what if I had been Raymond Francis McMillan (Chapter 23), born with no control of my facial muscles, drooling constantly, and, because of my appearance, rejected by my parents and placed in an institution for the mentally retarded for nearly 20 years? After I was released from the institution at the age of 21, and left to fend for myself in the world, would I have written the words that he wrote?

> I promised myself to be so strong that nothing could disturb my peace of mind. To give so much time to the improvement of myself that I have no time to criticize others. To be too large for worry, too noble for anger, too strong for fear and too happy to permit the presence of trouble.

I don't know whether I would have been able to write anything like that, or to live my life accordingly. I know only that the fact that someone could write those words, after having been through what Raymond went through, has been an inspiration to me and will be for the rest of my life.

EPILOGUE—April 1st, 1999

As I anticipated this day, my 80th birthday, in my heart of hearts I desired only one present—to once again sit around our dining room table and look into the faces of our six children.

When I was in high school, I read Thornton Wilder's play Our Town, and I have seen it performed on stage many times. In the final act the deceased daughter is granted her wish to return from her grave to spend just one more day with her family. Her fellow cemetery dwellers try to discourage her, but she insists and is granted her wish. She finds her mother busy with kitchen chores and her brothers and sisters getting ready for school and involved in their own individual activities—all heedless of her presence and of one another. In vain, she implores them to look at one another, enjoy one another's company,

The whole family together, 1999. Top row: Meg, Bobby, me, and Ginny. Bottom row: Tom, J. Link, Kathy, and Rick.

and appreciate the riches of their lives and the fact that they are all together again. But they do not listen, do not hear her message. She sadly returns to her grave.

Although today I have a peace that almost "surpasses all understanding," I am aware of the Biblical warning: "But lest anyone who thinks he is standing upright watch out lest he fall." We are all so blessed with The Grace of God and the beauty of our Earth, given unconditionally. It almost hurts.

Joseph E. Murray, M.D.

ENDNOTES

Chapter 4

1. The Surgeon-in-Chief, Elliott C. Cutler, was a Brigadier-General and in charge of the entire surgical military operation in the European Theater during World War II. With him were Dr. Robert Zollinger and Dr. J. Englebert Dunphy. Drs. J. Hartwell Harrison, Chilton Crane, Thomas Botsford, and Donald Matson were in the Pacific serving in Australia and New Guinea.

    Dr. Cutler, Dr. Cushing's successor as Surgeon-in-Chief at the Peter Bent Brigham Hospital, was overseas while I was an intern, so I never knew him as an active surgeon. He was slim, fast-moving, vigorous, and a true patriot. During one of his lectures, I recall him saying, "Your country always comes first." He was a born leader!
2. The skeletal staff at the Brigham included Drs. Francis C. Newton as Acting Surgeon-in-Chief, William Quinby, Franc Ingraham, John Homans, and David Cheever.

Chapter 5

3. James Barrett Brown was one of that pioneering group of plastic surgeons from Barnes Hospital at Washington University in St. Louis—the cradle of plastic surgery in the United States. S. Vilray P. Blair, the first plastic surgeon at Barnes, had organized the American Board of Plastic Surgery, originally as a part of the newly developed American Board of Surgery under Dr. Evarts Graham, Chief of Surgery at Barnes. Within a few years the Plastic Board became a separate entity. Brown became Blair's first Associate Plastic Surgeon. Louis "Bill" Byers became the third member of the legendary "B, B, & B" galaxy.
4. While in Britain, Dr. Brown had been a tentmate of Dr. Loyal Davis, a Chicago neurosurgeon and the father of former First Lady Nancy Reagan.
5. After graduating from Harvard Medical School in 1933, Dr. Cannon returned to his midwestern origins and selected Barnes Hospital for his surgical residency. He worked as a Plastic Surgical Fellow with Byers under Brown before returning to his work on the faculty of HMS until his retirement.
6. Dr. Bradford Cannon published a retrospective article describing in greater detail the medical response to the Cocoanut Grove tragedy

    > The whole staff of the Massachusetts General Hospital was immediately called to deal with the injured, but we were deprived of the help of many who had gone to war with MGH Base Hospital No. 6. In addition to caring for people's fluid and respiratory needs, the surgical teams dressed all

burned surfaces with a bland ointment impregnated in a fine-meshed gauze. There was no mention of tannic acid. The deep-pink skin color, caused by the fixation of carbon monoxide by hemoglobin, misled a number of staff unfamiliar with burns. Failure to note the absence of skin blanching on pressure led to misunderstanding and delay in planning long-term care. After national interest in the outcome of this catastrophe subsided, the surgical house staff returned to their routines. I, however, was informed that the task of caring for the survivors was now mine. I gladly accepted. For the next three or four months, I had sole care of the ten survivors with major burns, which involved frequent dressings, grafting, and, in one patient, a remote flap to protect exposed extensor tendons of the hand.

(*JAMA* 1990;263[6])

Another article on this subject was later published by Coleman, Moore, Cope, and Cannon in the *Harvard Medical Alumni Bulletin* (1991/92;65[Winter]:10–19).

7. Twenty years later, Wally Reed established the first free-standing Day Ambulatory Surgicenter in Phoenix, Arizona, which rapidly became a model nationwide.
8. Some of these casts are on permanent display at the National Archives of Plastic Surgery at the Countway Library of Medicine at Harvard Medical School in Boston.
9. Ed Link is recognized as the originator of flight simulation. He was later awarded the Lindbergh Award from the New York Museum of Science. At the awards ceremony he acknowledged the lifelong guidance and help of his older brother, George Link, my wife Bobby's father. Ed went on to found the Harborbranch Oceanographic Institute in Fort Pierce, Florida, with substantial support from Seward Johnson, of Johnson & Johnson, Inc.
10. Andy Moore later became the first plastic surgery chief at the University of Kentucky in Lexington and was much beloved by his patients, colleagues, and friends. Milt and Pat Edgerton were also close friends of ours. Milt became Chief of Plastic Surgery at The Johns Hopkins Hospital and later developed an outstanding program at the University of Virginia in Charlottesville.

Chapter 6

11. At the end of the war, Dr. Brown realized that there was a need for providing continuity of care for the many patients who were still hospitalized. He got in touch with President Truman, a fellow Missourian, who authorized him to persuade a group of two dozen qualified surgeons to volunteer for extended army service. The "incentive" was a promotion by direct order of the Secretary of War. Dr. Cannon volunteered and remained on duty until the Spring of 1947.
12. Dr. Herb Conway returned from the Pacific Theater of War with a strong interest in plastic surgery. At New York Hospital, he established a respected plastic surgery residency program with a research component involving wound healing and transplantation biology. He was an imaginative, energetic man, whose "take charge" personality intimidated most residents; however, those of us who worked hard, and showed initiative and talent, found him to be a real friend.

Chapter 7

13. I particularly remember and cherish Dr. Leroy Vandam and Dr. Robert Smith, who headed anesthesia services at the Brigham and the Children's Hospitals. Dr. Wallace A. Reed of Phoenix, Arizona, is another treasured anesthetist colleague dating back to Army days.
14. Conway H, Murray JE: Indications for reconstruction at the time of surgical excision of cancer of the oral cavity. *Cancer* 1953;*VI*:46.

Chapter 8

15. During World War II, the Cushing Army Hospital was an active plastic surgical center, one of the eight in the Zone of the Interior. It was originally located in Framingham, Massachusetts; in 1952 it was moved to South Huntington Avenue and renamed the Boston VA Hospital.
16. While serving as a dentist in England during World War I, Dr. Varastad Kazanjian developed innovative methods of caring for jaw injuries. He was internationally known for his accomplishments. After the war he received his M.D. from Harvard Medical School. While Kazanjian was a student at Harvard, he was spotted in the audience by a visiting British luminary who was lecturing to a group of students. He interrupted his lecture to acknowledge him and proceeded to tell the other students how many patients Kazanjian had treated and rehabilitated during the war. Dr. Kazanjian was one of the kindest physicians I ever knew, and he went out of his way to help me get established in Boston.
17. As a prepequisite for accepting a professorship at the Harvard Medical School, Harvey Cushing insisted that the Surgical Research Laboratory be physically located in the Harvard Medical School quadrangle. The lab spawned Dr. Cushing's studies on the circulation of the cerebrospinal fluid, Dr. Elliott Cutler's studies in cardiac surgery, studies in immunosuppression and transplantation under Dr. Francis D. Moore, and many others. Harvey Cushing became the first Surgeon-in-Chief at the Peter Bent Brigham Hospital.
18. Dave Hume and I started our surgical residencies at the Peter Bent Brigham Hospital on the same day—January 1, 1944. I left for active duty after the first nine nine months, while Dave stayed at the hospital for two additional nine-month appointments. He then served on active duty in the Navy until the war ended on V-J Day, August 15, 1945. Therefore, he was able to return to the Brigham before I did. Dave was the surgeon recruited for the transplant program organized by Dr. Thorn and Dr. Moore, and coordinated by Dr. Ben Miller, a nephrologist from Philadelphia. They also selected Dr. John Merrill, a nephrologist, was chosen to supervise the use of renal dialysis, (i.e., the artificial kidney). (I was amused when I recently received a letter from Dr. Robert Forster, who had been a medical resident with John, recalling John's unhappiness with this assignment.)

Chapter 9

19. Dr. Harrison was a pillar of strength and decency, with vast experience in surgery of the kidney, ureter, and bladder. Although not directly involved in

transplantation research, he provided a wealth of experience, knowledge, and balanced judgment concerning patient care. Under his hand, donor nephrectomies for the very first transplants were done without complication.

Chapter 10

20. F.R. Lillie was a founder of the Marine Biological Laboratory in Woods Hole, Massachusetts.
21. Milan Hašek built up a large research group in Prague, Czechoslovakia, and made valuable contributions to the field of immunology despite inadequate technical support in his native country. A hearty, friendly man, Milan stayed with us in our home after some of the transplant conferences. Sadly, Milan and his wife, Vera, who was also a transplantation immunologist, were not allowed to travel together to the United States, and political constraints in the Soviet Union hindered their further progress in the field. I was saddened to hear of Milan's suicide in 1984. The affection and esteem in which he was held by his students and colleagues resulted in a memorial volume called *Realm of Tolerance*.
22. Fortunately, these specially designed sterile transplant rooms became unnecessary once chemical immune suppression became available (Chapter 6).
23. Dr. E. Donnall Thomas and I shared the 1990 Nobel Prize in Medicine for our "discoveries concerning organ and cell transplantation in the treatment of human disease." Don and I were both residents at the Brigham in the late 1940s and early 1950s—he in Medicine under Dr. Thorn, and I in Surgery under Dr. Moore. We knew of each other's work but never worked jointly on a project. I learned of Don's Nobel selection from a reporter who finally caught up with me in a San Francisco hotel three days after the announcement. The reporter asked if I knew the co-recipient, "a Dr. Don Thomas from Seattle." Naturally, my wife Bobby and I were overjoyed with the news.

Chapter 11

24. Thomas Starzl, together with David Hume, were the first transplant surgeons to publish their successful results with large series of successful patients. These vast experiences were very valuable in establishing transplantation, since we preferred to study individual patients sequentially.

Chapter 12

25. Others who made notable contributions included Ross Sheil from Sydney, Australia; Allen MacDonald from Halifax, Nova Scotia; Gil Deithelm from Cornell/New York Hospital; Max Dubernard from Lyons, France; Simon Simonion from Philadelphia; and Andre Govaerts from Brussels, Belgium.
26. Years later, after I received the Nobel Prize, I received a heart-warming letter from the patient's widow. After congratulating me on the prize, she thanked me and the entire medical staff for our kindness to both her husband and herself throughout the ordeal. She expressed gratitude that she and her husband felt for having been able to play a part in the ultimate success of kidney transplantation.

Endnotes

Chapter 13

27. Murray, J.E., Merrill, J.P., Harrison, J.H., Dammin, G.J., and Wilson, R.E.: Prolonged Survival of Human Kidney Homografts by Immunosuppressive Drug Therapy. New England Journal of Medicine *268*:1315, 1963.

Chapter 15

28. The Christian Medical School in Vellore, India, is an outstanding medical school founded by Dr. Ida Scudder, the daughter of missionaries. As a child growing up in India, she could not wait to come go to the U.S. She entered Cornell Medical School and, upon graduation, became a Park Avenue obstetrician/gynecologist. While caring for her affluent New York patients, she reflected on the women in India who had no place to go for medical care. At that time (the early 1900s), all doctors were male, and culture forbade males touching females. Ida returned to India to start the all-female Christian Medical School. It which soon became a leading school institution. Men were admitted after WWI, and today the student body is about equally divided between men and women. It is supported by multiple Protestant missionary groups worldwide.

Chapter 19

29. John Woods spent a year following his plastic surgical residency in our research lab. He then returned to the Mayo Clinic as Chief of Plastic Surgery and also head of their transplantation program. Mutaz Habal is an established plastic surgeon in Tampa, Florida, and is currently the editor of *The Cranial Facial Journal*.

Chapter 20

30. The new medical school was administered by Farouk Saiidi, Harvard Medical School Class of '39.

Chapter 23

31. When I was in grade school, I occasionally accompanied my mother when she visited the Wrentham State School, where she was a Trustee. I recall going around with her and the headmaster seeing the "inmates." In my innocence, I asked him "Are all the children here retarded? How can you tell?" He responded, "Yes, they *all* are."

Chapter 24

32. As a form of self-administered psychotherapy, I recorded the details of this episode for in the *Harvard Medical School Alumni Bulletin* a ("Finding Creativity in Adversity," Harvard Medical School Alumni Bulletin/Winter 1986–87/Vol. 60, No. 4, p. 19).

CHRONOLOGICAL BIBLIOGRAPHY

1946   Brown, J.B., Cannon, B., Lischer, C.E., Davis, W.B., Moore, A., and Murray, J.E.: Further Reports on the Use of Skin and Cartilage from the Ear. Plastic & Reconstructive Surgery *I*:130.

1947   Cannon, B., Lischer, C.E., Davis, W.B., Chasko, S., Moore, A., Murray, J.E., and McDowell, A.: The Use of Open Jump Flaps in Lower Extremity Repairs. Plastic & Reconstructive Surgery *II*: 335.

1953   Conway, H., and Murray, J.E.: Indications for Reconstruction at the Time of Surgical Excision of Cancer of the Oral Cavity. Cancer *VI*: 46.

Cannon, B., and Murray, J.E.: Further Observations on the Use of the Split Vermilion Bordered Flap. Plastic & Reconstructive Surgery *XI*:497.

Favour, C.B., Murray, J.E., Wemyss, C.T., Colodny, A., and Miller, B.F.: Serum complement Levels in Dogs Undergoing Kidney Homotransplantation. Proceedings of the Society for Experimental Biology and Medicine *83*:353.

Cannon, B., and Murray, J.E.: Application of Plastic Surgical Principles to the Treatment of Cancer. Journal of the American Geriatrics Society *I*: 715.

1954   Cannon, B., and Murray, J.E.: Medical Progress – Plastic Surgery: Facial Injuries. New England Journal of Medicine *250*:17.

Murray, J.E., Lang, S., and Miller, B.F.: Observations on the Natural History of Renal Homotransplantation in Dogs. Surgical Forum *5*:241.

Murray, J.E., Lang, S., and Miller, B.F.: Functional Status of Single Autotransplanted Kidneys in the Dog. Federation Proceedings *13*:888.

1955   Murray, J.E., Merrill, J.P., and Harrison, J.H.: Renal Homotransplantation in Identical Twins. Surgical Forum *6*:432.

1956   Merrill, J.P., Murray, J.E., Harrison, J.H., and Guild, W.: Successful Homotransplantation of the Human Kidney Between Identical Twins. Journal of the American Medical Association *160*:277.

Murray, J.E., Lang, S., Miller, B.F., and Dammin, G.J.: Prolonged Functional Survival of Renal Autotransplants in the Dog. Surgery, Gynecology and Obstetrics *103*:15.

Murray, J.E., and Cannon, B.: Skin Grafts for Chronic Wounds of the Lower Extremity. Journal of the American Medical Association *161*:1462.

Cannon, B., and Murray, J.E.: Medical Progress: Plastic Surgery: Tissue and Organ Transplantation. New England Journal of Medicine *255*:900.

Thomas, L., and Murray, J.E.: A Study of Consecutive Skin Homografts in the Dog. Surgical Forum 7:622.

1957 Dammin, G.J., Couch, N., and Murray, J.E.: Prolonged Survival of Skin Homografts in Uremic Patients. Annals of the New York Academy of Science *64*:967.

Porter, K.A., and Murray, J.E.: The Survival of Transfused Marrow in the X-irradiated Rabbit as Indicated by Sex Differentiated Leukocytes. Surgical Forum *8*:142.

1958 Porter, K.A., and Murray, J.E.: Successful Homotransplantation of Rabbit Bone Marrow After Preservation in Glycerol at -70 degrees C. Cancer Research *18*:117.

Porter, K.A., and Murray, J.E.: Long Term Study of X-irradiated Rabbits with Bone Marrow Homotransplants. Journal of the National Cancer Institute *20*:189.

Couch, N., Cassie, G.F., and Murray, J.E.: Survival of the Excised Dog Kidney Perfused in a Pump-Oxygenator System: 1. Circulatory Changes in the Hypothermic Preparation. Surgery *44*:666.

Porter, K.A., and Murray, J.E.: Homologous Marrow Transplantation in Rabbits After Triethylene Thiophosphoramide. American Medical Association Archives of Surgery *76*:908.

Murray, J.E., Merrill, J.P., and Harrison, J.H.: Kidney Transplantation Between Seven Pairs of Identical Twins. Annals of Surgery *148*:343.

Murray, J.E.: Evaluation of Endocrine Transplants. Transplantation Bulletin *5*:343.

Porter, K.A., Moseley, R., and Murray, J.E.: Studies in Bone Marrow Homotransplantation in X-irradiated Rabbits. Annals of New York Academy of Sciences *73*:819.

1959 Cannon, B., Randolph, J.G., and Murray, J.E.: Malignant Irradiation for Benign Conditions. New England Journal of Medicine *260*:197.

Cassie, G.F., Couch, N., Dammin, G.J., and Murray, J.E.: Normothermic Perfusion and Replantation of the Excised Dog Kidney. Surgery, Gynecology and Obstetrics *109*:721.

Murray, J.E., Wilson, R.E., Sadowsky, N., Dealy, J.B., and Corson, J.: Skin Grafts in Irradiated Rabbits Treated with Marrow from Single and Multiple Donors. Biological Problems of Grafting *12*:354.

Brooke, M.S., Covaerts, A., and Murray, J.E.: The Immunology of Sub-Lethally X-irradiated Rabbits. Surgical Forum *10*:853.

Dammin, G.J., and Murray, J.E.: Criteria for Acceptance of Skin Grafts. Transplantation Bulletin *6*:429.

1960 Hoye, S.J., Hoar, C.S., and Murray, J.E.: Extracranial Meningioma Presenting as a Neck Tumor. American Journal of Surgery *100*:486.

Murray, J.E., and Cannon, B.: Basal Cell Cancer in Children and Young Adults. New England Journal of Medicine *262*:440.

Murray, J.E., Merrill, J.P., Dammin, G.F., Dealy, J.B., Walter, C.W., Brooke, M.S., and Wilson, R.E.: Study on Transplantation Immunity after Total Body Irradiation: Clinical and Experimental Investigation. Surgery *48*:272.

Merrill, J.P., Murray, J.E., Harrison, J.H., Friedman, E.A., Dealy, J.B., and Dammin, G.J.: Successful Homotransplantation of the Kidney Between Non-Identical Twins. New England Journal of Medicine *262*:1251.

Balankura, O., Goodwin, W.E., Murray, J.E., and Dammin, G.J.: Study of the Homograft Reaction by Retransplantation of the Canine Kidney. Surgical Forum *11*:24.

1961 Murray, J.E.: What's New in Surgery: Plastic Surgery. Surgery, Gynecology and Obstetrics *112*:242.

Piomelli, S., O'Connor, J., Behrendt, D., and Murray, J.E.: Survival of Skin Homografts in Radiation Chimeras. Transplantation Bulletin *27*:431.

Couch, N., McBride, R., Dammin, G.J., and Murray, J.E.: Observations on the Nature of the Enlargement and Regeneration of Nerves and the Function of Canine Renal Autografts. British Journal of Experimental Pathology *42*:106.

Calne, R.Y., and Murray, J.E.: Inhibition of the Rejection of Renal Homografts in Dogs by BW 57–322. Surgical Forum *12*:118.

1962 Murray, J.E., Balankura, O., Greenberg, J.B. and Dammin, G.J.: Reversibility of the Kidney Homograft Reaction by Retransplantation and Drug Therapy. Annals of New York Academy of Sciences *99*:768.

Murray, J.E., Merrill, J.P., Dammin, G.J., Dealy, J.B., Alexandre, G.P.J., and Harrison, J.H.: Kidney Transplantation in Modified Recipients. Annals of Surgery *156*:337.

Smith, G., Calne, R.Y., Murray, J.E., and Dammin, G.J.: Anatomic Observations on the Renal Vessels in Man with Reference to Kidney Transplantation. Surgery, Gynecology and Obstetrics *115*:682.

Calne, R.Y., Alexandre, G.P.J., and Murray, J.E.: A Study of the Effects of Drugs in Prolonging Survival of Homologous Renal Transplants in Dogs. Annals of New York Academy of Sciences *99*:743.

Vandam, L., Harrison, J.H., Murray, J.E., and Merrill, J.P.: Anesthetic Aspects of Renal Homotransplantation in Man. Anesthesiology *23*:783.

1963 Hodges, C.V., Pickering, D.E., Murray, J.E., and Goodwin, W.E.: Kidney Transplant Between Identical Twins. Journal of Urology *89*:115.

Murray, J.E., and Harrison, J.H.: Surgical Management of Fifty Patients with Kidney Transplants Including Eighteen Pairs of Twins. American Journal of Surgery *105*:205.

Alexandre, G.P.J., Murray, J.E., Dammin, G.J., and Nolan, B.: Immunosuppressive Drug Therapy in Canine Renal Homografts. Transplantation *1*:432.

Murray, J.E., Merrill, J.P., Harrison, J.H., Dammin, G.J., and Wilson, R.E.: Prolonged Survival of Human Kidney Homografts by Immunosuppressive Drug Therapy. New England Journal of Medicine *268*:1315.

Goldwyn, R., Murray, J.E., and Constable, J.: Ameloblastoma of the Jaw: A Clinical Study. New England Journal of Medicine *269*:126.

Murray, J.E., Reid, D., Harrison, J.H., and Merrill, J.P.: Successful Pregnancies Following Human Renal Homotransplantation. New England Journal of Medicine *269*:341.

Cannon, B., and Murray, J.E.: Open Grafting of Raw Surfaces. Presented at the Third International Congress of Plastic Surgery, New York City, October, 1963, p. 1147.

Cannon, B., Murray, J.E., and Arregui, J.: An Evaluation of Ischiectomy in the Treatment of Pressure Sores. Transactions of the Third International Congress of Plastic Surgery, New York City, October, 1963, p. 1147.

Dammin, G.J., Murray, J.E., Merrill, J.P., Harrison, J.H., and Tompkins, Z.M.: Accelerated Patterns of Rejection in the Renal Homografts and Their Significance. Proceedings of the Second International Congress of Nephrology, Prague, August, 1963, p. 189.

Merrill, J.P., Murray, J.E., Takacs, F.J., Hager, E.B., Wilson, R.E., and Dammin, G.J.: Successful Transplantation from a Human Cadaver. Journal of the American Medical Association *185*:347.

1964 Murray, J.E., Merrill, J.P., Dammin, G.J., Harrison, J.H., Hager, E.B., and Wilson, R.E.: Current Evaluation of Human Kidney Transplantation. Annals of New York Academy of Sciences *120*:545.

Murray, J.E., Lawrence, K., Kingsbury, P., and Friedman, P.: Critical Surgical Problems in the Treatment of Oral and Laryngopharyngeal Cancer. New England Journal of Medicine *270*:650.

Human Kidney Transplant Conference: Summary of Proceedings. Transplantation *2*:147 and 581.

Murray, J.E., Sheil, A.G.R., Moseley, R., Knight, P.R., McGavic, J.D., and Dammin, G.J.: Analysis of the Mechanism of Immunosuppressive Drugs in Renal Homotransplantation. Annals of Surgery *160*:449.

Sheil, A.G.R., Moseley, R., and Murray, J.E.: Differential Skin and Renal Homograft Survival in Dogs on Immuno-Suppressive Therapy. Surgical Forum *XV*:166.

Lawrence, K., Murray, J.E., and Friedman, P.: Influence of Cervical Node Metastases on Therapy and Prognosis of Lingual Cancer. American Journal of Surgery *108*:461.

Murray, J.E., Gleason, R., and Bartholomay, A.: Second Report of the Human Kidney Transplant Registry. Transplantation *2*:660.

Murray, J.E.: Moral and Ethical Reflections on Human Organ Transplantations. The Linacre Quarterly *31*:54.

1965 Couch, N., Luck, R.J., Takacs, F., Harrison, J.H., and Murray, J.E.: The Protective Effect of Hypothermia in Kidneys Transplanted from Living Donors. Surgery, Gynecology and Obstetrics *121*:1085.

Murray, J.E., Gleason, R., and Bartholomay, A.: Third Report of the Human Kidney Transplant Registry. Transplantation *3*:294.

Murray, J.E.: Organ Transplants: A Type of Reconstructive Surgery. Canadian Journal of Surgery *8(4)*:340.

Murray, J.E.: Plastic Surgery—An Integral Part of General Surgery. Symposium on Surgical Education. American Journal of Surgery *110*:61.

Veith, F., Luck, R.J., and Murray, J.E.: The Effects of Splenectomy on Immunosuppressive Regimens in Dog and Man. Surgery, Gynecology and Obstetrics *121*:299.

Murray, J.E., Gleason, R., and Bartholomay, A.: Fourth Report of the Human Kidney Transplant Registry. Transplantation *3*:684.

Murray, J.E.: The Deer's Antlers, Popliteal Aneurysm and Plastic Surgery. Plastic & Reconstructive Surgery *36*:145.

Wilson, R., Bernstein, D.S., Murray, J.E., and Moore, F.D.: Effects of Parathyroidectomy and Kidney Transplantation on Renal Osteodystrophy. American Journal of Surgery *110*:384.

1966 Murray, J.E., and Goldwyn, R.M.: Definitive Treatment of Intractable Plantar Ulcers. Journal of the American Medical Association *196*:99.

Murray, J.E., and Wilson, R.E.: The Role of Organ Transplantation in Biological Research. Annals of the New York Academy of Sciences *129*, Art. 1:585–0597.

Murray, J.E.: Organ Transplantation: The Practical Possibilities. Presented before the Ciba Symposium, London, England, March, 1966, and published in Ethics in Moral Progress. J. & A. Churchill, Ltd., London, pp. 54–77.

Tilney, N., and Murray, J.E.: The Thoracic Duct Fistula in Human Renal Homotransplantation. Surgical Forum *XVII*:234.

Veith, F.J., Murray, J.E., and Miller, M.: Massive Skin Grafts in Dogs Under Immunosuppressive Chemotherapy. Surgery *59*:594.

Murray, J.E.: Transplantation and Hemodialysis: I. Recipient's Response to Transplantation. Journal of the American Medical Association *198*:305.

Moseley, R.V., Sheil, A.G.R., Mitchell, R., and Murray, J.E.: Immunologic Relationships Between Skin and Kidney Homografts in Dogs on Immunosuppressive Therapy. Transplantation *4*:678.

Retik, A., Dubernard, J.M., Hester, W., and Murray, J.E.: Study of the Effect of Intra-Arterial Immunosuppressive Therapy in Canine Renal Allografts. Surgery *60*:1242.

1967 Gleason, R., and Murray, J.E.: Report from the Kidney Transplant Registry. Analysis of Variables in the Function of Human Kidney Transplants. I. Blood Group Compatibility and Splenectomy. Transplantation *5*:343.

Gleason, R., and Murray, J.E.: Report from the Kidney Transplant Registry. Analysis of Variables in the Function of Human Kidney Transplants. II. Immunosuppressive Regimens. Transplantation *5*:360.

Tilney, N., and Murray, J.E.: The Thoracic Duct Fistula as an Adjunct to Immunosuppression in Human Renal Transplantation. Transplantation 5:1204 (Part 2).

Retik, A.B., Hollenberg, N., Rosen, S., Merrill, J.P., and Murray, J.E.: Cortical Ischemia in Renal Allograft Rejection. Surgery, Gynecology and Obstetrics 124:989.

Strober, S., and Murray, J.E.: Studies of the Enhancing Properties of Plasma of Murine Parabionts. Transplantation 5:1371.

Murray, J.E., Wilson, R.E., and O'Connor, N.: Evaluation of Long-Functioning Human Kidney Transplants. Presented before the American College of Surgeons (October). Surgery, Gynecology and Obstetrics 124:509.

Murray, J.E., and Barnes, B.A.: Introductory Remarks to Kidney Transplantation. Transplantation 5:824 (Part 2).

Murray, J.E.: Religion and Medicine: Ethical Implications of Renal Transplants. Journal of the American Medical Association 200:187.

Lawrence, K.B., Murray, J.E., Constable, J.D., and Rybka, F.J.: Extrinsic Laryngeal Carcinoma: A Clinical Evaluation of 124 Patients. American Journal of Surgery 114:503.

Murray, J.E., Barnes, B.A., and Atkinson, J.: Fifth Report of the Human Kidney Transplant Registry. Transplantation 5:752.

Murray, J.E.: Cosmas and Damian (Letter to the Editor). Journal of the American Medical Association 202:214.

Rosen, S.M., Truniger, B.P., Kriek, H.R., Murray, J.E., and Merrill, J.P.: Intrarenal Distribution of Blood Flow in the Transplanted Dog Kidney: Effect of Denervation and Rejection. Journal of Clinical Investigation 46:1239.

1968 Tilney, N.L., and Murray, J.E.: Operative Technique and Physiologic Effects of Chronic Thoracic Duct Fistula in Man. Annals of Surgery 167:1.

Diethelm, A.G., Dubernard, J.M., Busch, G.J., and Murray, J.E.: Critical Re-Evaluation of Immunosuppressive Therapy in Canine Renal Allografts. Surgery, Gynecology and Obstetrics 126:723.

Dubernard, J.M., Carpenter, C.B., Busch, G.J., Diethelm, A.G., and Murray, J.E.: Rejection of Canine Renal Allografts by Passive Transfer of Sensitized Serum. Surgery 64:752.

Wilson, R.E., Hager, E.B., Hampers, C.L., Corson, J.M., Merrill, J.P., and Murray, J.E.: Immunological Rejection of Human Cancer Transplanted with a Renal Allograft. New England Journal of Medicine 278:479.

Murray, J.E., Wilson, R.E., Tilney, N.L., Merrill, J.P., Cooper, W.C., Carpenter, C.B., Hager, E.B., Guttmann, R., Hampers, C.L., Dammin, G.j., and Harrison, J.H.: Five Years' Experience with Immunosuppressive Drugs: Survival, Function, Complications, and the Role of Lymphocyte Depletion by Thoracic Duct Fistula. Annals of Surgery 168:416.

Murray, J.E., and Swanson, L.T.: Mid-Face Osteotomy and Advancement for Craniosynostosis. Plastic & Reconstructive Surgery 41:299.

McFarland, R., and Murray, J.E.: Etiology of Motor Vehicle Accidents. New England Journal of Medicine *278:*1383.

Advisory Committee of the Kidney Transplant Registry (Joseph E. Murray, M.D., member): Sixth Report of the Human Kidney Transplant Registry. Transplantation *6:*944.

Report of the Ad Hoc Committee of the Harvard Medical School to Examine the Definition of Death (Joseph E. Murray, M.D., member): A Definition of Irreversible Coma. Journal of the American Medical Association *205:*337.

Moore, F.D., Busch, G.E., Harken, D.R., Swan, H.J., Murray, J.E., and Lillehei, C.W.: Special Communication – Cardiac and Other Organ Transplantation. Journal of the American Medical Association *206:*2489.

Murray, J.E. (Chairman, Task Group IV): The National Effort and Regional Program. Bethesda Conference Report. Cardiac and Other Organ Transplantation. American Journal of Cardiology *22:*896.

1969 Swanson, L., and Murray, J.E.: Partial Glossectomy to Stabilize Occlusion Following Surgery for Prognathism. Oral Surgery, Oral Medicine and Oral Pathology *27:*707.

Wilson, R.E., Hampers, C.L., Katz, A.J., Bernstein, D.S., Wachman, A., Merrill, J.P., and Murray, J.E.: Management of Secondary Hyperparathyroidism in Renal Allograft Recipients. Transplantation Proceedings *1:*206.

Eisendrath, R.M., Guttmann, R.D., and Murray, J.E.: Psychological Considerations in the Selection of Kidney Transplant Donors. Surgery, Gynecology and Obstetrics, *129:*243.

Advisory Committee of the Human Kidney Transplant Registry (Joseph E. Murray, M.D., member): Seventh Report of the Human Kidney Transplant Registry. Transplantation *8:*728.

Advisory Committee of the Human Kidney Transplant Registry (Joseph E. Murray, M.D., member): Description of Kidney Transplant Function During the First Year. Transplantation *8:*728.

1970 Tilney, N.L., Atkinson, J.C., and Murray, J.E.: The Immunosuppressive Effect of Thoracic Duct Drainage in Human Kidney Transplantation. Annals of Internal Medicine *72:*59.

Glen, A.C.A., Cooper, W.C., Boak, J.L, Murray, J.E., and Munro, H.N.: DNA and RNA Measurements on Thoracic Duct Lymphocytes of Patients Undergoing Renal Transplantation. Transplantation *9:*83.

Alexander, J.L., Dmochowski, J.R., Murray, J.E., and Couch, N.P.: Successful 24 Hours

Renal Perfusion—Preservation with Monitoring by Surface Electrometry During Storage Interval. Surgery *67:*944.

Woods, J.E., and Murray, J.E.: Reconstruction of the Cervical Esophagus. Plastic & Reconstructive Surgery *46:*43.

Woods, J. E., Murray, J.E., and Vawter, G.F.: Hand Tumors in Children. Plastic & Reconstructive Surgery *46:*30.

Murray, J.E., and Baker, T.J.: Esthetic Surgery and the Plastic Surgeon (Letter to the Editor). Plastic & Reconstructive Surgery 46:389.

1971 Leake, D., Doykos, J., Habal, M.B., and Murray, J.E.: Long-term Follow-up of Fractures of the Mandibular Condyle in Children. Plastic & Reconstructive Surgery 47:127.

Advisory Committee of the Human Kidney Transplant Registry (Joseph E. Murray, M.D., member): Eighth Report of the Human Kidney Transplant Registry. Transplantation 11:328.

Murray, J.E., Swanson, L.T., Cohen, M., and Habal, M.B.: Correction of Midfacial Deformities. Surgical Clinics of North America 51:341.

Barnes, B.A., Murray, J.E., and Atkinson, J.C.: Transplant Survival and Patient Activity Data from the Human Kidney Transplant Registry. Transplantation Proceedings 3:303.

Birtch, A.G., Carpenter, C.B., Tilney, N.L., Hampers, C.L., Hager, E.B., Lebine, L., Wilson, R.E., and Murray, J.E.: Controlled Clinical Trial of Antilymphocyte Globulin in Human Renal Allografts. Transplantation Proceedings 3:762.

Murray, J.E.: Organ Transplantation (Skin, Kidney, Heart) and the Plastic Surgeon. Plastic & Reconstructive Surgery 47:425.

Tilney, N.L., and Murray, J.E.: Severe Temporary Deterioration of Renal Transplant Function Following Meningococcemia. Transplantation Proceedings 3:1118.

Murray, J.E., and Klein, E.: Plastic Surgical Treatment of Facial Skin Cancer. Journal of Surgical Oncology 3:269.

Murray, J.E., and Barnes, B.A.: Organ Transplant Registry. Journal of the American Medical Association 217:1546.

1972 Habal, M.B., and Murray, J.E.: The Natural History of a Benign Locally Invasive Hemangioma of the Orbital Region. Plastic & Reconstructive Surgery 49:209.

Murray, J.E., Matson, D.D., Habal, M.B., and Geelhoed, G.W.: Regional Cranio-Orbital Resection for Recurrent Tumors with Delayed Reconstruction. Surgery, Gynecology and Obstetrics 134:437.

Habal, M.B., and Murray, J.E.: The Surgical Treatment of Life-Endangering Chronic Aspiration Pneumonia. Use of Epiglottic Flap to the Arytenoids. Plastic & Reconstructive Surgery 49:305.

Hollenberg, N.K., Birtch, A.G., Rashid, A., Mangel, R., Briggs, W., Epstein, M., Murray, J.E., and Merrill, J.P.: Relationships Between Intrarenal Perfusion and Function: Serial Hemodynamic Studies in the Transplanted Human Kidney. Medicine 51:95.

Leake, D., Murray, J.E., Habal, M.B., and Swanson, L.T.: Custom Fabrication for Mandibular Reconstruction. Oral Surgery 33:879.

Habal, M.B., McComb, J.G., Shillito, J., Jr., Eisenberg, H.M., and Murray, J.E.: Combined Posteroanterior Approach to a Tumor of the Cervical Spinal Foramen. Journal of Neurosurgery *37*:113.

Habal, M.B., Meguid, M.M., and Murray, J.E.: The Long Scarf Syndrome – A Potentially Fatal and Preventable Hazard. Journal of the American Medical Association *221*:1269.

Habal, M.B., Birtch, A.G., Kountz, S.L., Stephens, B., and Murray, J.E.: Renal Allografting in the Patient with Juvenile Diabetes Mellitus. American Journal of Surgery *124*:682.

Murray, J.E.: Annual Discourse—Organ Replacement, Facial Deformity, and Plastic Surgery. New England Journal of Medicine *287*:1069.

1973 Habal, M.B., and Murray, J.E.: Argentaffin Adenoma of the Trachea. American Journal of Surgery *125*:336.

Habal, M.B., and Murray, J.E.: Orbital Reconstruction after Radial Resection. Archives of Surgery *106*:352.

Swanson, L.T., Habal, M.B., Leake, D.L., and Murray, J.E.: Compound Silicone-Bone Implants for Mandibular Reconstruction. Plastic & Reconstructive Surgery *51*:402.

Jaffe, N., Filler, R.M., Farber, S., Traggis, D.G., Vawter, G.F., Tefft, M., and Murray, J.E.: Rhabdomyosarcoma in Children: Improved Outlook with a Multidisciplinary Approach. American Journal of Surgery *125*:482.

Habal, M.B., and Murray, J.E.: Cranio-Orbital Resection and Neck Dissection for a Recurrent Mixed Tumor of the Lacrimal Gland. Plastic & Reconstructive Surgery *51*:689.

Habal, M.B., Snyder, H.H., Jr., and Murray, J.E.: Chondrosarcoma of the Hand. American Journal of Surgery *125*:775.

Murray, J.E.: Invited Editorial Comment on Spiro, R.H., Strong, E.W.: Epidermoid Carcinoma of the Oral Cavity and Oropharynx—Elective vs. Therapeutic Radical Neck Dissection as Treatment. Archives of Surgery *107*:382.

1974 Murray, J.E.: The Advice of John Staige Davis to Medical Students (Letters to the Editor). Plastic & Reconstructive Surgery *53*:582.

Swanson, L.T., and Murray, J.E.: Mid-face Correction for Craniofacial Dysostosis. Malformation Syndromes *X(7)*:189. (Birth Defects: Original Article Series, The National March of Dimes Foundation.)

Swanson, L.T., and Murray, J.E.: Mandibular Reconstruction in Hemifacial Microsomia (Chapter 29). In Tanzer and Edgerton (Eds.): Procceeedings of Symposium on Reconstruction of the Auricle, Volume 10. Meeting of Educational Foundation of American Society of Plastic and Reconstructive Surgeons, in collaboration with American Society for Surgery of the Hand, Committee on Continuing Education, New York, NY, November 2–4, 1972, C.V. Mosby, St. Louis.

Murray, J.E.: Some Biologic and Philosophic Thoughts of a Surgeon (Chapter 32). In Littler, Cramer, and Smith (Eds.): Proceedings of Symposium on

Reconstructive Hand Surgery, Volume 9. Meeting of Educational Foundation of American Society of Plastic and Reconstructive Surgeons, in collaboration with American Society for Surgery of the Hand, Committee on Continuing Education, New York, NY, November 2–4, 1972, C.V. Mosby, St. Louis.

Moore, F.D., Merrill, J.P., and Murray, J.E.: Life and Contributions of David Hume. Transplantation Proceedings *VI*:153.

1975 Vecchione, T.R., Habal, M.B., and Murray, J.E.: Further Experiences with the Arytenoid-Epiglottic Flap for Chronic Aspiration Pneumonia. Plastic & Reconstructive Surgery *55*:318.

Murray, J.E., Swanson, L.T., Strand, R.D., and Hricko, G.M.: Evaluation of Craniofacial Surgery in the Treatment of Facial Deformities. Annals of Surgery *182*: 240.

1976 Murray, J.E., and Goldwyn, R.M.: Plastic Surgery in Adolescence. In Gallagher, Heald, and Garell (Eds.): Medical Care of the Adolescent, 3rd edition. Appleton-Century-Crofts, New York, p. 678.

Murray, J.E., Tilney, N.L., and Wilson, R.E.: Renal Transplantation: A Twenty-Five Year Experience. Annals of Surgery *184*:565.

Murray, J.E.: On J. Engelbert Dunphy's Annual Discourse "On Caring for the Patient with Cancer" (Letter to the Editor). New England Journal of Medicine *295*:1435.

1977 Hall, J.E., Denis, F., and Murray, J.E.: Exposure of the Upper Cervical Spine for Spinal Decompression by a Mandible and Tongue-Splitting Approach. Journal of Bone and Joint Surgery *51–A*:121.

Jaffe, N., Murray, J.E., Traggis, D., Cassady, J.R., Filler, R.M., Watts, H., and Weichselbaum, R. H.: Multidisciplinary Treatment for Childhood Sarcoma. American Journal of Surgery *405*:413.

Mulliken, J.B., Healey, N.A., and Murray, J.E.: An Experimental Study of Hematoma and Flap Necrosis. Surgical Forum *28*:531.

1978 Mulliken, J.B., Murray, J.E., Castaneda, A.R., and Kaban, L.B.: Management of A Vascular

Malformation of the Face Using Total Circulatory Arrest. Surgery, Gynecology and Obstetrics *146*:168.

Kaban, L.B., Mulliken, J.B., and Murray, J.E.: Sialadenitis in Childhood. American Journal of Surgery *135*:570.

Murray, J.E.: Comment on Optimal Size of Resection Margin for Thin Cutaneous Melanoma. Surgery, Gynecology and Obstetrics *145*:691 and *147*:915.

1979 Murray, J.E., Kaban, L.B., and Mulliken, J.B.: Craniofacial Abnormalities. In Ravitch, M.M. (Ed.): Pediatric Surgery (Vol. 1), 3rd edition. Year Book Medical Publishers, Chicago, pp. 233–248.

Murray, J.E.: Ethics in Transplantation. Transplantation Proceedings *XI*(1).

Belfer, M.L., Harrison, A.M., and Murray, J.E.: Body Image and the Process of Reconstructive Surgery. American Journal of Diseases of Children *133*:532.

Murray, J.E., Mulliken, J.B., Kaban, L.B., and Belfer, M.: Twenty-year Experience in Maxillocraniofacial Surgery. Annals of Surgery *190*:320.

Murray, J.E.: Respect and Love of This Profession and Specialty. Plastic & Reconstructive Surgery *64*:390.

1980 Upton, L., Mulliken, J.B., Hicks, P.D. and Murray, J.E.: Restoration of Facial Contour Using Free Vascularized Omental Transfer. Plastic & Reconstructive Surgery, *66*:560.

1981 Murray, J.E. (Moderator): Panel on Transplantation. Transplantation Proceedings *13(Suppl. 1)*:72.

Mulliken, J.B., Glowacki, J., Kaban, L.B., Folkman, J., and Murray, J.E.: Use of Demineralized Allogeneic Bone Implants for the Correction of Maxillocraniofacial Deformities. Annals of Surgery *94*:366.

1982 Mullliken, J.B., and Murray, J.E.: Natural History of Vascular Birthmarks. In Williams, B. (Ed.): Proceedings of Symposium on Vascular Malformations and Melanotic Lesions. C.V. Mosby, St. Louis, p. 58.

1983 Upton, J., Schuster, S.R., Colodny, A.H., and Murray, J.E.: Testicular Autotransplantation in Children. American Journal of Surgery *145*:514.

Belfer, M.L., Harrison, A.M., Pillemer, F.C., and Murray, J.E.: Appearance and the Influence of Reconstructive Surgery on Body Image. Clinics in Plastic Surgery *9(3)*:307.

1984 Murray, J.E., Kaban, L.B., and Mulliken, J.B.: Analysis and Treatment of Hemifacial Microsomia. Plastic & Reconstructive Surgery *74*:186.

Boyd, J.B., Mulliken, J.B., Kaban, L.B., Upton, J. III, and Murray, J.E.: Skeletal Changes Associated with Vascular Malformations. Plastic & Reconstructive Surgery *74*:789.

1985 Bennun, R.D., Mulliken, J.B., Kaban, L.B., and Murray, J.E.: Microtia: A Microform of Hemifacial Microsomia. Plastic & Reconstructive Surgery *76*:859.

1986 Mulliken, J.B., Kaban, L.B., Evans, C.A., Strand, R.D., and Murray, J.E.: Facial Skeletal Changes Following Hypertelorbitism Correction. Plastic & Reconstructive Surgery *77*:7.

Murray, J.E.: Finding Creativity in Adversity: A Surgeon Ponders the Truths and Consequences of Three Episodes of Illness. Harvard Medical Alumni Bulletin (Winter 1986–1987) *60*:19.

Murray, J.E.: Decisions on the Frontlines of Surgery. Harvard Medical Alumni Bulletin (Summer 1986) *60*:18.

1988 Murray, J.E.: The Past, Present and Future: Renal Transplantation Before Starzl. Transplantation Proceedings *XX (Suppl. 1)*:339.

Murray, J.E.: The Many Faces of Surgery (Presidential Address). Archives of Surgery *123*:543.

1990 Murray, J.E.: The First Successful Organ Transplants in Man. Nobel Lecture (December 8, 1990), Les Prix Nobel, The Nobel Foundation, 1990/1991.

1992 Murray, J.E.: The Role of Surgeon-Scientists in Medical Progress (edited version of the I.S. Ravdin Lecture in Basic Sciences, presented October 23, 1991, during Clinical Congress in Chicago.) American College of Surgeons Bulletin 77:23.

Murray, J.E.: Reflections on Plastic Surgery. 60th Annual Scientific Meeting of the American Society of Plastic and Reconstructive Surgeons, Inc., Plastic Surgery Educational Foundation, and American Society of Maxillofacial Surgeons, in Seattle, Washington, September 25–26, 1991. Plastic & Reconstructive Surgery (May).

Murray, J.E.: Human Organ Transplantation: Background and Consequences. Science *256*:1411.

1993 Murray, J.E.: Role of the Surgeon in Scientific Medical Progress. Annals of the Academy of Medicine *22*.

1995 Murray, J.E.: Organ Transplantation and the Revitalization of Immunology. In Immunology: The Making of a Modern Science. Academic Press, New York.

1996 Murray, J.E.: Animals Hold the Key to Saving Human Lives. Los Angeles Times February 5.

Murray, J.E.: The Joy and Solace of Surgery. Harvard Medical Alumni Bulletin (Autumn, 1996) Vol. 16.

2000 Murray, J.E.: Reflections on Plastic Surgery at the Approach of the Millennium. Plastic & Reconstructive Surgery *106*:454.

2001 Murray, J.E., Merrill J.P., and Harrison, J.H.: Renal Homotransplantation in Identical Twins. (Reprinted from Surgical Forum *VI*:432, 1955, with commentaries by Joseph E. Murray and Charles B. Carpenter.) Journal of the American Society of Nephrology *12*:201.

INDEX

6-mercaptopurine (6-MP), 105–106, 107, 109

"Actively Acquired Tolerance of Foreign Cells," 91
Albasi, Virgil, 52–58, 60
Albro, Martha, 119
Alexandre, Dr. Guy, 109
Allografts, 8–9
American Association of Plastic Surgeons, 44, 155
American College of Surgeons (ACS), 96, 120, 143, 165, 223
  Forum Committee, 143, 165
American Doctor's Odyssey (Heiser), 24
American Surgical Association, 142
Anaceron, 174
Anesthetists, 54–55
Angell Veterinary Hospital, 113
Animal experimentation, 113
Arnold Arboretum, 35
Arrowsmith (Lewis), 24
Art of the Soluble, The (Medawar), 16
Aspiration pneumonia, 174, 175
Autografts, 8
Azathioprine (Imuran), 108, 109, 113, 114, 115

Baloun, Jay, 125, 127–133, 134, 136, 139
Becker, Iylene, 173–180
Beecher, Dr. H., 120
Belfer, Dr. Myron, 188, 193, 196
Bench scientists, 64
Bergan, Dr. John, 120
Beth Israel Hospital, 215

Bilateral otoplasty, 205
Billingham, Rupert, 91, 121
Biological Basis of Individuality, The (Loeb), 16
Birtch, Alan, 143
Blodgett, Dr. James B., 33, 35
Blood flow, 63, 81
Body image development, 196–197
Boland, Major Frank, 42
Bone marrow cells, 94
Boston City Hospital, 61
Boston Lying-In Hospital, 28
Boston Surgical Society, 165
Boston Symphony Orchestra, 29
Boston Veterans Administration Hospital, 13, 60
Boylston Society, 27, 28, 62
Brand, Dr. Paul, 141, 200, 218
Brent, Leslie, 91
Bricker, Dr. Gene, 43
Brigham. *See* Peter Bent Brigham Hospital
Brigham & Women's Hospital, 137, 215, 216, 225
Brigham/Harvard program, 109
British National Trust, 216
Brown, Dr. James Barrett, 8, 9, 12, 39, 42, 43, 44, 45, 69
Bunnell, Dr. Sterling, 141
Burn treatment, 8
Burroughs-Welcome, Ltd., 105, 109

Calne, Dr. Roy, 106, 109
Cancer, 51, 52–53, 59
  in children, 127
Cancer surgery, 46–47, 53, 55–58, 60

Index

Cannon, Dr. Bradford, xxii, 8, 9, 12, 13, 14, 40, 42, 43, 44, 45, 48, 49, 59, 60, 61, 89, 126, 144, 165, 188, 190, 194
Cannon, Ellen, 40
Cape Poge, 168–170
Carlisle Barracks, 39, 44
Carpenter, Dr. Charles B., 117
Carrel, Dr. Alexis, 24, 225
Castaneda, Dr. Aldo, 215
Chappaquiddick Island, 96, 167, 168, 170, 216, 217
Chelsea Naval Hospital, 61
Chemical immune suppression, 105–114
Children's Hospital, Boston, 30, 46, 60, 61, 126, 128, 133, 137, 138, 144, 145, 147, 173, 175, 179, 181, 187, 191, 208, 215, 216, 225
  Craniofacial Clinic, 187, 188–190
Christian Medical School, India, 141, 142, 200
Cocoanut Grove fire, 40
Cohn, Dr. Larry, 208, 211, 212
Collins, Dr. John, 208, 211, 212
Conant, James, 31
Conway, Dr. Herb, 49, 53, 54, 57, 58
Cope, Dr. Oliver, 40
Cosmas, 68
Cosmetic surgery, 199–206
Craniofacial Center, 137, 216
Craniofacial Clinic, 187, 188–190
Craniofacial surgery, 153, 155
Crikelaire, George, 181
Crippled Children's Program, 60
Crouzon's syndrome, 147, 151, 156
Curiosity, 226, 227
Curley, Dr. George F., xix, 27, 37
Cushing, Dr. Harvey, 145
Cushing Veterans Administration Hospital, 59, 60
Cutler, Dr. Elliott C., 33, 36, 45–46, 145

Dameshek, Dr. William, 105
Damian, 68

Dammin, Dr. Gustave, 77, 93, 121
Dana-Farber Cancer Center, 127, 208
Davis, Dr. William B., 45
Death, definition of, 120–121
"Definition of Irreversible Coma, A," 120
De Kruif, Paul, 24
DePasquale, Antonio, 21, 22, 52
Dialysis, 64, 79
Dingman, Dr. Reed, 170
Dogs, as experimental transplant models, 65–67, 92–93, 94, 106–107, 109, 110
Double mouth, 183–184
Doucette, Mel, 115–117
Drug-induced immunological tolerance, 105

Edgerton, Dr. Milton, 43, 44, 45, 166
Elion, Dr. Gertrude, 105, 106, 109, 224
En bloc excision, 55
Enders, Dr. John, 95
Endoscopic liposuction, 206
Eriksson, Dr. Elof, 215
Ervin, Norma Murray (sister), 49
Ervin, Tom, 49
Eyler, Don, 44

Facelift, 205–206
Farber, Dr. Sidney, 126–129, 139
Faxon, Dr. Henry, 60
Federico, Lisa, 190, 191–193, 194
Ferrebee, Dr. Joe, 98
Foch Hospital, 100, 107, 163
Foster, Wanda, 90
Four-dimensional approach, 194
Fowler, Dr. Benjamin, 44
Fox, Dr. Henry M., 77
Framingham State College, 22
Framingham Union Hospital, 61

Garton, Dr. Gosten, 221
Germasian, Dawn, 125, 136–139
Gillies, Sir Harold, 149, 150
Goldthwait, Jerry, 29
Goldwyn, Dr. Robert M., 170

Graham, Dr. Walter, 44
Gross, Dr. Robert E., 30, 144, 145, 187
Gustav IV, King of Sweden, 221

Habal, Mutaz, 175, 176, 179
Hale, Dr. Worth, 24
Halo brace, 151
Hamburger, Dr. Jean, 100, 107
Harrison, Dr. Alexandra Murray, 188
Harrison, Dr. J. Hartwell, 76, 77, 78, 80, 89, 99
Harvard Committee on the Definition of Death, 120
Harvard Dental School, 171
Harvard Medical School, 14, 24, 27–31, 63, 98, 126, 170, 215, 216, 225
    Alumni Fund, 219
    ␣Anatomy Lab, 130
    Surgical Research Lab, 62, 126, 143
Hasˇek, Milan, 92
Hasˇek, Vera, 92
Head & Neck Society, 58
Heiser, Victor, 24
Helm, Edith, 86, 90
Hemifacial microsomia, 190
Herrick, Richard, 69, 73–87, 89
Herrick, Ronald, 69, 73–80, 86
Herrick, Van, 76
Herrick, Virginia, 76
Hertig, Dr. Arthur, 28
Hickey, Jimmy, 158–162, 207
Hippocrates, 174
Hippocratic Oath, 212
Hitchings, Dr. George, 105, 106, 109, 224
Hitler, Adolf, 23
Holy Cross College, 24, 151
Huggins, Dr. Charles B., 225
Hume, Dr. David M., xxii, 35, 65, 66, 119
Hunter, John, 90–91, 174

Imagination, 227
Immune response, 64
Immunological tolerance, 91
Imuran. *See* Azathioprine

India, surgery performed in, 141
Ingraham, Dr. Franc, 144
Innervation, 63–64
International Conference on Human Kidney Transplants, 118–119
International Plastic Surgical Conference, Rome, 152
International Society of Transplantation, 92
International Transplantation Conference, Munich, 152
Iran, teaching in, 181–186
Isabella Stewart Gardner Museum, 29

Jaffe, Dr. Norman, 133–134
Jimmy Fund, 127, 133
Johansson, Bengt, 181
Journal of the American Medical Association, 120

Kaban, Dr. Leonard B., 188, 189
Kapper, Natalie, 193–196
Kazanjian, Dr. Varastad, 60
Keyhole operative technique, 150, 155
Kidney Research Laboratory, 76, 78
Kidney transplantation, 16, 61–69
    allogenic (non-identical-twin), 99–103
    cadaveric donor, 115–117
    in identical twins, 73–87
    medical and ethical issues, 76–79, 118
    perfecting surgical technique, 64–69
    setting standards, 119
Kocher, Dr. Emil T., 225
Kolff, Dr. William, 62
Kolff-Brigham Kidney, 62, 79
Kudarduskas, Dr. E. M., 74
Küss, Dr. René, 100, 107

Ladd, Dr. William E., 30, 61, 187
Leahy, Joan, 189
Lewis, Edward B., 184, 190
Lewis, Sinclair, 24
Lillie, F.R., 91
Lincoln, Abraham, 20, 210

251

Lindbergh, Charles, 23
Link, Edwin A., 36, 42
Link, George T., 36
Link Aviation Company, 36
Link Organ Company, 36
Link Trainer, 36, 42
Lischer, Dr. Carl, 43, 45
Littler, Dr. J. William, 44
Loeb, Dr. Leo, 16
Loman, Gladys, 95–96, 113
Longfellow, Henry Wadsworth, 21
Lower, Dr. Richard, 165
Lowery, Jack, 34
Lymph flow, 63

MacCollum, Dr. Donald, 30, 60, 61, 144, 187
MacDonald, Dottie, 188–189
Mannick, Dr. John, 93–94, 98, 215
Man the Unknown (Carrel), 24
Marine Hospital, Chicago, 75
Marshall, John, 20
Martha's Vineyard, 96–97, 166–170, 216, 217, 219
Martin, Dr. Hayes, 47–48, 58, 131
Mary Imogene Bassett Hospital, 93
Massachusetts Crippled Children's Clinic, 190
Massachusetts Eye & Ear Infirmary, 128
Massachusetts General Hospital, 28, 30, 31, 60, 215
Matson, Dr. Donald, 61, 95, 113, 114, 127, 129, 130, 131, 144
Mayo, Will, 204
Mazzahari, Dr., 136
McCall, Virginia, 41
McMillan, Raymond Francis, 207–212, 228
Medawar, Sir Peter, 16, 89–90, 91, 93, 106, 110, 118, 119, 120, 121
Medical doctor, three essential ingredients of, 226–227
  curiosity, 226, 227
  imagination, 227
  persistence, 227

Meigs, Dr. Joe, 28
Memoirs of a Small-Town Surgeon (Wheeler), 24
Memorial Hospital, New York City, 46–49, 53, 58, 155, 175
Mendel, Gregor, 184
Menkin, Valy, 27
Merrill, Dr. John, 65, 66, 76, 78, 82, 84, 89, 92, 94, 107–108, 115–116, 117, 121
Merton, Thomas, 86
"Metabolic Care of the Surgical Patient," 46
Meyer, Alphonse (Al), 29, 34
Microbe Hunters (De Kruif), 24
Microsurgery, 138
"Mid-Face Osteotomy and Advancement for Craniosynostosis," 152
Miele, Marilyn, 156–158, 161
Miller, Dr. Benjamin F., 66
Miller, Dr. David C., 76
Moebius syndrome, 207
Monks, Dr. George, 170–171
Monks Lectureship, 170–171
Moore, Dr. Andrew M., 8, 9, 12, 43–44, 45
Moore, Dr. Francis D., 31, 40, 46, 48, 61, 62, 64, 79, 80, 83, 86, 92, 94, 96, 143
Moore, Peggy, 44
Mt. Auburn Hospital, 60–61, 190
Mulliken, Dr. John, 188, 189, 218
Murphy, Walter, 147–152, 155, 156
Murray, Ginny (daughter), 49, 79, 142, 181, 223, 224
Murray, James (grandfather), 19
Murray, Joseph E.
  childhood, 23
  education
    Milford public schools, 23–24
    Holy Cross College, 24
    Harvard Medical School, 27–31
  introduction to surgery, 30–31
  later years, 213–228
  marriage, 37, 43–44

INDEX

military service in World War II, 28–29, 31, 36, 39–44
Nobel Prize in Medicine, 20, 219, 221–226
organ transplantation, 73–122
plastic surgery chosen as main interest, 143
private practice, 59–62
reconstructive surgery, 125–212
research activities, 62–69
retirement, 218–219
stroke patient, 216–218
surgical internship, 33–34, 35–36
surgical residency, 45–49
vacationing at Martha's Vineyard, 96–97, 166–170, 216, 217, 219
Murray, J. (Joseph) Link (son), 96, 223
Murray, Kathy (daughter), 168
Murray, Mary DePasquale (mother), 21–22, 23
Murray, Meg (daughter), 49, 96, 223, 224
Murray, Norma (sister), 19
Murray, Rick (son), 141, 168, 181, 185, 219, 224
Murray, Theresa (Taft) (grandmother), 19
Murray, Tom (son), 141, 168, 181, 185, 224
Murray, Virginia ("Bobby") Link (Mrs. Joseph E.), 24, 29–30, 34–35, 36–37, 39, 40, 42, 43, 44, 49, 79, 85, 96, 126, 128, 141–142, 166, 167, 168, 169, 170, 181, 185, 186, 189, 216, 217, 218, 223, 224
Murray, William Andrew (father), 19–20
Murray, William A., Jr. (brother), 23
Mussolini, Benito, 23

Najarian, John, 119
National Institutes of Health (NIH)
   Immunobiology Studies Section, 165
   Surgical Studies Section, 165
National Kidney Register, 119–120
Neckar Hospital, 100, 107

New England Conservatory of Music, 29
New England Deaconess Hospital, 215
New England Journal of Medicine, 117
Newton, Dr. Francis C., 36
Newton D. Baker General Hospital, 36, 39
Newton-Wellesley Hospital, 61, 85
New York Academy of Science Transplantation Conferences, 92
New York Hospital, 49, 52, 53, 60
Nobel Committee, 223
Nobel Prize in Medicine, 20, 219, 221–226
Normal School, Framingham, 22
Nüsslein-Volhard, Christiane, 184

Orbital rhabdomysarcoma, 128, 132
Orbital sarcoma, 133, 136
Organ transplantation, 63–64, 73–122
Ortiz-Monasterio, Fernardo, 181
Ossanlou, Dr. Cyrus, 181, 182
Our Town (Wilder), 229–230
Owen, Ray, 91

Packard, Vance, 96
Papanicolaou ("Pap") smear, 28, 62
Parmenter, Dr. Richard, 169
Pasteur, Louis, 226
Pediatric plastic surgery, 61
Pedicle, 41, 61, 134
Penn, Dr. Jack, 152, 163
Persistence, 227
Peter Bent Brigham Hospital, xxii, 28, 30, 31, 33, 34, 35–36, 45–46, 49, 61–62, 63, 73, 92, 94, 97, 98, 106, 115, 117, 121–122, 126, 137, 144, 145, 147, 170, 175, 181, 187, 207, 210, 215, 216
   kidney transplant program, 61–62, 92, 95, 121–122
Pillemer, Dr. Francine Cohen, 188
Plastic and Reconstructive Surgery, 152
Plastic surgery, 34, 48, 49
   attitude toward, 170
Plastic Surgical Travel Club, 166

Porter, Dr. Ken, 109
Practice of medicine as life of service, 227–228
Prince Bertil (Sweden), 221
Princess Lillian (Sweden), 221
Public Health Service Hospital, 75
Public Sailing Club, 29

Queen's Hospital, Tehran, 181, 182, 183

Radiation/bone marrow protocol, 94–96, 97, 105, 107–108
Reconstruction
   of burns victim, 10–13
   facial, 53
Reconstructive surgery, 15, 53, 59
Reed, Wally, 40
Rejection of organ, 64, 67, 69
   reversible, 112
Rhinoplasty, 202–203
Riordan, Dr. Daniel, 44
Riteris, Andrew, 99, 100
Riteris, John, 97, 99–103, 105, 108
Robbins, Dr. Fred, 95
Robin, E., 78
Rockefeller Institute, 225
Roosevelt, Franklin Delano, 23
Rosenberg, Isadore, 39
Royal Society of Medicine, 90

Sabin vaccine, 95
Sacco, Nicola, 22
St. Elizabeth's Hospital, 61
St. Goar, Dr. Walter, 217
St. Mary's Hospital, London, 109
Salk vaccine, 95
Sarcoma, 127
Schwartz, Dr. Robert, 105
Scribner, Dr. Belding, 64
Self, Dr. Ed, 168
Services for Handicapped Children, 60
Shillito, Dr. John, 173
Silva, Foster, 168, 169
Sloan-Kettering Cancer Institute, 46
Society of Hand Surgeons, 44

Stalmacher, Captain, 6
Starzl, Dr. Thomas, 94, 100–101, 119, 122
Surgical Research Laboratory, 62, 126, 143
Swanson, Dr. Lennard T., 144, 147, 148, 149, 151, 152, 156, 187
Swensen, Dr. Orvar, 35
Symphony Hall, 29

Tagliacozzi, Gasparo, 15, 204
Terasaki, Paul, 120
Tessier, Dr. Paul, 152, 153, 155, 156, 162–163, 171, 181, 182, 188
Thomas, Dr. E. Donnall, 94, 98, 221
Thomas, Dr. Jackson, 126
Thorn, George W., xxii, 30, 31, 61–62, 64, 65, 66, 92
Tilney, Dr. Nicholas, 219
Time magazine, 89
Toby, Donald, 113–114
Tracheo–epiglottic flap, 176–177
Transplantation, 16
   feasibility of, 16, 90
Transplant centers, 119
Treatment of Facial Fractures (Dingman), 170
Truman, Harry, 20
Trustees of Reservations, 169, 216
Tufts Medical School, 105
Tyler, Dr. Rick, 216, 217

Uniform Anatomical Gift Act, 120
University of Alabama Medical School, 216
University of Pittsburgh, 94
University of Washington, Seattle, 64
Upton, Dr. Joe, 134, 138, 188, 189
Urine flow, 81

Valley Forge General Hospital, xxii, 3–4, 8–13, 39–44, 45, 53, 58, 59, 62, 142, 165, 199, 226
Vanzetti, Bartolomeo, 22
Vecchione, Tom, 179
Vitale, Maria, 21

Walker, Phil, 35
Walter, Dr. C.W., 62
Washington, George, 20
Welch, Kathy, 127, 139
Weller, Dr. Thomas, 95
Wellesley College, 22, 168
Wellesley Country Club, 141
West Roxbury Veteran Administration Hospital, 59, 60
Wheeler, John Brooks, 24, 33
Wieschaus, Eric F., 184

Wilder, Thornton, 229
Wilhelm, Dr. Norbert, 35
Wilson, Dick, 143
Wint, Frank, 125–136, 138, 139
Woods, Charles, 3–17, 44, 48, 131, 228
Woods, John, 175
Wrentham State School, 158, 207, 208, 209, 210

Zukoski, Dr. Charles, 106